W9-BVV-434

The Great CHICAGO FIRE

ILLUSTRATED EDITION

ROBERT CROMIE

Introduction by

Paul M. Angle

RUTLEDGE HILL PRESS

Nashville, Tennessee

Published in Nashville, Tennessee, by Rutledge Hill Press,
211 Seventh Avenue North, Nashville, Tennessee 37219

Typography by D&T/Bailey Typesetting, Inc., Nashville, Tennessee

Book design by Bruce Gore, Gore Studio, Inc.

Hand tinting on back of cover by Schwalb Creative Communications, Inc.

Illustrations designated "Andreas" are from *History of Chicago From the Earliest Period to the
Present Time* by A. T. Andreas, published 1886 by The A. T. Andreas Company, Chicago.

Illustrations designated "Sheahan/Upton" are from *The Great Conflagration: Chicago: Its
Past, Present and Future* by James W. Sheahan and George P. Upton, published 1872 by
Union Publishing Co., Chicago, Philadelphia, and Cincinnati.

Library of Congress Cataloging-in-Publication Data

Cromie, Robert, 1909–
    The great Chicago fire / Robert Cromie : Introduction by Paul M.
Angle. — Illustrated ed.
        p.   cm.
    Originally published: New York : McGraw-Hill, 1958.
    ISBN 1-55853-264-1 — ISBN 1-55853-265-X (pbk.)
    1. Fires—Illinois—Chicago—History—19th century.   2. Chicago
(Ill.)—History—To 1875.   I. Title.
F548.42.C8   1993
977.3'11041—dc20   93-30996
                                                          CIP

977.3
11041
Crom

Printed in Mexico

1 2 3 4 5 6 7 8 – 98 97 96 95 94 93

INTRODUCTION

One dark night,—when people were in bed,
Old Mrs. O'Leary lit a lantern in her shed;
The cow kicked it over, winked its eye, and said,
There'll be a hot time in the old town tonight.

—QUOTED IN THE CHICAGO EVENING POST.
AUTHOR ANONYMOUS

 MANY A bombing raid in World War II took more lives and destroyed more property than any of the great disasters of modern times. Yet the bombing raids are forgotten, except by those who lived through them, while the disasters live in the collective memory. And no disaster seems to make an impression as lasting as one caused by fire. Chicago offers a case in point. On July 24, 1915, the excursion steamer *Eastland* turned over in the Chicago River, taking 835 people to their deaths. The toll was three times as large as that of the Chicago Fire. Yet the *Eastland* is largely forgotten, while the Fire is the great benchmark in the city's history.

Perhaps the reason for the fascination of fire-caused catastrophe is the universality of experience with the destructiveness of this element. Relatively few people are ever exposed to the horrors of tornadoes, floods, and earthquakes, but everyone who has seen a building burning—and who hasn't?—knows what fire can do.

Everyone, therefore, can imagine a holocaust like the Chicago Fire. Yet even this stupendous tragedy did not obliterate individuals. We know what happened to literally hundreds of people, from fire marshals to infants-in-arms, on October 8 and 9, 1871. In this respect the Fire differs from Chicago's third great disaster, the Iroquois Theater fire of December 30, 1903. On that afternoon 571 persons, mostly women and children, died in less than half an hour. That there were acts of heroism we may be sure—some are in the record—yet the tragedy was so short-lived, and so many of those who were involved lost their lives in it, that no one could write a full-scale book about it.

Mr. Cromie has demonstrated, on the other hand, that a full-scale book can be written about the Chicago Fire. In fact, one could collect a sizable shelf of books which already have been written. Accounts of the disaster started to come from the presses soon after the rubble had cooled; they continued to come in 1872. Since then others—mainly reminiscenes and contemporary letters—have appeared at frequent intervals. But it was not until 1940, when H. A. Musham's "The Great Chicago Fire" came out in the *Papers of the Illinois State Historical Society,* that we had the benefit of a detailed and analytical work written from a present-day perspective. Even this excellent monograph left something to be desired, for the author was more concerned with the work of the fire department than with the fire as a community convulsion. Besides, Musham's study was published in a small edition and distributed only to certain libraries and to members of the Illinois State Historical Society. For several years it has been almost unobtainable. Mr. Cromie's book, therefore, fills a real gap in the literature of the subject.

But to say this, and only this, would be to do the author less than justice. Mr. Cromie has formed conclusions and expressed judgments, as one writing eighty-seven years after the event certainly should. If some of the men who drove themselves to the limit of endurance on the night of October 8–9, 1871, could read what he has written, I think they would be pleased. I confess my own gratification that he has kept Mrs. O'Leary in the story, despite his reservations about her famous cow.

By emphasizing personal experience—the approach one would expect from a well-qualified reporter and feature writer—Mr. Cromie has achieved a high degree of realism. Any reader can identify with dozens of people as the fire runs its inexorable course. Mr. Cromie has also highlighted one of the most admirable of human traits: man's refusal to yield to an impersonal force even when it appears to be irresistible. Chicago firemen, worn out when the fire began, never gave up, though they soon knew that they had no chance of bringing it under control. Thousands of individuals risked their lives—and some lost them—in their efforts to save members of their families and their property. And before the ruins had ceased to smoke, the inconquerable spirit asserted itself and led to the work of rebuilding. Within four years, as Mr. Cromie has pointed out, few traces of the catastrophe could be found, and the city had gained close to a hundred thousand inhabitants.

For many years Chicagoans took pride in this refusal to be overcome by disaster, considering it to be one of the unique qualities of their city. World War II, however, proved that our predecessors of 1871 and 1872 had no monopoly of this virtue. Churchill's defiance of the seemingly irresistible German war machine; the inarticulate decision of millions, both in England and on the continent, never to surrender to death and destruction; the determination of residents of bombed cities to rebuild homes and factories and make new lives, prove that the spurning of catastrophe is a trait that characterizes all mankind. Even so, Chicago and its recovery from the Fire of 1871 remains one of the most spectacular exemplifications of this quality.

To Mr. Cromie's narrative I wish to add a brief epilogue on a subject beyond the limits he set himself. He points out that Joseph Medill, by campaigning on the issue of fire prevention, was elected mayor in 1872. But I live in a large frame house that was built in the burned district in 1875, and many of my neighbors occupy frame structures erected later. In fact, the area is so vulnerable to fire that the Chicago Fire Department dispatches five pieces of apparatus in response to every alarm, and throws them in fast. Thus slowly do we human beings turn experience to advantage!

PAUL M. ANGLE
CHICAGO HISTORICAL SOCIETY
1958

Preface to the Illustrated Edition

When Robert Cromie first talked to us about writing *Illinois Trivia,* which we published in 1992, he asked if Rutledge Hill Press would like to republish his 1958 book, *The Great Chicago Fire.* Originally published by McGraw-Hill Book Company, it had been out of print for several years.

Discussion with authorities on the literature about the Fire confirmed what we believed: Cromie's book was acknowledged to be the best narrative history of the Great Fire. Our vision for the new edition was to combine some of the best illustrations available with Cromie's very readable text to make a book that communicated both the disaster of the Fire as well as the hope and energy of the people of Chicago as they rebuilt their city.

Joy Mackenzie created this illustrated edition by researching and selecting the photos. Jim Bailey, Julia Pitkin, and Stephen Woolverton put together the type and illustrations with extra care to make them look as good as possible. Particular thanks goes to Andrea Mark and the Chicago Public Library, Martin Baldessari for research, Jack Levin for the use of his stereopticon slides, Caroline Stark and the Nashville Public Library, and Amy Lyles Wilson.

The Publishers

ACKNOWLEDGMENTS

A WRITER I never met—the late Isaac Rosenfeld of Chicago—would have been the author of *The Great Chicago Fire* but for his untimely death. His widow very kindly permitted me the use of his notes and provided a list of those who had answered his published appeal for original material. This information was invaluable in the preparation of this book.

Among the many persons with whom I had personal contact, no one was of more assistance than the entire staff of the Chicago Historical Society. The feeling of being welcome, which all researchers using that unique institution surely experience, is fostered by everyone within its walls, from guards to Director.

Since it is manifestly impossible to identify everyone who works at the Historical Society, I must be content with mentioning Betty Baughman, the reference librarian, who is trustworthy, loyal, helpful, friendly, courteous, kind, obedient, cheerful, thrifty, brave, clean, and reverent—but especially helpful; Margaret Scriven, the chief librarian; Mrs. Paul Rhymer, who obligingly let me inspect every fire print in the place; Blanche Jantzen, who did the same with the manuscripts; and Walter Krutz, photographer for the Society, who was kind enough to make available previously unpublished wet-plate negatives by John Jex Bardwell, a Detroit photographer of ninety years ago.

Special thanks also are due Lloyd Wendt and Herman Kogan, who provided material about Field and Leiter's store, obtained during research for one of their several books; Mrs. Grace Henderson of Evanston, who loaned me an account of the fire written by her father, the late Charles Anthony; Dorothy S. Johnson, a former colleague on the *Tribune;* Mrs. F. T. Haskell of Gladstone, New Jersey;

and Mrs. Charles S. Mack of New York, who was born the morning of October 7, 1871.

Also to Virginia Marmaduke, who publicized the writing of the book during her radio show and turned up several sources of information; Fanny Butcher and Charles Collins of the *Tribune;* Mrs. Solomon A. Smith of Chicago, author of *The Fire Dragon,* who lent her notes; Alan D. Whitney of Winnetka, whose mother lived through the fire; and several survivors with vivid memories of the disaster, among them Mrs. Emma Busse and her sister, Minnie, George H. Cuny, and Mrs. Edwin Corse, all of Chicago.

Gary Sheahan, a *Tribune* artist, provided the information on his grandfather, Judge Joseph Gary; and Hamilton Allport of Chicago made available an autobiography of Henry E. Hamilton. Also of assistance were T. B. Hilton of Hopewell Junction, N.Y.; Louise C. Maas of Berwyn, Ill.; Mrs. John Vieregg of Deerfield, Ill.; L. M. Bennett, advertising manager for Joseph T. Ryerson and Co.; Mrs. Robert W. Crosby, Columbia City, Ind.; Florence C. Roberts of Rockford, Ill.; Mrs. Donald R. Brown, Sheffield, Ala.; Florence Maisch, Fox Lake, Ill.; Mrs. Roland R. Dunn, Waukegan, Ill.; Mrs. Milton Levinson, Los Angeles; Mrs. Erma Wentland of Oshkosh, Wis.; Mrs. Melville Modjeska, Villa Park, Ill.; and Alice McClelland, Western Springs, Ill.

Others who loaned material or were otherwise helpful were Mrs. Joseph N. Seng, Mrs. Olive A. Flanagan, Mrs. Paul Leschuk, Mrs. Louis Wirth, Edward J. Kleker, Bernard DeRemer, Ernest C. Hasselfeldt, all of Chicago; Philip J. More of Evanston, Ill.; Mrs. August Ott, Forest Park, Ill.; Sarah S. Lyon, Huntsville, Ontario, Can.; Mrs. Patricia Walker, Cicero, Ill.; and Mrs. Cornelius J. Guerino, Palos Park, Ill.

Aid also came from Ernest J. Lanigan of the National Baseball

Hall of Fame in Cooperstown, N.Y.; Mrs. Emma VanInwagen of Evanston; Mrs. E. J. Dicken, Philip Kane, Adele H. Pritam, and Mrs. Emma E. McCashin, Chicago; Al A. Ulbrich, Bloomington, Ill.; Mrs. Laurence M. Klauber, San Diego, Cal.; Mrs. Harry Conant, Dover, Ill.; and Marion E. Wells, librarian of the First National Bank of Chacago.

Mrs. Ethel Hardy, of Chicago, niece of William Brown, the 1871 fire-alarm operator, filled in some missing details of the events of the Sunday night, and Ruth Tomboulian of Ithaca, N.Y., supplied material concerning her grandfather, a ship's officer who was in the Chicago River when the fire broke out. James W. Jardine, commissioner of the Department of Water and Sewers, made some contemporary records available.

The list goes on, because people were so kind: Mrs. Oliver Flanagan, Mrs. J. A. Riley, Mrs. W. F. O'Donnell, Evelyn Eagle and Mrs. Walter R. Eagle of Chicago; John Sullivan of the United States Weather Bureau office; Mrs. A. J. Magnus, Muscatine, Ia.; Catherine Hochlener, Chicago; Mrs. Emelie Fessel, Indianapolis; Vera Mae Pipher, Homewood, Ill.; Curtis C. Page, Cornell University; Mrs. Frank Leesey, Lorain, Ohio; John M. Hartley, Gig Harbor, Wash.; and Mrs. George Noble of Chicago.

In conclusion I must acknowledge information obtained from scores of books, plus the interest and assistance of those two excellent booksellers, Richard Barnes of Chicago and Donald LaChance of Evanston. Also I am most grateful to Paul M. Angle of the Chicago Historical Society, who not only gave valuable advice but also wrote the Introduction.

There always is the uneasy feeling that someone who helped has been overlooked. If this is so, I apologize for the inadvertence.

Good heavens—I mustn't forget to mention the help of my wife, Alice, who did a large amount of typing and made some excellent suggestions.

ROBERT CROMIE

The Great CHICAGO FIRE

ILLUSTRATED EDITION

CHAPTER 1

You could tell a Chicagoan in any city in the world, for he would not talk a minute scarcely until he would let you know he was from Chicago.

—REVEREND C. A. BURGESS

THEY CALLED it the Garden City, or the Queen City of the West, or the Gem of the Prairie. It was the largest, the richest, the most impressive city in the heartland of the nation; it was the crossroads of the Middle West, the robust symbol of the country's expansion and wealth.

Chicago had grown with incredible speed from humble origins. Sixty-eight years before, all that existed on the site was a stockaded trading post, Fort Dearborn, situated on marshy ground near Lake Michigan. It was a small way station along the trade route stretching from the Lakes to the Gulf of Mexico.

During the War of 1812 the small garrison was destroyed and its population wiped out by an Indian attack. When the village of Chicago was formally organized, in 1833, there were fewer than 100 inhabitants.

In the year 1871, more than 300,000 people lived within the boundaries of Chicago, which encompassed an area six miles long from north to south and three miles wide from the Lake shore west. It was the industrial, commercial, and cultural center of the Middle West, surpassing all its fellows west of the Appalachians, and rivaling the great cities of the East.

The bulk of Chicago's wealth came from the same sources as that of old Fort Dearborn. Indians paddling down the river in fur-laden canoes no longer played a part in the city's commerce, but its prosperity still depended on its location. Chicago remained strategically placed astride the roads of trade. All railroads—or almost all—led to Chicago. Twenty-one mainline tracks came into the city, and an average of 100 passenger trains and 120 freight trains entered or left every day. More than 16 million bushels of wheat passed each year through the massive grain elevators scattered along the banks of the river. The Union Stockyards had been established a few years before on the southern outskirts, and there were already twenty-one packing houses in the city. Chicago was an important place for buying things, storing things, selling things, and shipping things. Through it passed the newly tapped riches of the nation.

But the real reason for Chicago's preeminence was its position on the Lake.

IN 1871, CHICAGO, LESS THAN 50 YEARS AWAY FROM ITS DAYS AS A SMALL SETTLEMENT, WAS ONE OF THE NATION'S MOST PROGRESSIVE CITIES. AMONG ITS PRIZED ATTRACTIONS WAS CROSBY'S OPERA HOUSE, BUILT, TO QUOTE A CONTEMPORARY ACCOUNT, "ON A SCALE OF MAGNIFICENCE AND BEAUTY NOT HITHERTO ATTEMPTED IN THIS COUNTRY." IN 1868 THE REPUBLICANS HELD THEIR PRESIDENTIAL CONVENTION HERE, NOMINATING ULYSSES S. GRANT. WITH ITS NEIGHBOR, THE NOTED MUSIC PUBLISHING FIRM OF ROOT AND CADY, THE OPERA HOUSE STOOD AS AN ELEGANT SETTING FOR AN EVER-CHANGING KALEIDOSCOPE OF FINE CARRIAGES, HORSEBACK RIDERS, YOUNGSTERS, DOGS, HOOP-SKIRTED DAMSELS, AND MEN IN WORK CLOTHES OR TOP HATS. (CHICAGO PUBLIC LIBRARY)

Before the railroads became the leading method of transport, the Great Lakes were the natural pathway to the West. And even after the country was linked by the railroads from coast to coast, the ships, barges, and boats on the Lakes and on the Illinois and Michigan Canal continued to do much of the hauling, both heavy and light. Chicago had the advantage of a natural canal, the gentle Chicago River, running right into its heart. In 1871, steam had not yet cut the masts from the Lake shipping, so that on the city skyline would appear, above the roofs and down the streets to the river and the Lake, the delicate tracery of rigging.

The river divided the city into three parts. It forked about half a mile west of the Lake, and its two branches ran northwest and south, forming a rough T shape, the base of which was the Lake shore. Between the Lake and the southern arm of the T lay the South Division—usually called the South Side—which contained the main business section of the city, as well as the worst of its slums. Facing it across the river's trunk and lying between the North Branch and the Lake was the North Division, where many of Chicago's early settlers had made their homes, and which was still the city's finest residential district. West of the forks was the West Division, containing both an industrial section concentrated near the river and the crowded frame homes of the working class.

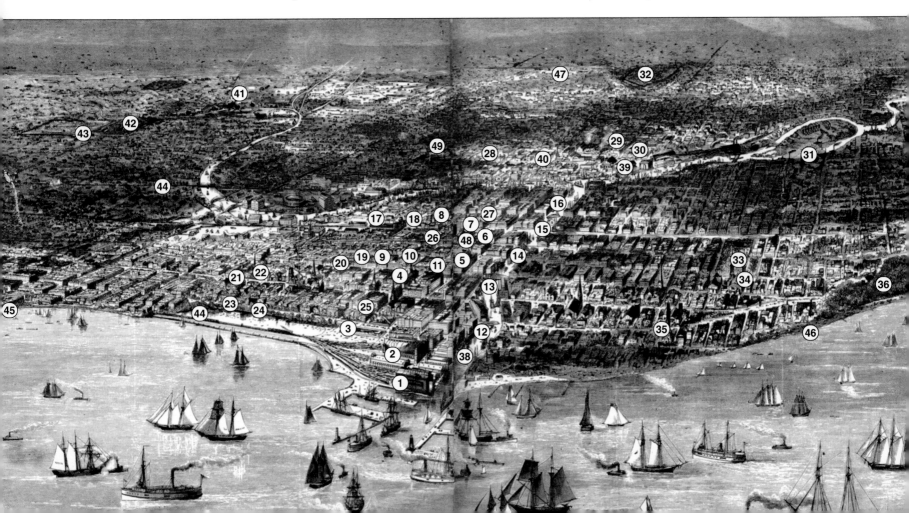

The three parts of the city were joined by twelve bridges, spaced at about two-block intervals over the various branches of the river. These bridges were generally made of wood, and supported by twin arches. They pivoted on a fixed pier in the middle, where a bridgetender sat at the controls of a steam engine, which turned the bridge to let ships go by. Since traffic was heavy on the river, this meant that the horsecars, buggies, wagons, and pedestrians were often left in impatient lines at the approaches. To relieve the congestion, two tunnels augmented the bridge connections from the South Side to the other divisions.

On the east, Lake Michigan lapped the city's doorstep. To the north, west, and south, the outskirts of Chicago dwindled into farmland and open prairie. In 1871, the city showed every sign of bursting through its limits and threatened to spread out in all directions except where the land lay under water.

As a matter of fact, some of Chicago's major recent civic improvements *did* lie under water. After decades of an indifferent water supply, drawn from unreliable wells and a none-too-sanitary river, the city government had, four years before, undertaken the construction of a new waterworks, drawing fresh water through a two-mile tunnel under the Lake bed. The eastern-most householder in Chicago was the tender of the Crib, an enormous open caisson with rooms built over it. This was the terminus for the Lake tunnel, and it contained the sluice gates for the water system, which in its day was a marvel of modern engineering.

Chicagoans marveled also at the un-accustomed purity of the water, since previously it had not been unusual for tiny fish to come wriggling through the taps. Franc B. Wilkie, a popular author of the day, expressed delight, bordering on shock, at the improvement:

"The cleansing properties of the new water are wonderful. Children whose faces have been washed in it have been lost and never found. Their mothers cannot recognize them. It is proposed to establish a place where lost children may be gathered, and where only the old water will be used in their ablutions. In time, it is expected that many young children, whom nobody knows, will be recognized by their parents."

Despite the pressure provided by the water tower, a neo-medieval structure housing a three-inch pipe some 130 feet high, the supply was still not wholly satisfactory all over town. The need for another pumping station was generally admitted. But the project was held up by heated arguments over certain alleged irregularities in connection with the proposed site. Which goes to show that Chicago shared the same benefits of civic democracy enjoyed by many another city of that period—or any period, for that matter.

Political difficulties notwithstanding, the city had made considerable recent progress with another of its major problems. This problem can be described in one word: mud. The site of Chicago, however convenient for commerce, was too nearly a swamp for the comfort of its inhabitants or the safety of its buildings. The streets, few of which were paved, became seas of mire in wet weather. In late winter and early spring this condition was constant. The story was circulated during this period that a traveler had been discovered in a notorious downtown mudhole, buried right up to his neck. "Don't worry," he was reputed

OPPOSITE: THIS PRE-FIRE VIEW OF CHICAGO FROM LAKE MICHIGAN LOOKS WEST. **1** CENTRAL ELEVATOR **2** GREAT CENTRAL DEPOT **3** WHITE STOCKING BASEBALL GROUND **4** BOOKSELLER'S ROW **5** TREMONT HOUSE **6** SHERMAN HOUSE **7** COURTHOUSE **8** BOARD OF TRADE **9** POST OFFICE **10** CHICAGO TRIBUNE **11** CROSBY'S OPERA HOUSE **12** RUSH STREET BRIDGE **13** STATE STREET BRIDGE **14** CLARK STREET BRIDGE **15** LA SALLE STREET TUNNEL **16** WELLS STREET BRIDGE **17** MICHIGAN SOUTHERN; C., R.I., AND P. **18** SITE OF OGDEN HOUSE **19** BIGELOW HOUSE **20** PALMER HOUSE **21** BARTLETT'S CHURCH (PLYMOUTH CONGREGATIONAL) **22** FIRST BAPTIST CHURCH **23** MICHIGAN AVENUE HOTEL **24** TERRACE ROW **25** DRAKE BLOCK **26** CHICAGO TIMES **27** SHERIDAN'S HEADQUARTERS **28** P., F.W., AND C. DEPOT; AND C., A., AND ST. L., **29** C., CIN., AND IND. CENT. DEPOT. **30** CHICAGO AND NORTHWESTERN **31** GASWORKS **32** UNION PARK **33** WASHINGTON SQUARE **34** DR. COLYER'S CHURCH **35** WATERWORKS **36** LINCOLN PARK **37** LAKE SHORE DRIVE **38** CHICAGO RIVER **39** NORTH BRANCH **40** SOUTH BRANCH **41** ENTRANCE OF CHICAGO RIVER INTO CANAL **42** UNION STOCKYARDS **43** DEXTER PARK **44** LAKE PARK **45** SOUTH SIDE **46** NORTH SIDE **47** WEST SIDE **48** BRIGGS HOUSE **49** GRAIN WAREHOUSE, NEAR WHERE THE FIRST FIRE BEGAN (HARPER'S WEEKLY, OCTOBER 21, 1871)

THE WIDELY-KNOWN SHERMAN HOUSE WAS
A SIX-STORY HOTEL BUILT IN 1861 AT
CLARK AND RANDOLPH STREETS IN THE
HEART OF THE BUSINESS DISTRICT. HERE
IT BECOMES THE BACKDROP FOR A PARADE
ADVERTISING A NEWLY-ARRIVED CIRCUS
WITH WHAT SEEMS TO BE KNIGHTS IN
ARMOR, FOLLOWED BY AN ELEPHANT AND
AT LEAST TWO DROMEDARIES. (CHICAGO
PUBLIC LIBRARY)

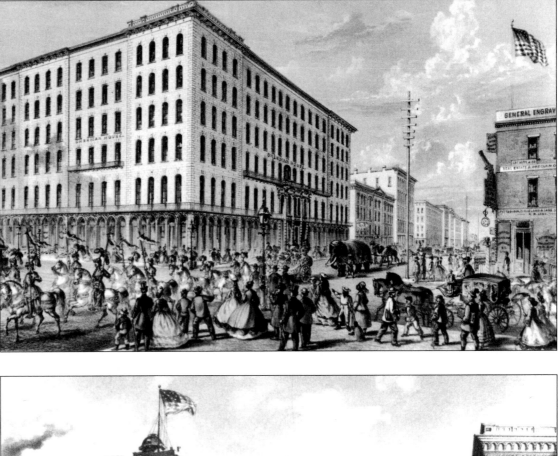

A FEW BLOCKS FROM THE SHERMAN
HOUSE WAS THE TREMONT HOUSE, AT
LAKE AND DEARBORN STREETS. BUILT IN
1850, THIS HOTEL WAS THE FIRST MAJOR
BUILDING IN CHICAGO TO BE LIGHTED
WITH GAS. IT WAS DESTINED TO HAVE A
LIVELY EXISTENCE AND TO BE A FAVORITE
STOPPING PLACE FOR THE CITY'S COMMER-
CIAL VISITORS. (CHICAGO PUBLIC
LIBRARY)

IN SPITE OF PROTESTS FROM OWNERS AND SCOFFERS WHO SAID THE IDEA WAS IMPOSSIBLE, THE CITY RAISED THE SIDE-WALK GRADE LEVEL SEVERAL FEET ALONG THE BUSINESS STREETS. THIS BLOCK OF BRICK AND STONE BUILDINGS ON LAKE STREET WAS RAISED INCH BY INCH. THE TREMONT HOUSE WAS RAISED WITHOUT DISTURBING THE GUESTS BY GEORGE M. PULLMAN, WHO DIRECTED THE WORK OF 1,200 MEN OPERATING 5,000 JACKSCREWS IN UNISON. (CHICAGO HISTORICAL SOCIETY)

to have told alarmed bystanders. "I'm riding a horse."

The level of the streets, particularly in the business section, had been raised little by little to help solve the drainage problem. Whole buildings had in some cases been raised also, to keep their doors above street level. In 1861 George Pullman, who made his name and fortune with the invention of the sleeping car, performed what experts said was an impossible engineering feat. He elevated the Tremont House, the largest hotel in the city, eight feet, using the efforts of 1,200 men and the power of 5,000 jackscrews. So smooth and gradual a job did he do that not a mortared joint was cracked, and most of the guests—for the hotel ran as usual throughout the operation—were unaware that anything uncommon was going on.

Another effort made to alleviate the mud problem of winter—and a correspond-ing dust problem of summer—was to pave the streets, and to build raised sidewalks even with or above the raised streets. A certain amount of progress had been made with the former, at least in the downtown area of the South Division, but by 1871 only 70 of the 530 miles of streets within the city limits were surfaced. Fifteen miles were covered with cobblestones or macadam. The other fifty-five were faced with pine blocks, fitted into the roadway as if they were bricks. The raised sidewalks, some of them several feet above the street, were also built of wood almost exclusively.

In fact, the city of Chicago was virtually a cenotaph to the great northern forests lying beyond the far end of Lake Michigan. One of its features that would have struck an observer most forcibly was the fact that the city was built almost entirely of wood. Chicagoans pointed with pride to majestic structures of brick and "Athens marble"

THIS SCENE AT CLARK AND WATER STREETS SHOWS THE HUSTLE AND BUSTLE OF THE CITY. THE BUILDING IN THE CENTER HOUSES A PUBLISHER, LAW OFFICES, AND AN ENTERPRISE THAT ADVERTISES "CARBONIC GRAIN DRYERS." ACROSS THE STREET ARE AN INSURANCE OFFICE, A JOB PRINTER, AND AN EXCHANGE OFFICE. THE TOWERING MASTS OF VESSELS MOORED IN THE RIVER ARE VISIBLE IN THE BACKGROUND. (ANDREAS)

which graced the blocks in the center of town. (Actually the Athens was in Illinois, and the marble was medium-grade limestone, but the effect was unquestionably impressive.) The most up-to-date buildings were beginning to use cast-iron plates and columns in their façades, a new fashion imported from the effete East. But these were by no means typical. Brick and stone and iron were marks of affluence and, although there was plenty of that in Chicago, it wasn't widely distributed. Among the substantial monuments of wealth were humbler structures either mainly or entirely of wood. The South Side slums and the West Side working-class district were enormous frame warrens, with wooden houses, barns, shacks, tenements, stores, warehouses, and small factories all jumbled together in cozy intimacy. In the richest part of the South Side, noble edifices of stone or

brick were interspersed with more homely wooden houses, shops, and stables; and, as befitted a great commercial city of the day, the streets and buildings were crowded with wooden signs and billboards. Even in the most elegant sections of the North Side, where marble lions and iron deer were prevalent, durable construction materials were still a mark of opulence rather than accustomed use.

It was even common to use wood in disguise. Most church steeples were built with a wooden framework, covered with tin or copper sheathing, and often shaped and painted to resemble the stone they were not. Even decorated cornices on the finest marble buildings were usually "sculptured" in this way. These can be too easily dismissed as the flashy posturings of a *nouveau-riche* city; there were practical reasons for these uses of wood. Aside from the fact that it was readily available in what then seemed like inexhaustible supply, wood also had the virtue of lightness, compared to the brick, stone, iron, and steel it imitated, and was far easier to work with. But because of the great amount of impermanent construction, and the swiftness of growth and change, the city looked like a stage which was never quite set, and whose scenery was constantly being shifted.

At the same time, Chicago was not simply an enormous false front—even though that was one of the many aspects of its character. Despite its comparative youth, and because of its tremendous vigor and variety, the city displayed as many different faces as there were human eyes to see it. One might notice the noisome red-light and saloon district at the foot of Fifth Avenue, just a few blocks from the best part of the business section, or observe the flimsy construc-

WHEN THE CUSTOMHOUSE WAS BUILT IN 1855, IT WAS PROCLAIMED TO BE CHICAGO'S FIRST "COMPLETELY FIRE-PROOF STRUCTURE" BECAUSE OF THE USE OF HEAVY WALLS AND WROUGHT-IRON BEAMS. IT WAS ALMOST DESTROYED IN THE GREAT FIRE. (CHICAGO PUBLIC LIBRARY)

THE UNION STOCKYARDS, A FEW MILES TO THE SOUTHWEST OF CENTRAL CHICAGO, OPENED CHRISTMAS DAY, 1865, AND SOON BECAME THE LARGEST IN THE WORLD. THEY INCLUDED A BANK, A HOTEL, AND A DAILY NEWSPAPER. THEY PROVIDED MATERIAL FOR UPTON SINCLAIR'S CRITI-CAL NOVEL THE JUNGLE, BEFORE BEING PHASED OUT IN 1971. (CHICAGO PUBLIC LIBRARY)

tion and gaudy tastelessness which characterized so much of its architecture, or tote up the beer and liquor consumption of a hard-drinking city—and come away with the impression (as many did) that here was a modern replica of one of the Sinful Cities of the Plain. But one might also get a quite different idea of Chicago from the well-proportioned, substantial lines of many North Side homes, the generous breadth of its streets, the number and popularity of its churches, and the prevalence of trees, lovingly nurtured even in the midst of the commercial district. One might also be impressed by the quality of the city's bookstores, especially those contained within

Bookseller's Row on State Street, or by the six modern theaters, or by the sixty-five private schools and colleges and six medical schools.

For behind the mask of raw youth, materialism, and vulgarity lay other, more substantial qualities, which were not so evident to the casual observer. These qualities were more often to be found in the citizens, perhaps, than in their city. For the source of all the hustle, haste, and hoopla was a spirit of enterprise, originality, and resiliency that could not be easily assessed. If this inner vitality tended to become obscured by the growing prosperity of the city, it was soon to be given an opportunity to prove itself.

CHAPTER 2

An alarm of fire during the evening caused no anxiety, for it was a thing of frequent occurrence.

—JOHN R. CHAPIN

GEORGE FRANCIS TRAIN, world traveler, author, and lecturer on moral subjects, gave a talk in Farwell Hall, an auditorium on the corner of Madison and Clark Streets, Saturday night, October 7, 1871. The topic of this address is not recorded, but one of the speaker's remarks proved memorable.

"This is the last public address," said Mr. Train, "that will be delivered within these walls! A terrible calamity is impending over the City of Chicago! More I cannot say; more I dare not utter."

Since events proved the speaker right in every particular, a reporter cornered him in Denver some weeks later and pressed him to explain his prophecy. But the prophet's hindsight was less precise than his foresight. "I knew that Chicago would be destroyed by fire or flood," he said suavely, "and on the night in question I had a presentiment that a terrible doom was overhanging the city."

Train's reckless pronouncements led the *Chicago Times* to dub him "The Prince of Blatherskites." It is likely that his prediction was designed merely to grip the attention of a restless Saturday night audience, yet plain common sense and the most casual observation could have told him that if Chicago was indeed in danger, that danger was fire.

The summer had been abnormally dry. Between July and October there had been only five inches of rain, falling in a few widely spaced showers. This was about a quarter of the normal amount. There had been less than an inch during the past month. The city was parched and dehydrated, and that first week of October was unusually warm for the season. The trees that lined the streets drooped in the relentless sun, their leaves gray with powdery dust.

TRAVELING AUTHOR-SPEAKER GEORGE FRANCIS TRAIN (HATLESS) SITS WITH FRIENDS ON A BALCONY OF THE TREMONT HOUSE IN 1865. SIX YEARS LATER, IN 1871, TRAIN'S ITINERARY BROUGHT HIM TO CHICAGO'S FARWELL HALL ON SATURDAY EVENING, OCTOBER 7. THAT NIGHT, THE NEW YORK AUTHOR MADE THE AMAZING PREDICTION THAT HIS SPEECH WAS THE FINAL ONE TO BE "DELIVERED WITHIN THESE WALLS! A TERRIBLE CALAMITY IS IMPENDING OVER THE CITY OF CHICAGO! MORE I CANNOT SAY; MORE I DARE NOT UTTER." SUNDAY'S <u>CHICAGO</u> <u>TIMES</u> CALLED TRAIN "THE PRINCE OF BLATHERSKITES." THAT EVENING, THE GREAT CHICAGO FIRE BROKE OUT. (CHICAGO HISTORICAL SOCIETY)

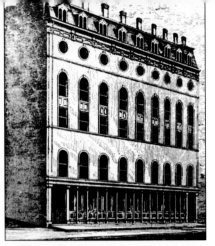

The buildings were like an enormous artificial forest, drying out in a sun-heated oven. Not only were most of the buildings made of wood, but even those of more substantial stuff almost without exception had wooden floors, window and door frames, and roofs. In fact, even those buildings labeled fireproof generally had roofs of wooden rafters and boards, over which was laid felt or paper covered with tar. The streets themselves were excellent avenues for the growth and spread of fire. The pine-block paving of several downtown streets was by no means fireproof, and the sidewalks were an even greater menace. Raised four and five feet in some places, these boardwalks were like gigantic andirons supporting a load of well-laid firewood. Once ignited, they would draw like chimneys through the open spaces beneath.

As if these running piles of kindling were not sufficient to carry flames from one place to another, fences of pine and hemlock were often placed along the streets or between lots. Not only did such fences form natural pathways for fire; in many instances they also closed off access to fire engines. This was a special problem along the river, where many of the streets came to dead ends and were fenced off at the nearest intersections to make more room for yards and buildings. Property owners in such locations could see no point in maintaining streets that didn't go anywhere, and the city made little effort to enforce the few zoning and street ordinances that then existed.

Not only the construction, but also the contents of the city's buildings made them ripe for burning. Even in 1871 Chicago was, as its famous native poet, Carl Sandburg, put it, "freight handler to the nation." The business districts were full of warehouses and stores, in which could be found aisle upon aisle of wooden shelves and cases, running from floor to ceiling, and as often as not containing inflammable goods. The multitude of railroad cars—both passenger and freight—which shuttled in and out of the city or lay in long lines in the railway yards—were made largely of wood, as were the boats on the river and the Lake, for the day of the steel ship had not yet arrived.

Moreover, Chicago had become a thriving center of woodworking industries: furniture factories, lumber mills, carriage and wagon factories (including the McCormick reaper works and George Pullman's sleeping-car factory), paint and varnish shops. The worst menace in these industries was the by-products: waste blocks, chips, shavings, and—above all—sawdust, which all of them manufactured in great supply, and which some were not overly careful to dispose of.

The seventeen grain elevators in the city were also potential torches. Most of them were made entirely of wood, and their contents were equally inflammable. But their main problem was size. By the standards of the day, and of the city they were in, they were huge. They ran the equivalent of four or five stories tall, and in a wind of any velocity their tarred or shingled roofs could not be reached by the streams of the most powerful engines of the fire department.

And since there was no available water power, all these industries depended upon the power of steam, which in turn depended on yards full of coal for boilers.

It might be said, with considerable justice, that Chicago specialized in the production, handling, and storage of combustible goods.

The peril of fire lurked in every home as well. This was particularly true in the poorer sections of the South and West Sides, crowded with flimsy frame houses on small fenced lots, but frame construction was not the monopoly of the poor. And no household, rich or poor, could get along without a good supply of stovewood and coal on hand, plus a bin of shavings and sawdust for tinder—especially with winter coming on. Kerosene often had to be kept on hand for lamps; the brighter, less smoky, and safer gaslight was used in the street lamps, but for home use was limited to those who could afford the substantial expense of the pipes and burners.

But a greater fire hazard than any of the foregoing, without exception, lurked in the barns and sheds that accompanied just about every house in the city, no matter how humble. In many of these were stored hay and other feed, not so often for horses—for even in this horse-drawn age, those who could afford to own them were in the minority—as for other livestock. The family cow—or the family goat, pig, sheep, or flock of chickens—was much more common then than now. If the householder was fortunate enough to have a horse, he also kept his buggy or wagon in the barn. Furthermore, the winter fuel supply was stored there, except for some stovewood and kindling kept close to the house. And in a time when basements in houses were less common than they are today, and attics were often pressed into service as bedrooms for large and expanding families, the barn was frequently used for the storage of odds and ends.

Of more than 600 fires reported in the year 1870, a goodly percentage were barn fires. A city ordinance forbade the use of candles or lamps, unless well secured in a lantern, in any area containing hay, straw, or other combustible material. But despite precautions, public or private, barn fires continued to break out sporadically, not because fire was often used in these buildings, but because their contents were so ripe for burning.

The danger of fire, while somewhat neglected, was not entirely ignored. Newspaper editorials gave it periodic attention, and the city fathers, generally more zealous in defense of the public purse than of the public safety, had nevertheless introduced several important reforms over the years. In 1858 the fire department had been changed from volunteer to professional, partly

because the volunteer companies had come to take a greater interest in fighting one another than in fighting fires. It had been not uncommon, when two volunteer companies met at the scene of a fire, for them to wage a pitched street battle for the "honor" of saving the property, only to discover after the melee that there was nothing left to save.

The morale of the professional department was high, despite the extreme demands made upon it. One reason for this was that the marshals, who actually led the men at fires, were customarily chosen from the ranks. Also, the pay was not bad. The chief marshal made two hundred and ninety dollars a month, the three assistant marshals about one hundred and fifty dollars. Foremen and engineers of individual engine companies earned one hundred. Pipemen, the firemen who tended the hose, and who were near the bottom of the scale, got seventy-five dollars. However low the figures may sound, these were steady jobs at decent wages in terms of 1871 dollars.

The city's main contribution to both the morale and the power of the department was the purchase, over a period of ten years, of seventeen steam-driven fire engines. Steamers, which replaced cumbersome hand-pumped engines, were of fairly recent adoption everywhere. Chicago's force was bigger and more up-to-date than most.

A steamer, very simply, was a coal- or wood-burning boiler, whose steam drove an attached force pump. Its intake pipe, or taper, was attached to a hydrant or other water source, and there was provision at its outlet for at least two hoses. The whole mechanism was mounted on a four-wheel carriage, and drawn by a pair (or more) of horses.

Such a description, however, fails to do the steamer justice. The upright cylindrical boiler, looking like an enormous milk can and shining with brass fittings and nickel plate, often stood higher than a man. Atop the pump, which extended forward from the boiler, a pressure head generally protruded, shaped like an enormous brass darning egg. The wheels and trim were brightly painted, and mounted somewhere on the machine was at least one bold brass-and-cut-glass carriage lamp engraved with the number of the engine.

Each of the engines had a departmental number, but was commonly known by its given name. Some were christened after Indian tribes, such as the *Waubansia* and the *Winnebago.* Several were honored with the names of politicians, such as the *Long John,* named after a tall former mayor, John Wentworth, and the *Little Giant,* for Stephen A. Douglas. Some were given titles of affection and respect, such as the *Economy.*

Careening toward a fire at a full gallop, the steamers made an impressive sight. Clouds of steam, smoke, and cinders chuffed noisily from the boiler stacks, while a path of gleaming clinkers marked their wake. A contemporary story was told of two Irishmen, lately arrived in this country and staying overnight at a hotel. One was awakened by fire bells, and reached the window in time to see two steamers round the corner. He shook his companion. "Pat, wake up!" he shouted. "They're moving hell! Two loads have gone by already!"

The steamers were augmented by twenty-three hose carts, four hook-and-ladder wagons, and two hose elevators. The hose elevator was a near relation of the hook and ladder, with a platform which could be lifted up about two stories, on which a pipeman could stand to direct a stream onto upper floors and roofs. This device was apparently of rather limited effectiveness; most firefighting was done at ground level.

Of greater significance was the newly renovated alarm system, a telegraphic network which supposedly brought alarms instantaneously to the central office in an upper floor of the courthouse. The signals, numbered to indicate location, were relayed to the fire stations, and tolled out on the great courthouse bell for good measure. The alarm boxes, formerly made of wood and operated by a complicated and easily bungled process of hand-cranking, were now sturdy iron containers for a simple lever which could be operated with one thumb.

Watchmen were on duty atop the various station houses during the hours of greatest danger, usually between 9:30 P.M. and 6 A.M. Another watchman stood on the courthouse tower, which provided a splendid view of the whole city. It was his duty to estimate the location of any unreported fires he saw and, via a speaking tube, to tell the fire-alarm telegraph office what signal should be rung.

Another weapon had lately been added to the arsenal against the ever-present danger. The Insurance Patrol had been inaugurated on October 2. It was headed by young Benjamin Bullwinkle, a former driver for the chief marshal. Financed by contributions from merchants and insurance companies, the patrol ranged through the business districts with chemical extinguishers mounted on a wagon, putting out small fires, preventing the spread of sparks from burning buildings, and salvaging property from doomed buildings.

Perhaps the most appropriate symbol of efforts made to defend the city against fire was that edifice of civic pride, the new waterworks, at the foot of Chicago Avenue. The pumping station and nearby water tower, built in a fearlessly romantic medieval style, with ornamental battlements, artificial turrets, and imitation arrow slits, were proper images of the city's vigor and self-confidence. If need be, the whole of Lake Michigan could be pumped into the waterworks and thence into the mains.

Yet, despite all these measures, much was left undone that ought to have been done. The department was administered by three elected commissioners who also had responsibility over the police department. Even had they been more dedicated to reform, they and the department were bound hand and foot to the city council by the long strings of the purse. The difficulty was not that the fire department was poor in quality; it was very good. But the force was spread so thin, and had such a difficult job to do, that it was not equal to a real

CHICAGO'S FIRE DEPARTMENT BECAME A PROFESSIONAL ONE IN 1857 WITH THE PURCHASE OF ITS FIRST PERMANENT STEAM ENGINE (TOP). IT WAS NAMED THE LONG JOHN IN HONOR OF LONG JOHN WENTWORTH (BOTTOM), THE CITY'S 6-FOOT 6-INCH MAYOR. (ANDREAS)

emergency. There were only 185 active firemen in the department, and the fire engines had to cover, on the average, more than a square mile of territory each.

The marshals pleaded in vain for more engines, fireboats on the river, enlargement of the water mains, and additional fireplugs. Regulations intended to alleviate fire hazards and prevent the spread of fire were ignored with impunity.

Worst of all, property owners staunchly resisted all efforts of the fire department, insurance men, and worried citizens to put teeth in the zoning laws and building code.

This first week in October had been a bad one for fires. On Saturday afternoon, September 30, the Burlington Warehouse A, on the lower South Side, caught fire from an undetermined cause. Fourteen engines responded to a third alarm, sounded when the flames went out of control. They could do little, however, except pour water on nearby buildings. Warehouse A was leveled, and one workman killed, in the city's worst fire in more than a year.

The following day there were four alarms, and the next day five. On October 3 half a dozen fires started and were put out. During the next three days a dozen more were discovered and finally beaten. But the department's men and equipment were becoming worn out. The steamers, in particular, had been overworked and were in sore need of overhaul. Hose was in short supply, and much of what was on hand was old and unfit for use.

On Saturday, October 7, shortly after Mr. Train finished edifying his Farwell Hall audience, an event occurred which for a while looked as if it might be the fulfillment of his pronouncement of doom. Actually, it was only an exhausting dress rehearsal for disaster.

A fire broke out in the Lull and Holmes Planing Mill, a small woodworking factory located on Canal Street near Van Buren, in the southern part of the West Side. The mill was in a neighborhood of lumberyards, a few cheap frame houses, and many saloons. Among the nearby combustibles (aside from the saloons) were a paper-box factory, two lumberyards—which also contained large coal piles—and the timber depot of an express company.

This area was known among insurance men as "The Red Flash," for reasons which may easily be imagined.

By the time the fire was spotted and reported, it had devoured its way out of the basement of the mill, and was licking hungrily north toward Jackson Street. It was abetted by a brisk wind, which rose as the fire grew hotter. This fire, though serious, was handled according to the routine procedures of the department.

The steamers within the area covered by the alarm arrived first. The *Little Giant,* one

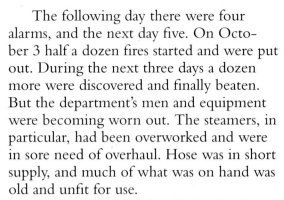

THIS SCENE ON LOWER CLARK STREET IN 1857 SHOWS WOODEN BUILDINGS, WOODEN SIDEWALKS, COMBUSTIBLE AWNINGS, AND WHAT APPEARS TO BE WOODPLANK STREETS. IT WAS AN INVITATION TO A FIRE. (ANDREAS)

of the older engines, whose house was a few blocks away, was one of the first. It pulled up to the corner near the mill, and the drivers unhitched the horses and led them out of the way of flying sparks. Meanwhile the pipemen attached the taper to the nearest plug. It is possible, in this part of the city, the hydrant was one of the churnshaped wooden ones, which were being replaced slowly by more modern cast-iron models. The engineer and stoker started the pump, and the engine began pouring 600 gallons of water per minute on the blaze.

Matthias Benner, assistant marshal, whose duties were largely confined to the West Side, came up soon after from a smaller fire in the South Division. The fire looked dangerous, so he sent in a second alarm.

The first alarm for a fire drew equipment only from the immediate area. In the event of a second alarm, other engines responded from nearby districts. The engines from areas lying farther away moved up to the vacated stations, so that no greater part of the city than necessary was left unguarded. A third alarm, signifying that a fire was out of control, brought all available men and equipment to the scene.

When the second alarm went out, other top officials of the department came rolling up in their personal wagons. John Schank, first assistant marshal, came from the South Side, and Lorens Walter, the second assistant, from the North. Chief Marshal Robert A. Williams himself appeared on the scene to direct the battle.

Williams was, if not entirely typical, an example of the best the department had to offer. A Canadian by birth, he joined the volunteer department in 1848, the year after he came to Chicago, and rose through the ranks. At forty-five, he was its top professional officer.

He was a powerfully built man: six feet tall, with wide-set brown eyes in a ruddy face. He sported a luxuriant spade beard and mustache. Nearly all the firemen followed the hairy fashions of the day, although how they managed to maintain a full growth is something of a mystery, considering the constant danger of brush fires and singes.

Williams's official uniform included a narrow, peaked cap and a long, belted coat with brass buttons. Another part of his regular equipment was his brass speaking trumpet, a device used by marshals and foremen to make their voices carry over the roar of flames and clatter of engines.

The chief marshal had a reputation for ability and conscientiousness, and for managing with very little sleep. One of his neighbors reported that when a night alarm rang, Williams's light went on immediately, and he was out of the house within two or three minutes. Furthermore, according to this admiring and watchful neighbor, Williams often went out two or three times the same night, several nights in succession, even in the worst winter weather.

Several engines appeared in answer to the second alarm at the rapidly spreading mill fire, and a third alarm proved necessary shortly afterward. The steamer *Chicago* followed Benner from the minor South Side fire. It took a position along the north face of the fire, in the path of the freshening wind. But the hose had barely been connected when several lengths burst. This was a common difficulty with the overstrained hose, but before it could be replaced the fire crossed the street and moved into the next block.

CANADIAN-BORN ROBERT A. WILLIAMS, THE CHICAGO FIRE MARSHAL, HAD DIRECTED A FIGHT AGAINST A FIRE ON THE WEST SIDE ON SATURDAY NIGHT. AND YET HE FOUGHT THE GREAT FIRE AS FIERCELY AFTER HE KNEW THE BATTLE WAS HOPELESS AS HE HAD WHEN IT WAS A SEEMINGLY CONTROLLABLE BLAZE. WILLIAMS, WHO WAS 45 IN 1871, JOINED THE FIRE DEPARTMENT IN 1848. (CHICAGO HISTORICAL SOCIETY)

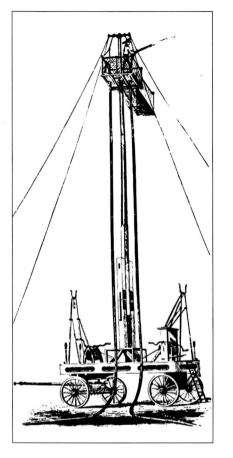

A HOSE ELEVATOR, MODERN VERSIONS OF WHICH ARE STILL IN USE, PERMITTED WATER TO BE THROWN FROM VARIOUS HEIGHTS AND WAS INVALUABLE IN RESCUE EFFORTS. (CHICAGO MUNICIPAL REFERENCE LIBRARY)

Williams and his assistant deployed their forces around the fire, with particular attention to the area into which the wind was blowing it. The strategy employed was fairly simple: Gather whatever engines were available, surround the fire, and pour water on the entire area—burned, burning, or threatened—for all the pumps were worth. Occasionally the hook-and-ladder companies and other firemen were directed to tear down fences, shacks, and doomed houses to keep them from feeding the flames.

The *Chicago*, while fitting new hose, suddenly found itself in great danger. Because hose was in short supply, and because pump pressure was limited, it was necessary to place the engines very close to the line of battle. As a result, they sometimes ran the risk of being ignited themselves. The *Chicago* was threatened when a building collapsed and sent flames shooting into the street. The crew were forced to flee for their lives, and it looked as if the engine would be lost. Fortunately a brief lull followed this first onslaught, and the men pulled their machine out of danger by hand. They continued to move it north and east to the river, near Adams Street, where it poured water on the giant National Elevator. This building was somehow saved, but for a time it seemed that the firemen would be forced into the river to escape the heat.

Citizen volunteers saw a threat to a line of passenger cars on the Pittsburgh, Fort Wayne, and Chicago tracks. Despite fierce heat they tore down an express company shed and saved several railway buildings and much of the rolling stock—the latter simply by moving it down the tracks and out of harm's way. The professional department was so undermanned, and had been in existence for so few years, that volunteer help was still expected to give a hand at big fires.

There was no dearth of prospective volunteers in the neighborhood, although few of them were of much help. Fires, big or small, were considered tops in entertainment, especially since most of the spectators did not have to pay the costs of production. A crowd quickly gathered, clogging up the streets and getting in the way.

The crimson glare against the sky drew thousands of onlookers. Many of them thronged down Clinton Street, halting half a dozen horse cars in their tracks near Adams Street. Jackson, Quincy, and Adams Streets were soon filled with sightseers, and the police finally had to block off Adams Street Bridge, not only because the mob was unmanageable, but also because the bridge was in grave danger of catching fire. The steamer *Titsworth* galloped across the span just as flames were breaking out. The horses' hair and the firemen's whiskers were singed, but the engine took up a position next to the bridge and halted the advance of the blaze in that sector.

Some of the South Side spectators left for their homes about midnight, a late hour for Chicagoans of that day, only to be confronted by a wave of new arrivals at Madison Street Bridge. The approaches to the bridge were out of the way of falling cinders, and became a favorite vantage point.

The rigging of ships in the river stood out in bold relief on the skyline. Sailors clung to the masts and crossyards, and every nearby rooftop was alive with spectators. The police tried without success to push back the crowds. Deputy Commissioner Sherman kept urging his men, "If they don't keep back, lock 'em up!"

The threat was totally ineffectual. Such

a mass arrest would have filled every jail in town, with prisoners left over.

Both volunteers and bystanders were in danger. The roof of a shed at Clinton and Jackson Streets collapsed under the weight of about a hundred and fifty spectators, and several of them were hurt in the fall. Others suffered minor injuries when a raised sidewalk gave way. Seven or eight men, fighting the blaze in a lumberyard near the river, appeared trapped between the flames and the water. They finally escaped by throwing planks into the river, leaping in after them, and paddling to safety on the east bank.

Residents in the area threatened by the fire followed their usual custom. They simply carried their household goods outdoors, stacked them haphazardly in the street, and went off to watch the fire. This stratagem, which sometimes saved their property, more often provided an excellent bridge for the flames from one side of the street to the other. Much of the salvage which lined the west side of Clinton Street, between Jackson and Adams, was destroyed as the fire swept over it to the east.

Lumber and coal piles beyond Clinton were soon alight, and frame dwellings on Jackson, as well as sheds, carpenter shops, and more woodpiles behind them, yielded quickly. In a wild twenty minutes, the area between Jackson, Adams, Clinton, and the river was covered with leaping flames. It was by far the largest fire that had ever ravaged Chicago.

Despite all the noise and excitement, the fire caught some persons unawares. A lone sleeper in a Jackson Street boardinghouse was roused by smoke to find the building on fire. Everyone else had moved out a day or so before, when the landlord's lease expired. The building's last tenant was evicted on the run, hatless, shoeless, with hair and beard scorched by the heat.

An old woman was seriously burned in another building nearby. She owed her life to a printer, Robert Campsie, who was also injured in the rescue. Firemen saved a small child, crying in terror in a blazing house, and a Clinton Street resident, George Goddard, was badly hurt in a fall from a roof, as he tried in vain to help a man trapped on top of a two-story building.

The saloon of Daniel Quirk was on the northwest corner of Adams and Canal, directly in the path of the flames when they threatened to cross Adams Street. Quirk was certain that the frame saloon would go. He faced the situation with nonchalance and generosity, setting up free drinks and handing out cigars to all his patrons. His guests were so appreciative that they went out and found some portable extinguishers, turning them on the walls when they began to smoke. Not only was the building saved; the fire was thus prevented from getting a foothold in the block.

By this time, every engine in working order was at the scene. The firemen fought with desperation, since the cordon of equipment surrounding the blaze was stretched to the breaking point. The engines fell back only when they were already actually bypassed and surrounded by the onrushing flames.

Dozens of hoses curled across the streets like fat snakes. Spectators sought shelter from the blistering heat, but the pipemen, like human salamanders, remained within twenty feet or so of the flames for several minutes at a time before dropping back for momentary relief.

At about 12:20 Sunday morning the

The fire smoldered all day Sunday, principally in the coal and lumberyards. The department was in no condition for an immediate return engagement. The men were exhausted to the point of collapse. Some had suffered slight burns, and many could barely see through eyes that were red and swollen from smoke and stung by cinders. Since in those days fires had to be fought at close range, the firemen were subjected to terrible physical suffering from smoke and heat.

Williams went home for breakfast during the early morning, leaving Benner in charge. Little remained to be done, except to clean up small lingering fires in the burned-out area.

With the daylight, too, John Develin, a sixty-three-year-old commission merchant, was able to reach what remained of his home on Jackson Street. He had been prevented from doing so earlier by the fierceness of the fire, and spent much of the night searching for his wife, who had been home alone with a badly swollen ankle.

Aided by some friends, he found Mrs. Develin at last in the ruins of their house, a "mere handful of burned bones."

Next day, in its story on the fire, the *Tribune* made, unwittingly, an ominous prophecy.

"For days past alarm has followed alarm, but the comparatively trifling losses have familiarized us to the pealing of the Courthouse bell, and we had forgotten that the absence of rain for three weeks had left everything in so dry and inflammable a condition that a spark might set a fire which would sweep from end to end of the city."

wooden portions of the Adams Street viaduct, over the railroad tracks, caught fire. Before the flames were smothered the wood burned away and the iron work in the lower part of the structure bent and twisted. But the fire was stopped from getting a fresh start above Adams Street.

By 3:30 A.M. the fire was under control. It was a costly victory. Four blocks were burned over almost completely. All that escaped were a few worthless houses and the National Elevator—which stood in the northeast corner of the ruined section. Nor did the fire department's equipment go unscathed. The steamer *William James* was heavily damaged on Canal Street, and the *Clybourne*'s hose cart was lost when an old firehouse was swept away.

CHAPTER 3

She occupied a little frame shanty on De Koven Street in the Bohemian quarter of the city. Her place was not indicated by a street number. Mrs. O'Leary knew she lived there, and nobody else cared.

—NEW CHICAGO

Even if it were an absurd rumor, forty miles wide of the truth, it would be useless to attempt to alter "the verdict of history." Mrs. O'Leary has made a sworn statement in refutation of the charge, and it is backed by other affidavits; but to little purpose. She is in for it and no mistake. Fame has seized her and appropriated her, name, barn, cows and all. She has won, in spite of herself, what the Ephesian youth panted for.

—CHICAGO EVENING JOURNAL

SUNDAY, OCTOBER 8, was unusually warm for October, and the West Side was enjoying a peaceful evening in contrast to the excitement of the night before. A few embers still flickered in the darkness, but most of the thousands of spectators who had come to visit the scene of the holocaust during the day had returned to their homes or were attending church services. Throughout the day, and into the evening, the city was refreshed by strong, though fitful, breezes.

The area for several blocks south of the industrial district destroyed Saturday night was occupied chiefly by hardworking Irish and Bohemian families of what now would be called the lower middle class. The streets were lined with modest frame dwellings, one or two stories high, with sheds or barns nearby, usually along alleys running parallel to the streets and halfway between them. No house in the entire section was without a plentiful supply of shavings from the numerous lumberyards and mills in the neighborhood, the ideal kindling for the woodstoves found in every kitchen. They were stored in the barns and sheds, or even stowed in open spaces under the raised foundations of the houses.

An obscure Irish family lived in a tiny shingled cottage at 137 De Koven Street. The head of the household was Patrick O'Leary, a laborer, who had bought the property for five hundred dollars in 1864.

In most respects the O'Learys lived very much like their neighbors, which is to say inconspicuously. Their property was a narrow strip in the middle of the block. It was 25 feet wide by 100 feet deep, and ran north from De Koven Street to an alley halfway between De Koven and Taylor. The O'Leary cottage did not even face upon the street, but lay directly behind another small shingled house, which Mr. O'Leary rented to Patrick McLaughlin, a railroad worker. The barn for Mrs. O'Leary's cows was at the other end of the lot, next to the alley.

Catherine O'Leary, a plump woman about thirty-five, kept five cows, a calf, and a horse. She ran a milk route in the neighborhood. Added to Pat's wages and the rent from the second cottage, the income from the milk made the O'Learys figures of downright affluence by the standards of the neighborhood. The animals were fed hay and grain stored in the barn. They were probably pastured elsewhere, since it is likely that whatever was in the O'Leary yard wasn't grass.

Around eight o'clock Sunday night Daniel Sullivan, a drayman, whose nickname was Pegleg for an evident reason, crossed the dirt street from his house to O'Leary's. He found the whole family in bed, except for the youngest and oldest of the children, whom the recumbent O'Leary ordered to retire. Sullivan took the hint and left after a short visit but, instead of going directly home, sat for a while on the wooden sidewalk across the street, leaning back against a high wooden fence. The night was warm and the wind seemed to have slackened somewhat.

Another neighbor, Dennis Rogan, also reported that the O'Learys were in bed about the same time. He dropped in on them about 8:30. When he asked Mrs. O'Leary why she had gone to bed so early, he was told she had a sore foot. Rogan also stayed only a short time, since Mrs. O'Leary had to be up to milk her cows at five, and O'Leary had to start work early. As Rogan left, he heard music coming from the McLaughlins', but did not stop to join the festivities. He was in bed by nine.

The McLaughlins were having a party in honor of Mrs. McLaughlin's brother, newly arrived from Ireland. They made up a party of nine. McLaughlin, an accomplished fiddler, had gone to bed early because he felt unwell, but got up again about 8:30 at the insistence of his wife. He played two tunes, while the Irish newcomer danced a polka with one of the women and a bout with the other.

The McLaughlins had gone out for supper. They served no refreshments at their own party, although one of the group went out for beer a couple of times during the evening. Frank Shults's saloon was at De Koven and Jefferson, half a block away.

Sullivan, meanwhile, sat against the fence in front of Thomas White's house, just east of his own, enjoying the night. The sound of the merrymaking at McLaughlin's came drifting to his ears.

After a few minutes the lonesome drayman decided to go home to bed. Then he saw a sudden spear of flame thrust through the side of O'Leary's barn.

Sullivan's reaction was swift and to the point.

He shouted, "FIRE! FIRE! FIRE!" at the top of his voice and ran clumsily across the uneven street. He scrambled up the embankment to the opposite sidewalk, went through the gate and along the areaway between O'Leary's and the Dalton cottage to the east. No lamp shone in O'Leary's house and Sullivan, his way lighted by the flames, moved directly toward the barn.

He was familiar with the layout of the stable. His mother kept a cow, and he often

THIS VERSION OF THE POPULAR BELIEF ABOUT MRS. O'LEARY SHOWS A SHATTERED LANTERN BEFORE THE BLAZE SPREAD. (ANDREAS)

THIS BROKEN KEROSENE LANTERN WAS SUPPOSEDLY FOUND IN MRS. O'LEARY'S BARN. EVEN IF IT DID EXIST, THE LANTERN DOES NOT PROVE ANYTHING. (ANDREAS)

bought feed for it from Mrs. O'Leary, taking it out of the barrels just inside the door. The loft held three tons of timothy hay, delivered only a few hours before. Two tons of coal and some kindling wood and shavings were in an attached shed at the southwest corner.

There were two doors. The one facing the yard was nailed back so it could not be shut. The back door was in two sections, the lower part fastened by a small catch. A new wagon, owned by the O'Learys, stood in the alley near the barn, and one of the five O'Leary cows was tied nearby.

The barn was burning briskly by the time Sullivan reached it, but he went through the south door and hurriedly loosened the ropes of two of the cows tethered against the west wall. He thought they would escape by themselves, but they stood unmoving. A horse and another cow were tied against the east wall, near the alley door, but Sullivan had no time to waste on them. He found the barn was growing fearfully hot, and bursting into flames behind him. He started in haste toward the alley door, feeling his way along the wall. Then his wooden leg slipped on the wet board floor, and he went down with a jarring thud.

The crippled man was in grave danger, but avoided panic. He scrambled up quickly and hobbled once more toward the alley door. Just before he reached it a half-grown calf, bellowing in pain and fright, lurched into him. The hair on its back was burning and a rope dangled from its neck. Sullivan grabbed the rope and tugged the calf out into the alley, their shadows dancing grotesquely before them. It was a close thing. The O'Leary house, about forty feet from the barn, was already beginning to smolder.

The neighborhood came suddenly awake. But the O'Learys slumbered on. Someone yelled to Dennis Rogan, already in bed, that the O'Leary barn was burning. Dennis leaped up and ran outdoors, darting into the alley behind O'Leary's in an effort to save their new wagon, but was beaten back by the heat.

He then ran to O'Leary's house and pushed open the door, screaming for O'Leary. That worthy came sleepily into the yard, "scratching his head as if there was a foot of lice in it." When he saw the flames he went hastily back.

"Kate!" he cried. "The barn is afire!"

Mrs. O'Leary emerged and began clapping her hands in anguish. Dalton's shed to the east and Murray's barn to the west were just catching fire. Four-year-old Mary O'Leary took her infant brother, James, from the house and handed him to a neighbor. The other O'Leary youngsters were hurried into the street. O'Leary, aided by six or seven neighbors and a delegation from the McLaughlin party, began pouring water on his little house.

Mrs. O'Leary, ignoring her sore foot, ran to the alley to try to save the new wagon, but could not get close to it. The cow which had been outside the barn had disappeared, probably set free by one of the neighbors. The O'Learys never saw it again. O'Leary later searched for it, but said he could not find it "anywhere in the world."

Later, in view of the developments, it became very important to many people to ascertain how the fire began. Perhaps the most popular theory was that an angry cow, disturbed several hours past milking time, kicked over a kerosene lamp and set the barn ablaze. There are several versions of this explanation.

In one version Mrs. O'Leary herself is supposed to have gone to the barn. Either she needed milk for a belated customer, or one of the cows was ill and she had gone out to care for it. In another version someone from the party at McLaughlin's sneaked into the barn without Mrs. O'Leary's knowledge, when it was decided to augment the beverage supply with some milk punch.

It might be assumed that Mrs. O'Leary *did* get out of bed and go to the barn, and that Sullivan, sitting across the street, failed to see the lamp that supposedly set off the blaze. It is necessary to conclude that—having set the barn afire, and menacing the animals which afforded a good share of the family's livelihood—the sturdy Irishwoman then ran quickly and quietly back into the house with no attempt to arouse the neighborhood, rescue the animals, or put out the fire. She had nothing to gain, either, since the property was uninsured.

The milk punch suggestion seems easier to defend, except that again Sullivan would undoubtedly have seen or heard anyone leaving the house. If someone from the front cottage did get out without being seen (since he might have been anxious not to have Mrs. O'Leary know her cow was being milked), it is unlikely that he would have watched the barn catch fire and done nothing to try to save at least the valuable livestock. The McLaughlins also claimed they had no whisky at the party, but only a couple of "growlers" of beer from Shults's saloon.

And who ever heard of an Irishman's using milk punch as a chaser for beer?

But Mrs. O'Leary's cow was quickly blamed in newspapers across the land, and some accounts even quoted her as bemoaning her losses, and ascribing them to the animal. In view of the quality of reporting in 1871, the fact that something appeared in print was no guarantee of its accuracy. The same papers also accused Mrs. O'Leary—almost point-blank—of having started the fire in revenge for having been taken off relief (although she seems never to have been on). They also ran *eyewitness* accounts of mass lynchings of incendiaries after the fire, asserted solemnly that 2,500 babies were born and died within two days after the fire, and warned of a mass invasion of the city by the out-of-town safecrackers, even mentioning a couple by name. The reporting in contemporary newspapers may be charged with a tendency to exaggerate.

The fire-origin theories didn't end there. There were dozens more, among them a number of "confessions" by persons admitting that they alone had started it.

ONE OF THE BUILDINGS STILL STANDING IN THE AREA WHERE THE FIRE BEGAN WAS THE O'LEARY COTTAGE. ITS SURVIVAL ANNOYED NEIGHBORS WHO LOST THEIR HOMES. (R.R. DONNELLEY & SONS CO.)

Some rumors had it that three men trying out a new terrier were after the rats in the O'Leary barn when someone dropped a lighted match; that a group of young men playing cards wanted milk for an oyster stew (October has an "R" in it) and the cow kicked over *their* lantern; that crackpots inspired by the "miserable harangues" of George Francis Train set the fire; or that the hay in the loft, although dry and delivered shortly before, ignited the barn by spontaneous combustion.

It was charged subsequently that Mrs. O'Leary was afraid to admit responsibility for the fire, because of the immense damage it had caused. But since there was no way of telling that this blaze was to be of any more consequence than the others which broke out daily throughout the city, there would have been no reason whatever for her to conceal its cause. She would have done what any other householder in the city would have done—run screaming for help.

This much is beyond dispute—the fire started in Mrs. O'Leary's cow barn on De Koven Street, and went on from there.

As for the cause, no one knows for sure. It is likely that no one ever will.

The rear of the O'Leary cottage caught fire several times during the next few hours, but each time the O'Learys managed to put it out before serious damage was done. Their next-door neighbors, the family of James Dalton, were not so lucky.

The Dalton lot was exactly like O'Leary's, lying beside it to the east. There was a shed, used as a summer kitchen, next to the O'Leary barn. An eight-foot wooden fence, possibly designed to keep the cows in their place, divided the two yards. The only difference between the properties was that the Dalton house was set back from the street

several feet farther than the O'Learys'; Dalton intended to add on to the front of it.

Mrs. Mary O'Rorke, Mrs. Dalton's mother, glanced from her room to see fire reflected on windows next door. She called in alarm, and the Daltons ran to the back of their house and peered out. The O'Leary barn was burning furiously. The fence between the yards soon caught, then the Dalton's summer kitchen, then the house. Mrs. O'Rorke barely managed to escape before the walls came tumbling in.

The Daltons had the dubious honor of being the first to be made homeless by the fire.

William Lee, who lived a couple of doors east at 133 De Koven, had wanted to accompany his brother-in-law and wife to their South Side home. The brother-in-law had a badly sprained ankle. But after reaching their wagon, he murmured an excuse and went back into his house, impelled by some elusive foreboding.

Their baby, a seventeen-month-old boy, began crying. Lee went into the bedroom to comfort the child. When he raised the window to fasten the blinds, he saw fire coming from the roof of the O'Leary barn. He shouted to his wife to take care of the baby, and ran to Bruno Goll's drugstore at Canal and Twelfth Street, about three blocks south. The fire was now about ten minutes old.

Lee was doing what apparently few in the neighborhood even thought of: he was turning in an alarm. Meanwhile, however, at least two local companies had spotted the growing blaze, and were on their way before any official warning was sent.

John Dorsey, foreman of the *America* hose cart, was standing in front of company quarters at 31 Blue Island Avenue, southwest of De Koven, about 9:15. William Fraser, a young baker, stopped to chat. Dorsey, who had been working most of the day on the fire of the night before, excused himself to go upstairs and change his boots. When he returned Fraser was staring toward the southeast.

"Dorsey," he asked, pointing toward the river, "what is that?"

"That is fire, by George!" Dorsey replied.

The foreman ran into the station to give the alarm. He hitched up the horses with the help of Fraser and Dave Manwell, the hoseman. Box 342, signifying a blaze some distance to the south, sounded before the *America* was a block from the station. Dorsey himself did not hear it, although others of the crew did. The *America* met Charley Anderson, the thirty-seven-year-old driver, at the corner of Harrison and Halsted Streets. He got on the hose cart and the volunteer, Fraser, on the reel. The *America* went at a gallop up Halsted to Polk, thence to Canal and down Taylor Street. It took a plug at the corner of Taylor and Clinton Streets, northeast, and directly in the path of the fire.

The *America* was the first piece of equipment at the scene, but the small stream of its unaided hose could not accomplish very much.

The *Little Giant* engine company, whose station was on Maxwell Street between Jefferson and Clinton, about six blocks south of O'Leary's place, also got a start on the official alarm. It was alerted by Joseph Lagger, the stoker, who spotted the flames from the lookout tower. Lagger shouted to Foreman William H. Musham, who roused the rest of the men. All were in bed except one, Michael Dolan, who was at

supper. The *Little Giant* was pulling into the street behind its four horses when the 342 alarm began sounding.

The men of the *Giant* were not fooled by the misleading alarm. They drove the engine directly to De Koven and Jefferson, took a plug at the southwest corner, and carried their hose between the houses on De Koven toward the blazing alley. The fire already had made considerable headway. Five or six barns and houses were burning. The wind was high and seemed to Foreman Musham to be increasing. The *Giant* began work two men short, since Dolan was absent and Pipeman Frank Howard had been on the sick list for a month. Dolan rushed up from dinner a few minutes later. The *Little Giant* was the first steamer at the fire.

Marshal Williams had spent a good part of the day sleeping off the ordeal of the ear-

lier fire. During the afternoon he had supervised the mopping-up operation on the remaining embers, and early that evening he had gone to another fire in the South Side, which was quickly put out. He then told the driver of his wagon to take him home.

The wind was rising. He had to tug down his uniform cap two or three times to keep it from blowing away. "We are going to have a burn," he told his driver. "I can feel it in my bones." His uneasiness remained strong when he got home. He told his wife: "I am going to bed early. I feel as though I have got to be out between this and morning, the way the wind is blowing."

He laid out his working clothes, so he could pull them on in a hurry. Mrs. Williams stayed up in the next room to read.

"I wish you would go to bed," he said somewhat irritably, "or close the door so I can get some sleep."

She shut the door between the sitting room and the bedroom. Williams fell at once into a sleep that was to be all too brief.

I run into the tower and whistled to the operator and told him to strike Box 342. This was my judgment.

—MATHIAS SCHAFER, INQUIRY STATEMENT

WILLIAM LEE, the O'Learys' neighbor, rushed into Goll's drugstore, and gasped out a request for the key to the alarm box. The new boxes were attached to walls of stores or other convenient locations. To prevent false alarms and crank calls, the boxes were locked, and the keys given to trustworthy citizens nearby.

What happened when Lee made his request is not clear. Only one fact emerges from the confusion: No alarm was registered from any box in the vicinity of the fire until it was too late to do any good.

According to Lee's account, Goll refused to give him the key, assuring him that an engine had already gone past. According to Lee, when he went home, it was just nine o'clock, before any of the firemen arrived. He was forced to evacuate his house. His wife, carrying the baby in its cradle, took refuge in a vacant lot near Sullivan's house, a block west. With them was the singed and disconsolate calf Sullivan had rescued from the O'Leary barn. The orphaned animal hovered close to them for comfort throughout the night.

Goll's account of what occurred in the drugstore is quite different from Lee's. He later declared that when a man in shirt sleeves ran in at about 9:05 reporting a fire, he himself turned in an alarm. Ten minutes later a second man came in and reported the fire was spreading, and Goll, according to himself, turned in the alarm again, although he assured the man that the firemen were on the way. At 9:30 Goll himself went to watch the fire.

What happened in the drugstore is perhaps immaterial. Whether or not alarms were sent, no alarm at all was recorded at the central alarm office until 9:40.

Furthermore, a tragedy of errors was taking place at the courthouse which dwarfed any previous mistakes into insignificance.

William J. Brown, the young fire-alarm operator in the courthouse, had sent a note to his sister Sarah that Sunday afternoon saying he would like her to bring him some supper, since he had to work late.

When evening came, sixteen-year-old Sarah and a friend, Martha Daily, brought food from the Blenis House at Randolph and Canal Street, where the Browns lived. The girls waited while Brown ate, and later lingered as he played his guitar.

About nine o'clock Sarah, peering from

the window, saw a glare in the southwest. She pointed it out to her brother. He blithely dismissed it as simply the reflection of embers from the Saturday night fire.

Meanwhile, on the cupola overhead, Mathias Schafer, the forty-year-old watchman, whose duty it was to scan the city for fires and order the proper alarm sent out to the station whenever he saw flames, whiled away the time chatting with a couple of visitors. They called his attention to what they thought was a blaze, but Schafer, knowing the area and having been fooled before, assured them it was the glow of the West Side Gas Works.

The visitors walked around to the east door and began asking questions about the big four-faced clock, installed a few months before as a gift from the Astronomical Society. Schafer answered as best he could, meanwhile lighting his pipe inside to escape the wind. When he had it going well, he

stepped out and scrutinized the streets stretching toward the Lake. Nothing was amiss.

Then he turned to the southwest and saw flames leaping against the darkness.

Schafer studied the blaze for a moment, concentrating to determine the location. Then he went inside the tower and whistled down the speaking tube. When Brown answered he told him to strike Box 342. This was at Canalport and Halsted, a mile or so southwest of the O'Leary cow barn.

Brown quickly obliged. This alarm—342—was the one heard by the crews of the *Little Giant* and the *America*. Fortunately they knew where the fire was from their own observations, and were not misled by the erroneous alarm. The watchman's mistake was nevertheless a major one, since other engines in the O'Leary district remained at home when the wrong signal was sent.

Schafer went out again, after speaking with Brown, and looked at the fire more closely with his spyglass. He decided it was nearer to Box 319, at Johnson and Twelfth. This was still some seven blocks from the point of origin of the fire, but close enough to summon the right equipment to the scene.

Schafer's original mistake, serious though it was, can be explained and even condoned. The O'Leary blaze was almost directly beyond the still-flickering coal piles set aflame by the Saturday night fire, when viewed from the courthouse tower. There also were tall buildings intervening to block the view and make an accurate estimate of distance almost impossible. The night was dark, since the moon was not scheduled to appear for several hours, and the atmosphere was both smoky and hazy.

Under these difficult circumstances, Schafer's first guess—that the fire was near Box 342, almost a mile from the O'Leary barn, but virtually in a direct line from the courthouse—wasn't a bad one. Furthermore, he recognized his own error and tried to remedy it as quickly as possible. His second estimate was fairly accurate.

He whistled for Brown once more and told him to strike Box 319. The younger man refused, explaining that since 342 was on the proper line he was afraid striking 319 would only lead to confusion! In consequence two powerful engines, the *R. A. Williams,* which could throw 700 gallons per minute, and the *J. B. Rice,* which could pump 900 gallons, did not respond to the first alarm, although the O'Leary barn was in their district.

The *Williams,* the department's newest steamer, was kept on West Lake Street near Clinton. It was about to pull out on a "still" alarm, one not reported through the regular warning system, when Box 342 came in. Since this designated an area outside their regular first-alarm range, the *Williams'*s men unhitched the horses.

The stubbornness of the youthful Brown—who was to declare pompously in a letter less than a month later: "I am still standing the watch that burned Chicago"— has no such defense as Schafer's error of perspective. His reason for not changing the signal at Schafer's request was arbitrary and foolish, since he must have known that Schafer's second estimate of the location was almost certain to be closer. His stubbornness also meant that equipment which should have been on the scene quickly failed to come for many minutes.

Brown sounded the first alarm around 9:30, and not long afterward Boxes 293,

295, and 296—the last the one at Goll's drugstore—were pulled and recorded at the courthouse in rapid succession. But Brown received no signal for a second alarm, a signal known only to department marshals and foremen. Some time before ten o'clock (Brown estimated it at about ten minutes after he sent the first alarm), he struck a second on his own initiative.

It was 342.

Reinforcements began coming in shortly after Brown sent out the first of his ill-judged signals. The first of these was the *Chicago,* a powerful steamer which had its house on Jefferson Street near Van Buren, about nine blocks north of the fire. If an accurate alarm had been sent in, it would probably have been one of the first pieces of apparatus on the scene. But a confusion in direction cost the steamer's crew several precious minutes.

The *Chicago* company was alerted by someone who poked his head into the doorway of its quarters on Jefferson Street near Van Buren and shouted the alarm. The watchman, Ira Mix, let the horses out, and sounded the bell to awaken the sleeping men. The heavy-eyed firemen came down at once. The alarm bringer cried that the whole corner was afire, but in his excitement pointed north instead of south. Before the two-horse team was hitched the gong sounded for 342, which indicated a blaze in the opposite direction.

The driver asked Foreman Chris Schimmels which fire to head for, and the twenty-seven-year-old ex-carpenter told him to go to the first one reported. The *Chicago* ran a block north, to the location indicated by the shouter, and found everything serene. Without stopping, the driver wheeled the galloping team around the

block to Van Buren, went west on that
street to Des Plaines and directly down
to the plug at Forquer and Jefferson. Its
hose led south to Taylor, then east to the
fire. Two or three buildings on Taylor, a
block north of De Koven, already were in
flames.

Benner, the assistant marshal in charge
of the West Side, was at his home on
Randolph when the alarm sounded for Box
342. He hurried to the corner of Randolph
and Jefferson, where his driver picked him
up. Benner observed that there must be a
mistake in the box number. They went at
once to Jefferson and Taylor.

Benner found the *Chicago*'s hose leading
east on Taylor and the *Economy*'s stretched
down the alley from Jefferson toward the
O'Leary barn. Benner ordered the *Economy*
to go north of the fire. At this time three
houses east of O'Leary's place were burning
on De Koven Street, as well as a large

brown house immediately to the west and
several barns along the alley.

Marshal Williams was deep in slumber
at his Randolph Street apartment in the
South Division when the O'Leary barn
ignited. His wife also had retired. The
alarm sent out by Brown registered on
instruments in the bedroom. The exhausted
marshal awoke at once, as he always did, but
not in time to avoid being jabbed sharply in
the ribs by a wifely elbow.

"Robert!" his mate said. "FIRE!"

Williams was in his clothes even before
the gong stopped striking. He pounded
downstairs and into the street, glancing at
the brightness in the southwest. Because of
the distance he decided there was no use
running, and forced himself to wait. A
moment later his wagon came along and he
hopped aboard.

The wagon rumbled across Randolph
Street Bridge from the South Division to

the West and had turned down Des Plaines before Williams, busy pulling on his belted rubber coat, noticed they were taking a roundabout route. They finally reached Taylor and Jefferson after going west to Halsted.

Williams leaped down, ran past the pipemen of the *Chicago* at the corner, and followed the *America*'s hose into a vacant lot on Taylor. The rear of buildings facing that street were on fire, as well as two barns, several outhouses, and a stretch of wooden fence. Since its arrival, the valiant crew of the little hose cart had fought a losing battle against the flames advancing with the wind through the middle of the block. The blaze had struck out north from the O'Leary barn, and spread east and west along a broad front on the south side of Taylor. Williams exhorted the two men handling the *America*'s pipe:

"Hold on to her, boys!"

He then ran east to Clinton Street to see if more equipment had arrived from that direction. He found nothing except the *America*, attached to the plug at the corner. The fire grew fiercer. Williams ran back to the pipemen in the vacant lot.

"Hang on to her, boys!" he cried. "She is gaining on us!"

At this point another engine appeared to reinforce the defenders along Taylor Street. It was the steamer *Illinois*, whose house was many blocks to the southwest, on 22d Street. The watchman had seen the fire and had called Foreman Mullen to look. The foreman had decided it was out of their district. Just then Box 342 sound-ed—one of theirs—so they hitched up and galloped off. At the corner of Halsted and Canalport, where the box was, a crowd directed them north. The engine ended up at a plug at Des Plaines and Taylor, and the hose was extended toward the flames at Jefferson.

Williams ran up impatiently from the center of Taylor, where the pipemen of the *America* were increasingly hard-pressed.

"Where is your water, Bill?" Williams shouted.

"It is coming, sir, coming," Mullen responded. He ran back down Taylor as fast as he could, but before he reached the engine the water came on. The *Illinois* was short-handed and Williams helped drag the hose in from Taylor far enough so that water could be thrown against the back of a building facing south on De Koven.

"Now," Williams said, "hang on to her here!"

The intense heat washed over the pipemen in unending waves, and Mullen protested:

"Marshal, I don't believe we can stand it here!"

"Stand it as long as you can," Williams cried, running out to Taylor again. He saw the houses on the north side of the street sending out warning plumes of smoke, and raced once more to the *America*'s pipe, where he told Driver Anderson:

"Turn in a second alarm! This is going to spread!"

Anderson protested that he didn't know the correct signal, and Williams instructed Foreman Dorsey to go instead. Dorsey ran for Box 296, at Goll's drugstore, opened the cottage-shaped box, and pulled down the hook with his thumb. He thought it was a first alarm, however, and failed to give the signal which would have made it a second. Dorsey testified later that he had not heard the alarm for Box 342 strike.

Anderson, meanwhile, left alone to

uncomfortably close to the flames, was an important link in a line of defense across the forward path of the fire along Taylor Street. Even then, no serious danger would have arisen, if it had not been for another of the many unhappy coincidences that seemed to conspire against the firefighters. For just at the moment when the *America's* hose went dry, another link in the chain of defense parted.

While the the hose from the *Illinois* had been wetting down the north side of Taylor, the *Chicago's* hose was attacking the flames in a row of two-story houses on the south side of the street, near the Jefferson corner. The streams from the *Chicago's* powerful pump easily reached the windows in the upper story. Then quite suddenly the water dwindled, until only a trickle poured from the nozzle. David Kenyon, the second pipeman, started back for the engine and met Schimmels on the way. The two found the engineer, Henry Coleman, starting to "pull!" the fuel from the firebox of the engine. Schimmels asked what the trouble was. Coleman replied there seemed to be something broken in the pump.

"Is there any danger of running the engine?" Schimmels demanded. "I do not know," answered Coleman. "I might run the engine and smash her all to pieces!"

"Smash her!" snapped Schimmels angrily. "Break her completely and then it is broke!"

Schimmels's grammar may have been faulty, but his meaning was clear. Coleman hit the balky pump a sharp blow with a hammer and started the engine. This un-scientific treatment was apparently effective. The engine gave no further difficulty. But other problems remained. The fuel

handle the pipe, was having a hard time of it until a friend, Charles McConers, came by and offered aid.

"Charley?" McConers observed, in what may have been the understatement of the night, "this is hot!"

"It is, Mac," agreed Anderson.

McConers left, but came back quickly carrying a wooden door, which he placed as a shield between Anderson and the flames. "I have it now," Anderson thought in sudden relief. "I can stand it a considerable time."

But McConers found the heat unbear-able. In less than a minute, or so it seemed to Anderson, he dropped the door, which now was ablaze. Anderson's clothes began to smoke, and his leather hat twisted on his head from the searing heat.

Then Williams returned.

"Charley," he told Anderson, "come out as fast as possible. Wet the other side of the street or it will burn!"

The marshal impressed some onlookers into helping with the hose, but before they pulled it out onto Taylor the water stopped.

The steamer *Waubansia* had come in from the south side and usurped the *America's* plug, a routine action when an engine whose steam-driven pump could throw a powerful stream had no water source handy except one already being used by a hose cart. The cart, of course, had no way of building up pressure and could send the water only as far as the force in the mains would permit. Hose carts were only an auxiliary to the steamers, and were used only when the latter were not available.

In this instance, the *America's* hose, while very low in power and therefore requiring its unfortunate handlers to stand

was almost gone. The crew was short of hose, and one of the sections had burst. Blankets were tied around the breaks, and held in place with heavy planks. These proved useless. The leaks were so bad that no pressure could be maintained in the hose. More precious minutes were wasted. Schimmels asked spectators for help, and they began chopping up fences and sidewalks for fuel. Finally some hose was delivered from the cart of a steamer laid up for repairs. Meanwhile the driver was sent back to the station for coal. This was no simple errand. The coal was in the basement. It had to be thrown into the street, then into a wagon.

While Williams dashed off to find out why the *America's* steam had quit, and while Schimmels and his crew were desperately trying to get the *Chicago* back into operation, the fire crossed Taylor Street. Four or five houses on the north side burst into flames. The hose of the *America* was attached to an outlet on the *Waubansia*, and steam was raised in the *Chicago*, but in an alarmingly short space of time the center of the block between Clinton and Jefferson was ablaze.

Anderson, left to broil at the end of the *America's* hose, finally emerged from the furnace he had been working in. He kept on going. A score of buildings on the north side of Taylor were ablaze, and he could stand no more. He abandoned the *America* to anyone who cared to try to use its weak stream, and spent the rest of those nightmare hours with other companies.

Up to this time, the situation had been precarious but not desperate. The fire had spread rapidly, but was mostly confined to the O'Leary block, and much of that block had not yet caught. There were at least five steamers, three hose carts, and a hook-and-ladder company at the scene.

This equipment was drawn up in a thin cordon surrounding the fire. To the southwest, the *Little Giant*, connected to the hydrant at De Koven and Jefferson, had its hose running toward the alley sheds and barns ignited by the O'Leary fire. The *Chicago* and the *Illinois* were north and a bit farther west, with their hoses running into Taylor Street. The *Waubansia* had replaced the *America* at Clinton and Taylor, the northeast boundary of the fire area. To complete the circle, the *Economy* was at a plug at Clinton and Bunker Streets, a block southeast of the fire, with its hose extended into the east end of the alley.

In addition, auxiliary units appeared to augment the efforts of the steamers. Besides the *America*, the *Tempest* and *Washington* hose carts were busy in the area, supplying hose to the steamers and helping to man the machines and pipes. Also the crew of the hook and ladder *Protection*, an early arrival, was attempting to create a firebreak by tearing down fences and sheds along the west end of the alley, near Jefferson Street. Williams and Benner were on the scene directing and coordinating the battle; and the two other assistant marshals, John Schank from the South Division and Lorens Walter from the North, quickly arrived to help out. Finally, more engines and men were on their way to the fire in response to the second alarm sent by Brown, which did inadvertent good as well as harm.

This organization ought to have been enough of a force to contain the fire within the block, under ordinary circumstances. But the circumstances were not ordinary. As one fireman later put it: "From the beginning of that fatal fire, everything went wrong!"

First of all, the fire of the night before had wrought great damage on the department. The men were exhausted from the ordeal, many of them suffering terribly from inflamed eyes and smoke poisoning—the occupational hazards of the profession. Few of them had had much sleep for two days. Sickness and injury made the undermanned force even more shorthanded. It is highly likely that, despite the heroic feats of individual firemen, the group as a whole was not performing with its customary speed and alertness.

The equipment was also tired. Two of the seventeen fire engines were being repaired, and many of the remainder were battered and in need of overhaul. The condition of the hose, which deteriorated rapidly with age, heat, and water, was especially bad.

Then there was the agonizing delay caused by the tardy—and wrong—alarms, which turned a minor neighborhood fire into a three-alarm blaze. And finally, with the momentary stoppage of water in the hose of the *America* and the simultaneous breakdown of the *Chicago*, the fire broke through to the north side of Taylor Street.

This in itself was not a catastrophe—except, of course, to the people who lived in the houses on the north side of Taylor. The fire was still not, properly speaking, out of control. But the thin line of men and equipment had to be stretched even thinner around the larger area on fire. Williams wanted to mass his forces north of the fire, and meet it face to face. But he dared not leave the rear—along De Koven and Jefferson Streets—unguarded, for fear the fire might burn back south and west against the wind.

The most crucial consequence of the spread of the fire was the increased heat, and with it the increased number of flying sparks, embers, and debris. The heat caused a powerful and ever-growing updraft, which in turn found an eager ally in the wind.

The wind deserves special mention. Perhaps more responsibility for the spread of the fire can be ascribed to it than to any other factor, except the natural inflammability of the city. The wind was fitful but strong all day, and freshened during the evening. Its general direction was northeast, on a line from the O'Leary barn into the very heart of the city.

Williams regarded with great uneasiness the stream of flaming particles passing high over the firemen's heads. There was nothing he could do. He could only hope that citizens in the blocks to the north would quench these dangerous torches when they landed, to keep new fires from springing up ahead of him. It was now about ten o'clock, a little over an hour since the fire had broken out.

James H. Hildreth, a former alderman, was in bed at his home at 574 Halsted Street when he heard alarms and the engines started jangling by. Hildreth, never one to be out of things, dressed and hastened toward the excitement. When he reached De Koven and saw the wind-driven flames he thought the fire spreading too fast to be controlled.

He hunted up Williams and told him the fire was getting out of hand and some of the engines should be moved north—gratuitous advice which Williams may have been weary of hearing by that time. Schank had already told him the same thing.

Williams patiently pointed out that the

OPPOSITE: MAP SHOWING THE AREA BURNED DURING THE GREAT CHICAGO FIRE. 0 SATURDAY NIGHT FIRE 1 LULL & HOLMES'S PLANING MILL 2 HOME OF MRS. PATRICK O'LEARY 3 GASWORKS 4 ARMORY 5 CONLEY'S PATCH 6 MICHIGAN SOUTHERN DEPOT 7 GRAND PACIFIC HOTEL 8 PALMER HOUSE 9 WABASH AVE. METHODIST CHURCH 10 MICHIGAN AVE. HOTEL 11 TERRACE ROW 12 TRINITY CHURCH 13 BIGELOW HOTEL 14 LAKESIDE PUBLISHING CO. 15 NIXON BUILDING 16 HONORE BLOCK 17 POST OFFICE, CUSTOMHOUSE 18 SHEPARD BUILDING 18A HORACE WHITE RESIDENCE 19 FARWELL HALL 20 OTIS BLOCK 21 REYNOLDS BLOCK 22 TRIBUNE BUILDING 23 MCVICKER'S THEATER 24 TIMES BUILDING 25 NEVADA HOTEL 26 CHAMBER OF COMMERCE 27 BRUNSWICK HALL 28 METHODIST CHURCH 29 PORTLAND BLOCK 30 COURTHOUSE 31 CROSBY'S OPERA HOUSE 32 ST. JAMES HOTEL 33 FIRST NATIONAL BANK 34 FIELD, LEITER & CO. 35 BOOKSELLER'S ROW 36 DRAKE-FARWELL BLOCK 37 SECOND PRESBYTERIAN CHURCH 38 FIRST CONGREGATIONAL CHURCH 39 AVERY'S LUMBER YARD 40 LIND BLOCK 41 SCHUTTLER WAGON FACTORY 42 BRIGGS HOUSE 43 METROPOLITAN HOTEL 44 METROPOLITAN BLOCK 45 SHERMAN HOUSE 46 WOODS' MUSEUM 47 MATTESON HOUSE 48 MARINE BANK 49 SHAY'S DRY GOODS STORE 50 TREMONT HOUSE 51 ILLINOIS CENTRAL R.R. LAND DEPT. 52 WRIGHT BROS. LIVERY STABLE 53 GALENA ELEVATOR 54 MCCORMICK REAPER FACTORY 55 CHICAGO HISTORICAL SOCIETY 56 ROBT. A. KINZIE RESIDENCE 57 HAINES H. MAGIE RESIDENCE 58 LAMBERT TREE RESIDENCE 59 WILLIAM B. OGDEN RESIDENCE 60 WALTER L. NEWBERRY RESIDENCE 61 ISAAC N. ARNOLD RESIDENCE 62 JULIAN S. RUMSEY RESIDENCE 63 GEORGE F. RUMSEY RESIDENCE 64 WATERWORKS 65 LILL'S BREWERY 66 NEW ENGLAND CONGREGATIONAL CHURCH 67 UNITY CHURCH 68 MAHLON D. OGDEN RESIDENCE 69 EZRA B. MCCAGG RESIDENCE 70 GURDON S. HUBBARD RESIDENCE 71 DAVID FALES RESIDENCE 72 DR. J.H. FOSTER RESIDENCE (R.R. DONNELLEY & SONS CO)

wind was blowing embers overhead into areas the firemen could not guard, then broke off the conversation since he had more important things to do. The persistent Hildreth, one of those self-appointed meddlers in everyone's business, was not satisfied. A full-blown scheme for defeating the flames was in his head and he meant to try it out if possible.

He then found Joseph Locke, the city engineer, and persuaded him it would be sound strategy to blow up a line of buildings in the fire's path, somewhat in the nature of the firebreaks used in valuable timberland to halt advancing flames. Locke agreed, and the two men again sought out the harried Williams to explain the plan. Williams protested that he had neither the power nor the powder to blow up other men's buildings. Hildreth, although himself

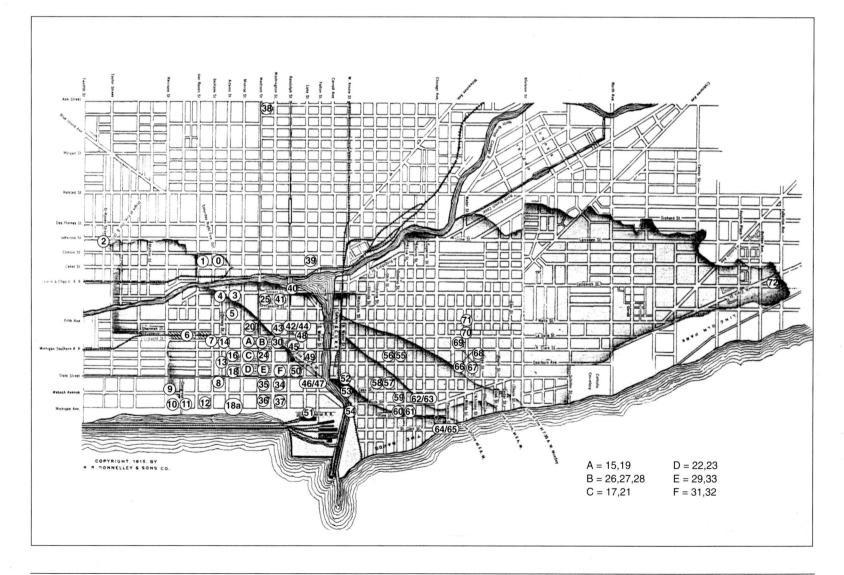

A = 15,19 D = 22,23
B = 26,27,28 E = 29,33
C = 17,21 F = 31,32

disturbed at the thought of destroying someone else's property, said he knew where powder was to be had. Williams told him to get it, perhaps figuring this errand would keep the importunate ex-alderman occupied elsewhere.

O'Leary and his friends still battled to keep his house from going with the rest of the neighborhood, but got scant help from the beleaguered firemen. One asked O'Leary what company carried his insurance, and when he admitted he was not insured at all, the fireman moved on. This solicitude for the welfare of the big insurance firms, a tender feeling no doubt nurtured by the companies themselves, was commonplace at the time. Later another pipeman gave the house "two or three splashes" before going on. O'Leary believed, as he put it some weeks after, that "my little shanty wasn't worth much. They didn't care about it." Nonetheless it survived with slight damage while more valuable buildings in the neighborhood were burned to the ground.

Two blocks or so north of the O'Leary place was an area covered with one-story frame dwellings, small barns, pigsties, corn cribs, and wooden sheds, all crowded together. Ewing Street, three blocks north of De Koven, was little more than a wider-than-usual alley, with boardwalks along it.

The nest of wooden buildings between Taylor and Ewing smoked, then yielded to the flames. The fire went roaring on, and the wind again stepped up its pace.

Along Ewing Street, a dust-haunted thoroughfare over which teams could pass only in fair weather, half-naked women were carrying bedding, cane-bottomed chairs, iron kettles, and other household treasures as they scurried for safety. Drays loaded with refugees and their hastily chosen belongings went swaying past in single file.

The flames leaped from shanty to shanty, and householders with no transportation came running out with their dearest possessions, which they then piled in the day-bright streets to serve as tidbits for the hungry flames.

Reporters had followed the engines in. Joseph Edgar Chamberlin of the *Evening Post* observed that the firemen were working "stupidly and listlessly." But he was not surprised. He attributed their apathy to the fact that they had labored so hard on the Saturday night fire and to "the whisky which is always copiously poured on such occasions." The Irishmen of that day were always being accused of overindulgence in liquor, and many of the firemen were Irish. The idea seems to have been as unjust as it was prevalent.

Gustavus Percy English, a night police reporter for the *Tribune,* had written a story on the Saturday night fire after an afternoon spent gathering facts, and started for his room at Adams and Fifth. He was barely out of the *Tribune* building when he heard the bells and saw a wavering light across the river. He whistled up the speaking tube and told Sam Medill, the city editor.

"You had better jump into a hack and see what it is," Medill suggested, with the casual disregard which all city editors have for other people's time.

English went by cab and on foot and followed the fire for a while, listing the doomed buildings, their occupants, and probable values. But when the flames began springing up too fast and in too many places, he lost track of their progress and returned to the office. Medill asked where the fire was.

"Everywhere," said English.

"Write it up," snapped the editor.

Williams rallied his forces along the new line around Ewing Street. Two more engines, the *Frank Sherman* (named for the general's brother) and the *Long John,* arrived to help out on this northern frontier of the burning area. Meanwhile the fire began to eat back against the wind, just as Williams had feared, endangering new areas to the south and west. A barn caught toward the west end of the alley between De Koven Street and Taylor. This ignited the Turner block, a row of five two-story buildings along the east side of Jefferson, from De Koven to the alley.

Shults's saloon was on the ground floor of the corner building, and the other ground floors also contained stores. Living quarters were above. These buildings caught from the heat of those burning nearby.

Matthew Turner, owner of the block, who had been leaving the Jesuit Church about nine o'clock when he first saw the fire, hurried to his property, but found the wind blowing away from it. He had considered it in no danger as late as ten o'clock. It caught a few minutes later. Vigilant Marshal Benner massed the streams of the

Little Giant, the *Chicago,* and the *Illinois* on this new peril, in order to keep the fire from getting out of the block and across Jefferson Street.

Benner himself was working on the second floor of the block. He pulled down part of the ceiling to pour water in under the roof, and sent Schimmels with Kenyon, the *Chicago* pipeman, into the north end of the building. They were halfway upstairs when they were driven into headlong retreat by the smoke and the buffeting heat. Kenyon fell all the way to the foot of the stairs. The flames had also broken through onto the roof where other firemen and volunteers waited with buckets of water.

Despite the bitter fight at this particular sector of the front, Benner felt that the fire was under control, both here and as a whole. He estimated—correctly—that he had stopped it from going farther west, and assumed that others would by this time, have halted it from its course to the north and east. Then he came down out of the building and met Schank.

The first assistant marshal told him to send to the north all the engines he could spare.

"John," the startled Benner asked, "where has the fire gone to?"

"She has gone to hell and gone," Schank replied.

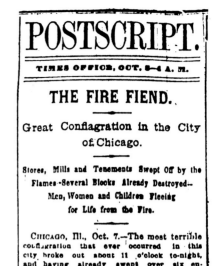

THE NEW YORK TIMES CARRIED A LONG ACCOUNT OF THE DISASTER UNDER THE HEADING "THE FIRE FIEND."

The firemen . . . might as well have attempted to arrest the wind itself, because at this time the wind and the fire were the same thing.

—HISTORY OF THE GREAT CONFLAGRATION

THE FIRE which had started in the O'Learys' barn was a bad one. More than an hour later it was still raging un-abated, having burned out the heart of one block and crossed over to another. But it was not yet as serious as the four-block holocaust of the night before. In spite of delays and errors, and the fatigue of both men and equipment, it still looked as if the fire might be brought under control.

What changed the situation was the circumstance of the wind. All day long, strong gusts had been blowing from the southwest. Although they abated slightly in early evening, the wind kept increasing as the fire spread, picking up larger and larger brands and hurling them across the sky.

This ominous vanguard from across the river soon awoke the South Side from its customary Sunday night tranquility.

One observer was walking along Clark Street, in the business district, about ten o'clock. A high wind blustered up the street from the south. The sound of singing was borne upon it, from a Methodist church near-by. Pedestrians were having difficulty making their way against the force of gusts that poured across the lawn of Courthouse Square.

A policeman was walking swiftly down the street near Monroe. A worried pedestrian asked him what he knew of the fire. The officer looked at him, but passed on without replying.

At Adams Street, a cluster of men stood in conversation, peering anxiously west. "It must be a damn big fire this time," one said. "You can't put out a high wind with water."

A mounted policeman rode toward them from the direction of the fire, and turned up Clark Street. The men called out to him, but he did not answer. The night was growing steadily brighter. Glowing cinders were falling in showers.

People peered apprehensively from their windows, and went out to gather on the sidewalks in tight, anxious groups. The roar of the wind sounded like the breaking waves of the Lake during a winter storm. As the "red snow" became heavier, the crowds grew larger and noisier. The sidewalks were so jammed that several pedestrians were forced to take to the middle of the street. There they had to dodge hard-driven vehicles clattering by in both directions.

At the courthouse, Schafer, from his vantage point on the tower, called down to

OPPOSITE: ON OCTOBER 28, 1871, THE LONDON ILLUSTRATED NEWS PUBLISHED THIS DRAWING OF THE FIRE IN FULL FURY AS IT MUST HAVE APPEARED FROM THE LAKE NEAR THE RIVER MOUTH.

Brown that the fire was still growing. About 10:20 Brown decided to pull a third alarm, once again on his own initiative. And, once again, he sounded the bell for 342. This time he could do no harm. Most of the engines were already at the scene, and those on the way no longer needed a signal to tell them where the fire was.

The steamer *Long John* had come across the river, in answer to the second alarm, from its station near the courthouse. Both sides of Taylor Street were on fire as far east as Clinton. The *Frank Sherman* joined the *John* near Ewing Street. These two engines moved south and worked with the *Waubansia* at Clinton and Taylor, attempting to halt the progress of the fire north and east.

The heat soon grew to such intensity that they were forced away. The *Waubansia* was pulled east to Canal by hand, for there was not enough time to bring up the steam. The man who grabbed the pole had to use his coattail as a pad to keep from burning his hands. The other two engines also retreated north and east, to take up a new line in the face of the advancing flames.

The fire worked its way toward Canal Street on the north side of Taylor. Williams bravely dashed down the flaming thoroughfare, hoping to find reinforcements to stem this fresh outbreak. He saw a hose stretching along the street from the east—undoubtedly that of the *Waubansia,* halted at the corner of Canal. Smoke and embers made it impossible for him to see the engine or its crew, and forced him to retreat. The *Waubansia* was also forced to flee, and headed two blocks north to Ewing Street.

The steamer *Titsworth* responded to the third alarm, coming from the South Side by way of the Madison Street Bridge. It could get no farther south than Ewing Street, and continued west to Jefferson, where it took a plug. The hose was dragged down as far as Forquer, but five lengths burst within ten minutes. The *Titsworth* was then forced to move along Jefferson Street several times in quick succession, always farther north.

Ewing Street east of Jefferson was by this time a giant bonfire. The home of W. M. Aulwurm was one of the first to burn in its block. Mrs. Aulwurm was awakened by the persistent chirping of the family canary. The family fled in haste. Seven-year-old Henry, barefoot and wearing only his nightshirt, carried the feathered sentinel in its cage.

When Police Captain Michael Hickey reached Canal Street from the South Side, he found several men from his precinct already there, under the command of Sergeants Lewis Lull and William Buckley. As a result of the Saturday night blaze, instructions had been given for such procedure in case of any major fire. Hickey and Captain George Miller ordered their men to help the firemen tear down sheds along Canal Street, persuade stubborn residents to leave their threatened houses, and aid in carrying out furniture. There was at this time no marked disorder.

Individual property owners often importuned the firemen for special help. Jacob Beiersdorf, owner of a furniture store on Canal, offered Benner a thousand dollars to save his building.

"You might as well offer a million," was the marshal's indifferent response, "for I could not stop it."

The fire reached both sides of Canal, and a lumberyard to the east also caught. An insurance man and several other citizens drew Benner aside and asked him to shift the *Waubansia* back from Ewing Street to Taylor, near the river, where several mills and lumberyards were still safe. Benner un-enthusiastically promised to do what he could.

Later on, when it looked as if the fire would burn south against the wind, Benner did send the *Little Giant,* which had remained at its post on the corner of Jefferson and De Koven Streets, east to the foot of Taylor, where the Chicago Dock Company property remained unscathed. As Foreman Musham prepared to move the engine, he was approached by a desperate citizen, who shouted an offer of two hundred dollars to "any man who will save my buildings!" Musham left a hose with some volunteers, but they soon abandoned it to the fire.

As the flames were devouring Ewing Street to the north and Canal Street to the east, the fire engines, of which there were about a dozen at the scene, were split into three main groups, each group working independently. The first, including the *Little Giant,* the *Chicago,* and the *Illinois,* was at work around the area of the original fire. Since the wind was blowing away from them the men were able to keep the fire from crossing Jefferson Street, and to push the southern boundary of destruction up from De Koven to Taylor. As the flames died down in this area, several of the engines moved north or east to points of greater danger.

The second group, including the *Titsworth* and reinforcements from outlying parts of town, was at work to the north and west of the fire. Its crews also were engaged in preventing the flames from crossing Jefferson, in which they were successful, but their efforts to stop the fire in its swift progress north were far less rewarding.

The third group, including the *Waubansia,* the *Long John,* the *Sherman,* and the *Economy,* hung on north and east of the blaze, retreating gradually before the fury of the wind-driven flames.

The lines of defense were scattered, but not totally disorganized. Most of the equipment was massed in the northern sector, where Marshal Williams hoped to halt the destruction in the area around Ewing Street.

Spectators on top of a lumber pile at the corner of Taylor and Canal saw embers soaring overhead, like blazing arrows on the wind. One missile flew up from a spot just north of Taylor and soared four blocks to a resting place on the cupola of St. Paul's Catholic Church, at Clinton and Mather.

The wooden steeple rose high above the street. Once fire had gained a foothold there, firebrands would be spread over an even larger area than before.

Williams was beginning to hope that the final victory on Ewing Street was near. Then he was told that St. Paul's was on fire, two blocks behind him. Fearing that the wind was so violent that no stream could reach the steeple, he sought out George Rau, foreman of the hook-and-ladder *Protection.*

"Go and put up your highest ladder," he ordered, "and I will get a stream down there just as quickly as I can."

William Bateham, himself a former fire marshal, and now alderman of the ninth ward, had seen the flames from his home at Silver and Harrison Streets about nine o'clock. He started for his two lumber mills, behind St. Paul's. On the way he met a friend, John Garrick, who had been inspecting his own property at the southwest corner of Clinton and Harrison.

Garrick had decided there was no cause for alarm, but turned back with Bateham when he noticed flaming fragments streaking through the sky. Garrick stopped at his place, and Bateham crossed to the shingle mill, the smaller and closer of the two mills on his property. He found the watchman already at work with a chemical engine, fighting sparks which were settling about him like a swarm of locusts.

Bateham, with his experience in the fire department, was far better prepared for this emergency than most citizens. He started a steam-powered pump kept for such purposes. With the help of some employees, also attracted by the fire, he fastened a hose to a nearby hydrant on Canal Street, to begin flooding the mill yard. In the yard were 1,000 cords of kindling, stacked 25 feet high, and 600,000 feet of furniture lumber for a factory in the attic of the shingle mill. Large objects whirled three to five hundred feet overhead, tracing a blazing path across the clouds.

More stacks of lumber were stored in the middle of the block, between the two mills. South of the larger mill stood the Roelle Furniture Finishing Company, fronting on Mather next door to the church.

The northwest corner of the block bounded by Harrison, Mather, Clinton, and Canal Streets was occupied by Charles Huntoon's old-fashioned rural house, a relic of the time when the area was open country. This stood well back from the street, on a large lot covered with trees. A small match factory was just north of the church, and a three-story boardinghouse stood at the corner of Harrison and Canal Streets, with a saloon on the ground floor.

It was a block made to order for burning—like the rest of the immediate neighborhood. Numerous two- and three-story frame buildings stood on the east side of Canal, and between the street and the river were stores, woodworking mills, saloons, furniture factories, lumberyards, paint shops, blacksmith shops, and wagon shops, many of these crowded together along the river for easy access to the Lake ships.

Most of these buildings were, naturally, of wood, and raised on piles from six to ten feet from the ground, providing an ideal draft underneath. As in the rest of the city, the sidewalks were raised, with no partitions under them. A person could walk upright beneath the planks from one end of the block to the other.

At first, the appearance of more fire engines on the scene gave hope that the fire on top of St. Paul's could be stopped before doing serious damage. Residents nearby shouted to the men on the steamer *Jacob Rehm,* as it came from the North Side in response to the third alarm. The *Rehm* pulled up and took a plug by the church. Rau and his men from the ladder truck ran up an old ladder they found in the churchyard. Some of the firemen went up with a hose and put out the flames.

They came down quickly, intending to continue toward the main fire. But a new blaze on the roof called them back. After it was extinguished Rau left, and two or three firemen began to lower the ladder. The ladder fell and broke.

There was no fire visible on the church for a few minutes. Then Engineer John Doyle of the *Rehm* saw flames on the roof for the third time. They leaped high on the east end, and began traveling back against the wind. The *Rehm* threw a stream from the street. It was not enough.

Schafer spotted the St. Paul's fire from

the courthouse. He told Brown to strike Box 287, at Van Buren and Canal, a good, close estimate. It was shortly before eleven by the courthouse clock.

The *Lincoln* hose cart, which had left the North Side on the third alarm, was passing St. Paul's when the driver saw the *Rehm.* The *Lincoln* stopped to help. The steamer *Fred Gund,* also from the North Side, came to a halt at Polk and Clinton. It had to wait to take water in relay from the *Rehm,* since there was no free hydrant available.

Foreman Dennis J. Swenie of the *Gund,* impatient at the delay, walked up to the *Rehm.* He found it throwing water on the church roof, and was told the hose would be brought down to the *Gund* as soon as St. Paul's was safe. Swenie returned to his engine, waited five minutes or so, then walked north once more. This time St. Paul's was burning inside.

Swenie immediately brought the *Gund* to Canal and north to Bateham's. He took away from Bateham the plug in front of the mill, and gave him a lead from the engine in return. The wind was so strong that Swenie was blown into the middle of the street, still clinging to the hose.

The wind had reached a new pitch of violence. The heat of the fire set up fresh gusts of turbulent air, which added to the near-gale force of the wind. It also created chaotic whirlpools and eddies, spreading flames and sparks in all directions. Many bewildered survivors later recalled that the wind and the fire seemed to come upon them from everywhere at once.

Benjamin Bullwinkle, twenty-four-year-old captain of the fire insurance patrol which had been activated only six days earlier, came down Canal Street with his men, methodically putting out small awning and roof fires with chemical extinguishers. When they reached the *Gund,* several members stopped to help.

Canal was crowded with teams and furniture. Bedding, piled in the street for safety, was burning. Firemen were busy carrying holy relics from St. Paul's, whose door was six or eight feet above sidewalk level. Planks had been laid from the entrance to some wooden horses on the walk to make an easier descent. One fireman, with a large statue of a saint on his back, came to the end of the last plank and found no one to relieve him of his burden.

"Where in hell shall I put this?" he asked in his exasperation.

The blaze in the church showed no sign of dying down. Williams hurried behind it and found Swenie, who had brought a hose in from Canal Street.

"Dennis," he asked anxiously, "cannot you work north of this? I am afraid it is going to get in ahead of us there."

Swenie, himself a former department chief, had the pipe taken up on the roof of a nearby building, from which water could be directed both north and south. Williams went back to the *Rehm,* which by now had a second hose playing on the church.

"Boys," he warned the *Rehm's* crew, "hang on to it or you will have to pull the engine away. Just as soon as it [the church] falls it will be all right."

A drugstore behind the *Rehm* flared up several times. The flames were smothered on each occasion. But the men working near the engine were in great personal dan-

ger. Smoke eddied from their clothing as well as from buildings nearby. Williams himself helped with one pipe, directing the stream to cool down the west side of Clinton Street. Doyle's mates brought him a door, which afforded scant shelter. A stream from another engine was being thrown on St. Paul's from the rear. But finally Williams told Doyle:

"John, you will have to take up. This place is getting too hot!"

Despite the searing heat, Doyle managed to fill the engine's boiler and to shut off the plug with a wrench. He helped one of the other men uncouple the hose, and took time to go into an alley to the north and throw a covering over one of his horses, which was being showered with sparks. The *Rehm* was pulled by hand a block to the west.

Great throngs of spectators stood on nearby streets, watching the losing battle for St. Paul's. An old Irishwoman asked one observer what was burning. He told her it was the church.

"Oh," she said cheerfully, "God will put it out."

A few minutes later, the roof fell in.

For a moment danger to the mills seemed ended. Then someone told Williams that Bateham's buildings were going. The marshal dashed around the flaming ruins to find the smaller mill and the match factory burning briskly, as was a stable next to the church. While the firemen's attention had been focused on the church, the flames had crept up Canal Street, turned west at Mather, and leaped across the street to the mill despite efforts of the crew of the *Gund* to hold them back.

Two other steam engines were brought into the mill area, but accomplished noth-

ing. The lumberyards caught. The fire was thick and heavy. It seized the old red mill, the larger of Bateham's, to the east. Williams told Leo Myers, foreman of the *Tempest* hose cart, "It is gone sure!"

"I am afraid it is," Myers agreed.

"If it has got to go," said Williams stubbornly, "we will try and cut it off at Harrison Street."

The marshal then headed north, to set up the next move in this deadly game of leapfrog. As he passed the *Gund,* he saw that lumber piled next to it on the sidewalk was burning. Williams paused long enough to order the engine moved north, then ran on. The fire outraced him to Harrison, where he met Commissioner James E. Chadwick.

"Don't you know the fire is getting ahead of you?" Chadwick asked uncharitably.

"Yes," Williams admitted sadly. "It is getting ahead of me in spite of all I can do. It is just driving me along."

The heat and smoke began to take their toll on the overtired, overburdened firemen. Foreman Schimmels of the *Chicago* brought the steamer back to its quarters and turned command over to Pipeman Michael Conway. Schimmels told his men he was "played out," and went home for a brief rest.

Conway had gone to his home on Jackson near Des Plaines about four-thirty that Sunday afternoon, bone-weary. His eyes were inflamed and swollen and, after bathing them, he tumbled into bed, too tired to eat. His wife had awakened him

A TRAGIC MOMENT DURING THE FIRE AS ENVISIONED BY AN ILLUSTRATOR FOR A GERMAN-LANGUAGE PUBLICATION. THE DRAMATIC CAPTION SAYS, "LOST! LOST! NO HOPE! EVERY AVENUE OF ESCAPE SHUT OFF. THEY PERISH IN THE CRUEL FLAMES." (DAS GROSSE IN CHICAGO)

about eleven o'clock, only because she feared their own home might burn. Conway went at once to the engine house.

After Schimmels put him in charge, Conway saw that there was little hose left. He drove a cart down Des Plaines Street in quest of some, returning with two or three lengths he found abandoned in the streets.

When Williams had seen the *Gund* in dangerous proximity to a pile of blazing lumber on Canal Street, neither he nor its crew realized how serious that danger was.

Foreman Swenie was some 450 feet from the engine, near the burning west part of Bateham's mill, when suddenly the water stopped at the pipe. Swenie hurried down the alley to see what was happening. He found the engine in danger of being over-whelmed by the flames from the lumber pile, and the rest of the crew driven back by the heat. No one could get near enough to the hydrant to uncouple the hose.

Ex-alderman Hildreth, who had been detoured for the time being from his search for gunpowder, was trying to help. He made several attempts to get to the hydrant, but retreated when his hair, eyebrows, and mustache were singed.

Finally Swenie crawled to the plug on his hands and knees, and got the hose disconnected. The *Gund* fled toward Van Buren Street, a block and a half north. The fire had nearly reached Harrison Street.

Hildreth persuaded Bullwinkle to take him to the South Side to find some explosives. Bullwinkle whistled for one of his crew, Charles Emory, who had been putting out awning fires in the neighborhood with a Babcock extinguisher, and they, with Hildreth and Bateham, headed north on the insurance patrol wagon toward the Lake Street Bridge.

Meanwhile the fire quickly burned out the area between the St. Paul's block and Ewing Street. The *Sherman,* having been forced to flee from Taylor and Clinton Streets, took up a position on Polk Street, and was fighting the flames approaching from Ewing. The area grew steadily hotter. The whiskers of Stoker George Leady and Engineer John Hohn were scorched, and the legs of the horses, which had been kept in harness, were burned. When the hose began to smoke and char, and a building behind them burst into sudden flames, they decided the time had come to make a run for it, and fled down Polk Street toward the river.

The *Gund* made a stand on the corner

LOOTING WAS WIDESPREAD. SOMETIMES THE BOOTY WAS A BARREL OF LIQUOR, SOMETIMES WHATEVER COULD BE FOUND IN A HOUSE ABANDONED BY ITS PANIC-STRICKEN OWNERS. SALOONS WERE INVADED AND LOOTERS GRABBED BOTTLES FROM THE SHELVES OR OVERTURNED WHISKEY BARRELS, SPILLING THE CONTENTS INTO THE STREET. (CHICAGO PUBLIC LIBRARY)

of Van Buren and Canal, carrying one hose down an alley behind Canal, and another along Canal Street itself. The *Long John* was nearby, at a plug between Harrison and Van Buren, and brought its hose through an open lot into an alley between Canal and Clinton. There Marshal Williams joined Foreman Alex McMonagle.

Before either engine could start pumping, however, a new fire exploded in the center of the block.

"Robert, we can't stay here long," observed McMonagle, a former shoemaker of apparently unshakable calm.

Williams gave his usual desperate answer:

"Hang on as long as you can!"

"I'll hang on as long as I can," McMonagle replied, "but I can't hang any longer."

Williams told him to turn the horses around and be ready to run when necessary. McMonagle then "hung on" so long that when the situation became untenable, the hose had to be dragged behind the engine in its flight.

The *Long John* passed the *Gund* and several other engines which had made a line on Van Buren. It went up Canal another half block, coming to a halt in front of the still-warm ruins of the Lull and Holmes planing mill.

West Side residents were growing more panicky and disorganized. Police Sergeant

Charles H. French hastened along the streets, warning those few householders who had not already fled to close their windows to prevent flying sparks from igniting bedding and draperies inside their homes.

Some refugees headed north a few blocks, then east into the South Division. Others wandered aimlessly along the railroad tracks between Canal and the river, carrying a few belongings in hastily wrapped bundles. Sergeant French, patrolling the area despite the heat and sparks, directed everyone he could toward the west, where there was a chance to breathe cooler air. There was no means of crossing the river in this area.

The building on Harrison Street owned by Garrick, Bateham's friend, was destroyed. Garrick was able to save nothing but a large American flag. He wrapped this around him, and walked home to safety through the crimson night.

As the area of destruction spread, law and order began to give way. Captains Miller and Hickey, who had been helping their men beat out sparks in the Bateham yards before they caught, had to leave to quell a fight in the nearby saloon, where roughs were trying to seize liquor without paying for it. And some time during the West Side blaze an expressman, Jacob Klein, was smashed on the head with a shovel. He had been trying to keep two men from stealing what he was carrying from a burning building. The blow proved fatal.

As had happened farther south, the progress of the onrushing flames was speeded east by the goods stacked in the center of Canal Street. Bureaus, tables, and chairs served as steppingstones from one block to the next, and the wind plucked burning mattresses off the street and hurled them against houses yet untouched by the fire. These buildings often went down before the harried firemen could get close to them with a hose.

The wind, still growing angrier, flung burning shingles, pieces of felt roofing, and other flaming omens of disaster across the river into both the North and South Divisions of the city.

Below Bateham's, back toward the glowing debris that had been O'Leary's barn, flames leaped high into the night. The holocaust glowed with every imaginable color—crimson and amber, pink and gold, curious shades of green and purple and blue.

Twenty blocks crackled and roared as churches, stores, manufacturing plants, substantial dwellings, shanties, barns, saloons, outhouses, railroad cars, mills, and bridges were consumed by the ravening fire. The firemen in its path were driven from corner to corner by an implacable tidal wave of flame. Often they escaped only moments before the last exit was closed.

The fire had come seven blocks northeast of its birthplace in less than three hours, traveling for the most part in twin columns between Jefferson and Clinton and Clinton and Canal, with the eastern flank moving faster. Most onlookers clung to the hope that it would halt beyond Van Buren, balked by the sixteen-acre desert created the previous night, and that it would not be able to jump the river to the east. But many looked with deep uneasiness at the sky, spangled now with countless windblown brands.

Bateham was worried as he left the blazing ruins of his factories. "The materials from this mill will fire the South Side," he said. "Nothing can stop it now."

CHICAGO'S FIREMEN FOUGHT GALLANTLY AGAINST IMPOSSIBLE ODDS. NONE FOUGHT MORE BRAVELY THAN THE CREW OF THE STEAMER FRED GUND, WHICH FINALLY DISAPPEARED UNDER A COLLAPSING BUILDING NEAR CANAL AND VAN BUREN. (CHICAGO HISTORICAL SOCIETY)

Several of the steamers working on Van Buren Street were forced to pull out or be overrun. In most cases they left their hose to burn, although there was no replacement anywhere. The men asked Williams what to do, but the marshal for the moment had nothing to suggest.

"God only knows," he responded.

McMonagle was running toward the *Long John* with a length of hose on his shoulder when next he saw Williams. At almost the same time he saw something else. He dropped the hose and shouted in dismay:

"Robert! The fire is on the South Side!"

"The devil it is!" said Williams. "Go for it! I'll be there in a minute."

Before he jumped into the *Washington* hose cart and headed for the new peril, Williams warned that the *Gund* must be moved again, and at once. He appealed to a crowd of spectators for aid.

The *Gund* had been trying to stop the fire from crossing to the east side of Canal and Van Buren. This was a futile task since there were liquor stores on two of the corners, and the fuel they provided made the atmosphere so hot the stream from the hose seemed to evaporate before it fell to the ground.

The onlookers whom Williams asked for help included Henry Hittorf, a West Randolph Street jeweler, who stood near the bridge with several friends. The group tried to haul away the engine, but the three firemen tending it could not get close enough to the hydrant to uncouple the hose. The volunteers stayed close by for several minutes. The heat became so intense that the firemen were forced to take shelter in the lee of the engine. They then fled. Some tried to return to get pieces of clothing thrown on the engine earlier, but could not reach it.

Foreman Swenie ran up. He ordered his men to make another attempt to pull the *Gund* away. The engine faced east, its wheels blocked by some loose pieces of coal. These were removed, just as a wave of fire from the corner drove the men back once more. They retreated about a hundred feet. When the heat ebbed, Swenie rallied them again.

They got within ten feet of the *Gund* before being forced away. They tried a third time, desperate and gasping for breath. As they neared the engine it started to roll. The hose had burned off at the plug, freeing it.

The front wheels struck the coal and cramped. The steamer swerved, then lurched across the street. It collided with a raised sidewalk, already ablaze. No one could get near it. A few minutes later a building at the corner of Canal and Van Buren collapsed. The *Gund* disappeared beneath a torrent of bricks.

At about this time Sergeant Kaufman, who was in charge of the United States Weather Signal office on La Salle Street, just west of the courthouse, sent in a report to Washington. He had seen the fire, and before leaving the office went onto the roof for a last look at the anemometer. It registered sixty miles an hour. Whether this was accurate or not, the fury of the wind almost carried both the gauge and Kaufman right over the edge.

CHAPTER 6

You couldn't see anything over you but fire . . .
No clouds, no stars, nothing else but fire.

—THOMAS BYRNE, HOSE ELEVATOR NO. 2

THE SOUTH side was a sort of peninsula, roughly rectangular in shape. On its east was the Lake, and the South Branch and main stream of the river separated it from the rest of the city. Within it were contained all the sharp contrasts of wealth and poverty, substance and squalor, which characterized the city as a whole.

Michigan Avenue, running north and south along the Lake front, had in recent years become one of the most stylish residential streets in town. Splendid town houses and terrace apartments overlooked the shore park and breakwater, beyond which the Lake extended to the horizon. Toward the northern end of Michigan Avenue, in Dearborn Park, was the small stadium of the Chicago White Stockings. Railroad tracks ran up along the breakwater to the Illinois Central depot standing near the site of Fort Dearborn. On land reclaimed from the Lake were several freight yards and two large grain elevators, like enormous shingled monuments marking the northeast corner of the division.

Behind Michigan Avenue, stretching from the river almost a mile south to Harrison Street, was the principal business section of the city. Wabash Avenue, formerly almost entirely residential, had become a commercial area from Madison Street to the river, and contained several large wholesale stores and warehouses. Many of the city's finest retail stores—including Field and Leiter's "marble palace," Carson, Pirie, and Company, and Bookseller's Row—were located on State Street, along with the mansard-roofed Palmer House, one of the tallest buildings in town.

On Dearborn Street stood many of the

NORTHSIDE RESIDENCES PROVIDE A STUN-NING BACKGROUND FOR THIS VIEW OF THE LAKE SHORE. MEN IN TOP HATS CONDUCT A DISCUSSION IN THE RAILROAD YARDS NEAR THE END OF THE TRACKS. (CHICAGO PUBLIC LIBRARY)

city's finest and most modern office buildings, including the Shepard, Honore, and
Reynolds blocks, the austere post office and
customhouse, and the *Times* and *Tribune*
buildings. On Dearborn and elsewhere such
substantial edifices were commonly built of
the popular white "Athens marble."

Near the center of the business district
was the courthouse, whose tall cupola
towered above surrounding buildings, a
conspicuous landmark on the Chicago skyline. In front of it stood the Sherman
House, one of the largest and most modern
hotels in the city, and behind it stood the
massive, tall-windowed Chamber of
Commerce building.

A point of special pride with their owners—and with the city at large—was that
several of these buildings were reputed to be
completely fireproof, including the *Tribune,*
the post office, the First National Bank at
State and Washington, and Field and
Leiter's.

The architecture of this district might

be described as unembarrassed eclectic.
Ornate façades, rounded windows, and
decorative gingerbread—both wrought iron
and carved stone—were extremely fashionable. Mansards were common, and there
was hardly a roof line not elaborated by
either ornamental cornices or false-front
pediments, or both. Traces of classic,
medieval, and Renaissance styles were
mixed into an exuberant and original pas-
tiche.

All these buildings were, comparatively
speaking, new. Many of them had gone up
in the boom of prosperity that came with
the Civil War and stayed on after. But even
this district was not completely built up.
Between impressive stone buildings were
vacant lots or temporary frame shops and
houses.

This section of town, whose property
valuation topped $340,000,000—more than
half the total worth of the city—encompassed virtually all the banks and larger
stores, all the theaters worth attending, all

the newspaper offices and bookstores, the largest railroad stations, almost all the important public buildings, most of the hotels, and several of the most substantial churches.

But there was another part of the South Side—very close to the business section but distinctly different in atmosphere—which was by no means so impressive. It was a narrow strip south of Randolph Street, running from Wells Street—recently renamed Fifth Avenue—west to the river. If the rich section directly north and east of it was the city's pride, this was the city's shame.

It was an area that might charitably be called industrial, except that most of it was the worst sort of slum. The lower part of Fifth Avenue, known as Conley's Patch, was particularly notorious. It was lined with squat frame buildings which housed brothels, dance halls, pawnshops, tawdry boardinghouses, and saloons. These were crowded together along the streets and narrow alleys, all tinder-dry. They were particularly open to attack since no one cared to defend them. Most of the people who actually lived in the neighborhood owned nothing worth saving except their lives.

The legitimate businesses which occupied the remainder of the area were of the sort that provided such excellent fuel for the fire on the West Side: woodworking mills, warehouses, small factories, lumberyards. Among the largest plants was the South Side Gas Works, which manufactured and stored illuminating gas for the whole division. In addition to the main plant and the large storage tanks, kept filled with explosive coal gas, the property contained several sheds and extensive coal piles.

When the fire reached the South Side, it did not make its start in the proud rich section, but settled in this squalid district which promised to be receptive to its advances.

The first buildings to go were not, as might have been expected, directly across the river from the West Side fire. The brands which set the Parmelee Stage and Omnibus Company building and Powell's roofing works ablaze jumped over the water and two intervening blocks as well.

The Parmelee building, a brand-new three-story structure, covered most of the block at Franklin Street and Jackson. The Powell works were a block north at Adams Street, next door to the gasworks.

The Parmelee building went quickly, despite the efforts of men posted on the roof. The $80,000 building was to have

CONLEY'S PATCH, A SLUM ALONG LOWER FIFTH AVENUE, WAS A NEIGHBORHOOD OF CHEAP SALOONS, PAWNSHOPS, BROTHELS, ONE-STORY SHACKS, AND UNAPPEALING BOARDINGHOUSES. IT WAS AMONG THE FIRE'S LEAST-MOURNED LOSSES. (CHICAGO TODAY)

THIS PICTURE FOR A STEREOPTICON SHOWS HOW COMPLETELY THE FIRE RAVAGED THE ILLINOIS-MICHIGAN CENTRAL DEPOT NEAR MICHIGAN AVENUE AND THE CHICAGO RIVER. (CROMIE COLLECTION)

opened for business three days later. The burning of the roofing plant was witnessed by Thomas Ockerby, night superintendent of the gasworks. Ockerby was one of the comparative handful of civilians in town who tried to outwit or outbattle the flames, and kept trying until no chance of winning remained.

He had come on duty at about 5:30 that afternoon. When the West Division fire began sending sparks across the river—not very long after its first outbreak—he sprang into action. He ordered his men to wet down barns and other buildings nearby, with a hose attached to a fireplug. He toured the saloons along Market Street, logical places in which to look for the local inhabitants, warning all he saw of the danger, and telling them to go home and see that their roofs didn't catch. Most important of all, he and Thomas Burtis, the assistant superintendent, saw to it that the gas in the tanks was transferred out of the division to reservoirs on the North Side, thus considerably reducing the chance of later explosion. Ockerby manipulated the valves himself, so that all gas generated from that time went directly north.

He then climbed to the top of a fairly tall building nearby to await developments. As he stood watching in the windy darkness, a blazing bit of debris, which he took to be a shingle, dropped into an open tar tank in the roofing-plant yard. The tar, incidentally, was a by-product bought from the gasworks, for use in roofing and paving.

Ockerby slid to the ground at once, and ran to a shed just west of the burning tank. He feared there might be horses in the shed, but none was there that night. He barely had time to drag out a buggy owned by the works superintendent; when he

returned for some harness, the shed already was wreathed in flame. The tar tank and the whole of the roofing works were burning lustily, and tar barrels behind the shed caught almost simultaneously.

The fire spread to other buildings, and Policeman Henry Ulrich, who had been standing in front of the gasworks when the firebrand landed, immediately began to rouse the neighborhood, or whatever portion of it still slumbered.

Within two minutes after the shed caught, one of the large gasholders began blazing. Ockerby sent men to its top with buckets of water, and ordered others to lead the horses from a company barn.

An employee told him that a fire engine had reached the corner. He ran out and asked the foreman to bring a hose into the yard to wet down the gasholders. The foreman said he would not go and would not send any of his men.

"It is perfectly safe," Ockerby protested. "I will go down there with you."

The other man was unconvinced.

"I do not take any man's soul in my hand," he replied. "You can take the lead in there if you want to."

Ockerby grabbed the hose and dragged it from Monroe Street down the alley and into the yard, where he directed a stream against the blaze. He remained at the pipe until the firemen shut off the water, reclaimed the hose, reeled it up, and went away, leaving the gasworks to burn without hindrance.

At an inquiry later on, no fireman ever mentioned this incident, which is perhaps understandable. At the same time, it was likely that no effort, however valiant, could have saved the gasworks for long from the onslaught of sparks and heat which continued from the west.

A general shift of firefighting equipment from the West to the South Side was taking place. Many engines were dislodged from positions along Van Buren and came over. Then the fire began to wane as it hit the burned-out area of the night before. Consequently, much of the force could be moved to face the new threat.

Unfortunately, the danger in the West Side had not sufficiently abated to free every engine, and several had to remain behind. Those that were able to go were too few and too late.

When Marshal Williams told Foreman McMonagle to take the *Long John* to the South Side, he himself jumped aboard the hose cart *Washington* and bounced along behind. He tried to pass the steamer on the Madison Street Bridge, but traffic was too heavy. He finally got around the *Long John* on the other side, by cutting down to Monroe and dashing down Franklin Street from there. He reached Adams Street to find the *Economy* there before him. It had crossed at Polk Street as the fire approached the river.

Williams found the gasworks already on fire. He ran into the yard, like the professional he was, ignoring shouts that he would be blown to bits. Everyone feared an explosion, even though there was little gas left on the premises. Williams quickly decided that the buildings were beyond salvation and ran out again.

Although Ockerby and his men had taken every precaution to reduce the chances of an explosion, the danger increased as the works burned. The pipes supplying the South Division were not shut off. When the last men were driven from the buildings, shortly after midnight, there was enough gas to give light for an hour or

so. Fortunately, when the buildings burned, the joints of the pipes melted, permitting the gas still coming from the works to leak out gradually, and ignite slowly. Since the rest of the gas had been transferred, through Ockerby's foresight, the dreaded explosion never took place.

About twenty minutes after the gasworks was in full blaze another flying brand landed on a three-story tenement nearby. It flared up "like a lucifer match," to quote one observer. This was in Conley's Patch. At 12:45 a third fire established itself in the southern part of the Patch, near the Van Buren Street Bridge.

The armory just south of the gasworks, used as police headquarters, also was burning, and a few moments later its magazine exploded. This provoked renewed cries that the gasworks were about to blow. Nothing happened, but few people waited to find out.

The ragged inhabitants of Conley's Patch poured through the streets in a frantic rush for safety. Rough men, hard-faced women, and pale children came swarming from their dismal homes. Many other South Siders, who had gone to the West Side to watch the fire, were now forced to fight their way back into the South Division against a stream of people heading the other way.

Eager as they were to escape, many from the Patch found the habits of a lifetime too strong to resist. They broke into stores and saloons, stole from passing wagons, and robbed weaker fugitives. Many also did what they could to add to the confusion by getting drunk as quickly and completely as possible. Some drank their way to blank-eyed unawareness before leaving the area, and were caught and killed by the enemy. It

A CASUAL-LOOKING GENTLEMAN SURVEYS THE RUINS OF THE UNION NATIONAL BANK, WEST OF THE CHAMBER OF COMMERCE. (JACK LEVIN COLLECTION)

was not until this hour that violence, theft, and general disorder became widely noticeable.

Among the losses on Fifth Avenue was a small, three-girl brothel owned by Lizzie Allen, née Ellen Williams. Lizzie had come to town from Milwaukee, worked for various madams until 1865, then invested her savings in a little place of her own. The stock was saved, but the shop was swept away.

Another landmark erased was Ramrod Hall, a one-story frame building on Quincy Street near Fifth, which was said to be the largest brothel in town. It was presided over by Kate Hawkins, who kept from thirty to sixty girls in line with a horsewhip. The Hall had been the scene of a wild free-for-all six months earlier. Kate tried to confine to quarters one of her employees, who announced she was leaving to get married. Friends of the bride-to-be, "a very lucrative piece of furniture" named Mary Woods, rallied around. By the time the police arrived, Ramrod Hall was a shambles. Now, fire did an even better job of wrecking the joint.

When Williams left the gasworks to the forlorn efforts of its employees, he came out a block north on Monroe. The cornices on the nearby Merchants' Union Express Company barn were burning, beyond reach of the wind-blown water from the *Economy*. He ordered the crew of the *Long John* to work there as well, but the fire repeated the tactics which had proved unbeatable on the West Side. It leaped over the defenders and kept on going.

One of the firemen told Williams that Fifth Avenue was on fire between Monroe and Madison, and he ran east to look. He returned to order the *Economy*, the *Long John*, the *Coventry*, a North Side steamer, and the *Brown,* just arrived from the West Side, to form a new line of defense along Madison Street. Other steamers continued to come up.

The body of flame beat its way up Market, Fifth, Franklin, and La Salle, the first four blocks east of the river, erasing everything in its path. The gasworks fire quickly enveloped the block directly west of it, then headed north, destroying the John V. Farwell stables and express company barns, containing almost a hundred helpless horses.

There were horses stabled all over the South Division, since they were in universal demand for livery and carting purposes, and few were in use on a Sunday night. Furthermore, horses are hard to handle during a fire, and most of the places they were stabled were shorthanded at that hour. That many horses died during the holocaust was unfortunate but inevitable.

While many fire engines remained on the West Side, those under Williams's direction vainly tried to stem the northeast course of the new fire, which was beginning to rival its predecessor. Tugs screamed in the river in an effort to get the bridges open, so they could tow shipping to safety in the Lake.

As the fire roared up the east bank of the river, the steadfastness and devotion to duty of Andrew Boyer, the sixty-year-old tender of the Madison Street Bridge, saved that wooden span from apparently certain destruction. When flames threatened the eastern end, he was urged to flee. Brave perhaps, and stubborn for sure, Boyer cried, "I *will* save my bridge!" and refused to budge.

He swung the bridge, which pivoted in the middle to let ships go by, over the water whenever the flames drew near. His two

sons waited anxiously below in a boat, in case their father was forced to leap for his life. They also rescued several persons who jumped or fell into the river, and ferried others across to safety on the West Side when the bridge was open.

The fire swept the eastern approaches at Madison and passed on to the north. The bridge remained.

Its escape was extremely lucky, for the river itself was no protection. Nearby, some tugs tried to get close enough to the burning tannery of the Chicago Hide and Leather Company to put a line on the brig *Fontinella,* which was moored there. But after the tugs were beaten back three times, the flames boarded the *Fontinella* and ate the mooring lines through. The brig then drifted unmanned into the stream, where fire ran up the rigging and along the deck, and turned her into a blackened derelict.

The fire, having made its way through the slums, moved to better lodgings. Having passed through the slums and marginal industrial sections, the heart of the business section lay before it. In particular, the courthouse was directly in its path.

Its first task was to leap over the line of engines on Madison Street, just one block south of the courthouse. The force of the wind blew a cornice off a building at La Salle and Madison Streets, where the *Coventry* was working. Awnings blazed at the third-floor windows of the Thomas building on La Salle, north of Madison. Two doors up, the house of the *Long John* was threatened.

Nearby on La Salle the four-story stone

and brick Oriental building was beginning to burn. Williams himself was helping man one of the *Coventry*'s hoses. He worked his way into an alley behind it. A frame carpenter shop, already ablaze, lay between him and the rear of the larger building. He smashed into the carpenter shop by way of a basement window, cutting his hand in the process. But when he had dragged the hose through, its stream proved useless. The wind cut it off ten feet from the nozzle.

A tenant in one of the third-floor offices of the Oriental block was dropping valuables to his partner and two friends on the sidewalk below. As the flames grew hotter, those on the street shouted to him to escape. He was unmoved.

"That is my stairway," he cried, pointing to a rope hanging from the window beside him. "Now don't you fret for me."

His position became untenable, and the rope was his only means of escape. He dropped a last load of books and some money from the safe, then started down the

rope as nimbly as a sailor. Before he reached the ground, the fire came through a window on the second floor and ignited the rope. It snapped and sent him tumbling to the sidewalk. The fall dislocated a shoulder. Despite his pain, the man was unruffled as he was helped to his feet. He patted the money he had saved.

"Guess that will settle the doc's bills," he said.

The *Long John*'s quarters were ignited by a blaze which jumped from a picture-frame factory on Monroe. The *Coventry* found itself threatened with the same fate as the *Gund*.

"Boys," Williams told the *Coventry*'s panting crew in characteristic understatement, "we'll have to get away from here!"

Some of Bullwinkle's men, sent over from the West Side, came by at this moment. Seeing the *Coventry*'s plight, they simply broke off the taper at the hydrant and freed the engine. Williams ordered the *Coventry* to the Sherman House plug, a couple of blocks north on Randolph Street, but because of the broken taper the engine was useless and had to drive off for repairs.

Hildreth, meanwhile, had finally obtained a wagonload of powder, after breaking into a magazine at State and South Water Streets. He moved some 2,500 pounds of explosive to the courthouse basement, then went hunting for Williams. After a fruitless search, he came back to the courthouse and ran across Mayor Mason.

Determined to save the city, Hildreth urged him to sanction the use of powder. The mayor, who had come to the courthouse around midnight, wrote out an order in phraseology suggested by Judge H. G. Miller.

"Who will see that this is carried out?" Mason asked.

"I will," said Hildreth, grabbing the paper. "Give it to me quick!"

Hildreth then resumed his search for Williams, since the order authorized him to use powder "under directions of the fire marshal." He found him nursing his hand in the alley behind the Oriental building. They walked to the northwest corner of Madison and La Salle and took shelter from the sparks in a doorway.

Hildreth read Williams the order and asked for suggestions.

"That gives you all the power you want," Hildreth urged. "You know the engines cannot stop the fire and we may as well stop it by blowing up buildings on some given line."

Williams surveyed the situation quickly. West of La Salle, the fire had already crossed Madison Street, and was approaching the Metropolitan block, beyond Washington Street and west of the courthouse.

"I don't know where to commence," Williams said thoughtfully. Then he looked again toward the courthouse. The Union National Bank, on the southwest corner of La Salle and Washington, lay directly between it and the path of the fire.

"You'd better take that bank on the corner," he said. Knowing the volatile nature of his companion, he added, "Be sure you have all the people out when you do."

Unfortunately, none of this registered on Hildreth. Either the roar of wind and fire drowned out the marshal's words, or Hildreth mistook his caution for reluctance. Believing that Williams would not cooperate, he ran back to the mayor and asked for another and more specific order. He entreated the mayor to write quickly. Judge

Miller caught some of Hildreth's evangelistic fervor.

"Do something, in the name of God!" he cried.

Hildreth outlined his plan, which was much the same as what Williams had proposed, and which he had not heard. The logical place to start was the Union National Bank, and then a line of buildings along the south side of Washington Street on both sides of La Salle might be leveled and the fire halted there. But he added dolefully:

"I fear it is too late now."

"Go on and do *something*," Mason urged.

Hildreth could not find any volunteers to help carry the powder out of the courthouse, which is not surprising. Police Sergeant Lull, who had crossed to the South Side with the fire, ordered eight or ten policemen to help. Lull cleared the building of occupants as the powder was taken into the basement of the bank build-

ing. He and Hildreth then kicked in the ends of the kegs and scattered the powder in rows from one keg to another.

They could hear walls falling nearby, and Lull became alarmed. He urged Hildreth to hurry. The two then took a long fuse, lighted it from a gas jet, and after watching it burn down about six inches, put it on the floor and ran. Six or seven minutes later the powder went off with a roar. It blew out all the windows but only one wall, the rear one. The interior of the building was exposed to the flames, hastening its destruction.

Hildreth was thoughtful, but not discouraged. With the doubtful Lull following at his heels, he went back to the courthouse for more powder. He meant to try again.

I was so glad to get away that I just walked down to the lake and looked it over as if I was looking into heaven.

—PRISONER FROM THE COURTHOUSE JAIL

THE MILLION-dollar courthouse was the showpiece of the city, a symbol of its fresh prosperity and civic pride. It was built of marble in a flamboyant style, with curved pediments and knobby balustrades ornamenting its roof. The center of the building was crowned by a two-story tower with a cupola, which contained the four-faced clock, installed that spring, the five-and-a-half-ton bell, and the fire watchman's platform. From the cupola protruded a tall flagpole. A contemporary guidebook, no doubt written by an envious outsider, described the building as "one of the homeliest of its kind in the country."

The central portion of the building had been built in 1853 and enlarged five years later by flanking wings of "Lockport marble"—limestone, that is—each three stories high above a half basement. Finishing touches were still being added to this construction.

The west wing held the offices of Mayor Mason, a former Illinois Central Railway official, who was finishing his two-year term that autumn. Also in the wing were the offices of the Board of Police and of the chief marshal, the fire-alarm tele-graph, and the other city departments. Since Chicago was also the county seat, the east—or county—wing housed courtrooms, county records, and, in the basement, the county jail.

According to the original design, the city wing should have cost $250,000 and the county wing $200,000. Because of "insecure foundations, and a buckling roof and other *et ceteras* of city contracting," the actual cost was much higher. At last count, the city wing alone had eaten up $467,000.

The building was considered virtually fireproof, despite the fact that its cornices and exposed tower were made of wood.

Courthouse Square was surrounded by an iron picket fence. Trees grew in front of the building, facing Randolph Street, along the walks which ran diagonally from the main entrance to the Clark and La Salle Street corners.

Schafer had been relieved of his duties by Dennis Deneen at eleven o'clock, but remained in the tower for another hour, watching flames take over block after block in the West Division. He left the courthouse about midnight, planning to take a closer look at the spectacle. On the street, the wind was so strong he could hardly move against it. A short distance from the courthouse he met George Fuller, night operator of the fire-alarm telegraph, who was on his way to relieve Brown. Fuller had stopped at Monroe and Clark for a midnight snack on his way to work.

Schafer decided to return to the building with Fuller, who took over for the feckless Brown at 12:30. Five minutes after that, several new boxes were struck. The first was No. 19 at Van Buren and Market, signaling the new outbreak on the South Side.

Suddenly Deneen shouted down the tube that one of the vents in the west wing was burning. He asked for an extinguisher.

Fuller relayed the information to the police office. Sergeant Vesey sent an extinguisher and a man to operate it. This small fire was quickly put out.

Shortly before 1 A.M. the fire was marching inexorably north up Market, Fifth, Franklin, and La Salle Streets, and branching out in flanking forays to gobble up the cross streets between these northbound avenues. It had not yet reached Washington in force, nor made a direct attack on the courthouse. While the flames were mopping up the West Division, where all resistance had been driven to the edges of the doomed area, they were advancing

both north and east in the newly occupied sectors of the South Side, and it soon became apparent that much of that part of town—from the river down to Harrison Street at least—could be saved only by a miracle. None occurred.

Sixty-six-year-old Mayor Mason had established temporary headquarters in the basement offices of the police commissioners. He began sending urgent wires to neighboring cities appealing for more fire engines, and sent his two sons out to bring back reports on the situation. It was here that Hildreth had found him, and got authorization for his explosive experiments. By this time the fire extended over so wide an area, and the firefighting equipment was so scattered, that the battle was all but lost.

Although Mason and several other officials did their best, there was no disaster plan to coordinate their efforts once the fire had gone out of control. As exemplified in Hildreth's attempts to get backing for the use of powder, everyone, including the police and fire departments, was playing by ear, and there was no one to direct the band.

However, to be fair to the city fathers and the fire department, it seems likely that any plan would have been blown away on the screaming southwest wind. It is impossible to imagine any remedy, other than a sudden downpour, to stop the fiery contagion which was spread hundreds of feet overhead, completely out of reach. Communication, too, would have been a major problem, especially since several of the bridges were gone or going.

Nevertheless, few of the official efforts to face up to the disaster showed much imagination. Courage, yes—especially among the firemen—and occasional instances of good common sense. But there were very few who tried to work out any fresh or original way of stopping the holocaust or salvaging property in its path. The one important exception was, perhaps, Hildreth. But his ideas were not—at least at first—very shrewd or well-organized.

Hildreth was undaunted by the fiasco of his first attempt at demolition. He and his reluctant police squad took more powder from the engineer's room, under the sidewalk in the courthouse, and started out the main door. A sudden blast of heat, pouring around the block from the west, drove them back. They headed for the east door instead, and went around by way of Clark to the Smith and Nixon building, across from the courthouse on Washington Street. Sergeant Lull's coat caught fire several times from flying sparks as he helped carry the explosive.

After the powder was deposited in the basement of a restaurant in the building, the others ran, leaving Lull and Hildreth to prepare the charge. They took more pains with this one, although Lull was unnerved at the casual way Hildreth scuffed through the spilled powder as they worked. Hildreth laid the lighted fuse on the floor at last, and ran through the door Lull was holding open for him.

The two raced down Washington to Dearborn Street. They warned passers-by to stand back. In a few moments the powder went off. It made a splendid noise, but accomplished little else. A hole was blown straight up through the center of the building, but not a wall fell. Even more discouraging, all the powder was gone. One of Mason's sons appeared to cheer up Hildreth, however, by telling him the mayor had sent for more.

The courthouse itself, taller than the average building and exposed to continual buffeting by the fire-laden winds, was in constant danger. The steamer *Chicago,* with Conway in charge in place of the exhausted Schimmels, moved along Clark Street, immediately east of the courthouse. The firemen saw flames on the roof. Conway asked Henry Coleman, the engineer, if a stream could be thrown that high. Coleman thought it could. The engine stopped and prepared to attach its hose to a plug at Clark and Washington Streets. But Conway then saw—by fire glow nearly as bright as day—figures come onto the roof carrying pails and brooms. He ordered the hose called up, and the engine moved on to buildings in more imminent danger.

The men that Conway saw included Schafer. They managed to keep the sparks beaten out for some time, although Schafer's clothing caught more than once. But they were gambling against fatal odds. A blazing piece of pitch or felt was blown through a broken window under the cupola. It landed in a pile of shavings, left by workmen who had been repairing the clock. Schafer saw rising smoke and shouted an alarm. He ran to the north side of the tower and went in through a door under the balcony as Fuller started up from below.

Schafer was unable to stifle the mushrooming flames and yelled to Deneen, who was still in the tower, to run for his life. Deneen, finding the way down the iron stairway barred by smoke and fire, slid down the banister, burning his hands and face and scorching his whiskers during the descent.

Fuller, who earlier had rung some of the smaller outside bells to awaken sleepers who might be in peril, sounded them again. Schafer dashed down to the opera-

tions room. He saw flames through cracks in the ceiling. The plaster was already beginning to fall. Schafer started the machinery which rang the big bell automatically, then ran. It was about 1:45 Monday morning.

The men in the upper portion of the building fled by way of the west wing, pausing only long enough to slam fireproof doors between the buildings, a thoughtful but futile gesture. Fuller headed for the *Titsworth* house, picked up a fire hat, and worked for hours with the engines before going home.

Schafer hurried to the basement and warned the jailer to clear the cells before the courthouse burned down. He came out on Randolph Street. Marshal Williams was directing the *Economy* as it played a stream on the Sherman House, immediately across the street. Williams asked Schafer to help, and Schafer, who had already done far more than duty required, nonetheless obliged.

Police Captain Hickey also worried about the prisoners. He went into the courthouse and urged that they be freed at once, saying he and several of his men would escort those charged with murder to the North Side and lock them up again. The storm of sparks around the courthouse grew thicker as Hickey argued. Men ran past with their coats on fire.

The prisoners in the jail, more than a hundred of them, paced their dark cells, listening to the tumult of wind, the crackling of flames, and the sound of the engines. They began to shout and bang on the bars. A cloud of smoke blew into the building, entering air holes at the top and bottom of each cell door, and the prisoners began screaming in terror.

W. K. Sullivan, a *Tribune* reporter, was

among a group of men who reached the burning courthouse as the prisoners inside were begging for freedom. The outer jail door was locked, so he and the others took a plank from the street and began crashing it against the door. This drew a stern reproach from County Commissioner Daniel Worthington. This old gentleman, noted for honesty and insistence on public economy, warned those manning the battering ram that they would be held responsible for any damage to the building.

At last, on written orders from Mayor Mason, the cells were opened and their occupants freed, with the exception of a handful of murderers, who were marched away under guard.

The punctilious Worthington was later censured for having refused permission for county records to be removed, on the grounds that the courthouse was "fireproof." William Hawkins Hedges, head of the city sewer department, managed to load a two-wheeled pushcart with plats and surveys from his office, and shoved the cart into the La Salle Street horse-car tunnel two blocks north. All he got was an "A" for effort. Later on flames were sucked through the opening, firing the records as they roared by.

One of the liberated men fainted from relief. Others were stunned by their freedom and moved as though in a daze. Most ran for safety, but a few paused long enough to take some of the jewelry which A. H. Miller, owner of the store at the corner of Clark and Randolph, opposite the courthouse on the east, was giving away in preference to leaving it for the fire.

Miller, whose home was in the North Division, had been summoned by one of his clerks as the fire approached the store. With the help of several employees he had filled two large wagons with his stock. As he and the others were about to leave, he was told by firemen that the wagons must not be driven over the hose. The clerks took what they could carry and started north on foot. Miller, seeing the newly released prisoners streaming by, invited them to take whatever was left. Some must have thought they had reached Paradise—tossed out of jail and plied with jewels.

The clerks had reached the State Street Bridge to the North Division before they realized Miller was not directly behind them. One hurried back to find his employer trapped under some fallen debris. He was dug out unhurt, and made his way home.

In the heart of the business district, frame shops and shanties provided kindling for stone banks and insurance buildings. A large livery stable caught fire in an alley across from the courthouse, and another alley, running south from the *Long John*'s house, also provided quick nourishment for the flames. In it stood a plumbing shop, a restaurant, a bathhouse, several carpentry shops, some tenements, and Wright's undertaking establishment. Here the fire overtook what was left of the luckless Mrs. Develin for the second time.

The main line of resistance was centered around the courthouse block, on Randolph Street to its north and Clark Street to its east. Williams was still trying desperately to stem the flow of flames from the southwest, and had several engines dumping water all over the area. He boarded the *Washington* hose cart, and went off in vain search of the *Coventry,* in order to get another stream on Miller's jewelry store. But that engine had gone to the North Side to replace its broken taper. Fledgling fires were hatching in nests formed by furled awnings at the jeweler's.

Williams didn't know—but might have guessed—that the fire had once more jumped over him. Parts of Lake Street, the next block north of Randolph, lined with wholesale warehouses, were beginning to catch. Fires were also reported toward the northern end of Dearborn, a block east of Clark.

Williams's despair would probably have become complete had he known that the infection in the air was spreading beyond the South Division entirely, and attacking likely prospects across the river.

The *Chicago* was on Randolph between Franklin and Fifth, where fire was spurting from basement windows. Conway, running from the engine to the pipe, saw a woman in one of the upper windows. She wore a white cloth on her head. He had the strange thought that she looked as though she were cleaning house.

He shouted to her to leave the house. She replied that she would in a minute. He threw a heavy stick at the window to emphasize his suggestion. She came down at once. The building began burning just as she stepped from the front door.

The *Chicago* concentrated on a blue-gray fire that raged in the cellar of the Charles Pick crockery store at 212 Randolph, until the heat drove the firemen to Randolph and Market. There Henry

Baker, owner of a woodyard in the alley off Market, offered Conway money to bring water back to his property. Conway protested that such a move would be useless.

"You change the stream," Baker said, "and I will give you two hundred dollars."

"Keep your money," Conway responded, "but I will change the stream to satisfy you."

He did so, but within a few minutes it became apparent that Conway was right. The woodyard burned with the rest.

Conway and his men then watched helplessly as the Washington and Metropolitan hotels went down, in the block directly west of the courthouse. He warned the others against approaching the Metropolitan House. It long had been regarded in the department as a death trap. The warning was sound. The Metropolitan collapsed into a shapeless mass "before you could count to twenty."

A man was hurled by the wind against a lamppost in front of the Pittsburgh and Fort Wayne office, on Clark Street across from the Sherman House, and man and post went over together. The former *Tribune* building, on Clark near Randolph, was ablaze, and embers from it ignited Woods' Museum, half a block east.

It was difficult for anyone to survive near Courthouse Square, where the wind whipped in with venomous fury and sparks fell in a golden storm. Foreman Swenie of the ruined *Gund,* a stout, red-faced man who loved baseball, found himself clinging to a telegraph pole to avoid being blown into the street. He couldn't round the Sherman House corner against the wind.

Two boarders from a rooming house at 110 North Dearborn came across the river into the South Division to see what was

happening. They were Frank J. Loesch, a Western Union bookkeeper, and William A. LeRow of LeRow, Peters and Company, manufacturers of wire mattresses.

They saw whisky barrels standing in the street at Monroe and Fifth, apparently awaiting removal. Several men rammed the barrels until the whisky spilled out into the road, and then threw themselves down and drank from the gutters.

Firebands began falling, and the two sightseers ran east on Monroe, then north on La Salle to Washington. They saw no one else in the block north of Madison, which was carpeted with live coals. Halfway down that street, LeRow suddenly cried out that he was suffocating. Loesch grabbed his collar, and held on until they reached Washington. There the air was a little better. LeRow revived but decided he had had enough and went home.

Loesch then went to the Western Union office in the Merchants' Insurance building. The manager and three or four clerks were putting account books into the vault. The employees worked by the light of the flames, since the gas was out. The

ONE OF THE POPULAR SOUVENIRS OF THE FIRE WAS BEFORE-AND-AFTER CARDS, CONTAINING TWO PICTURES OF THE SAME SCENE. THESE PICTURES FROM ONE SUCH CARD SHOW THE COURTHOUSE AND CITY HALL BOTH BEFORE AND AFTER THE FIRE. (CHICAGO PUBLIC LIBRARY)

AFTER THE FIRE, THE COURTHOUSE BELL BECAME A TARGET FOR SOUVENIR HUNTERS WHO FASHIONED THE METAL INTO RINGS AND SCARF PINS. THE BELL WAS EVENTUALLY SOLD AT AUCTION FOR 62-1/2 CENTS PER POUND. HERE A SIGHTSEEING YOUNGSTER SITS INSIDE THE BELL. (CHICAGO PUBLIC LIBRARY)

roof caught fire. Telegraph operators ran from the upper floors, and the Associated Press reporter stopped transmitting his story in midsentence. He had to go to a suburban railroad depot to finish it.

The final message sent that night over the Western Union wire read:

THE BLOCK IMMEDIATELY ACROSS THE STREET FROM THE TELEGRAPH OFFICE, ONE OF THE FINEST—

Loesch escaped to La Salle and ran up to Randolph. Everything below the corner of Washington and La Salle appeared to be burning, and the brownstone center part of

the courthouse was afire, the bell still clanging as the flames devoured the tower. The limestone of which the wings were built was melting and running down the face of the building at the southwest corner.

Smoke poured from the windows and ventilators of the courthouse. The great bell hammered out the warning of destruction which no one needed. It was tolling its own knell. Soon the whole massive structure was wrapped in flame. At 2:12 the hands slid down one of the clock faces. Three minutes later both tower and bell crashed into the basement with a shattering roar that could be heard in every part of town.

Mayor Mason stayed in his basement headquarters at the courthouse until the roof began to fall in, and then gave up the fight. He and his sons ran out of the building and north on Clark, which was by then the only escape route. Fire was sweeping in along the south and west, and it looked as if there might be flames to the east as well.

Mason finally reached the river and crossed over to the North Side. He walked well east of the flames, which were beginning to gain a foothold above the river, and returned to the South Side by way of the Rush Street Bridge. His own house was far to the south on Michigan Avenue, out of the path of the fire.

Mayor Mason apparently decided that nothing more could be done until the following day. He went home.

CHAPTER 8

The dogs of hell were upon the housetops . . . bounding from one to another.

—HORACE WHITE

THE SIX-story Sherman House, a hotel built only ten years before, stood directly north of the courthouse on Randolph Street. The main entrance was from Clark, up a broad flight of stone steps under a two-story portico. There was a railed observation tower on the flat roof, from which visitors could view most of the city. A second-floor balcony extended along both the Clark and Randolph façades, providing a pleasant private promenade above the dust and noise of the street.

When the flames moved northward from the courthouse, they overleaped the Sherman and ran toward Lake Street. Then they turned back to seize the hotel from the rear.

The woodwork began smoking an hour before the first slender finger of flame appeared at the third floor. Scores of men were fighting to keep the roof clean of sparks. But soon there were scarlet festoons at the windows, and clouds of smoke began scudding toward the northeast. The Sherman housed 300 guests that night. Several were women traveling alone, and five of these were known to be ill.

John R. Chapin, an artist for *Harper's*

Weekly, had come to town by train that afternoon and registered at the Sherman. He heard the fire alarm around ten o'clock while reading in bed, but paid no attention to it. He grew drowsy and turned out the gaslight about 10:30. He was awakened some hours later by the rattle of a key in the lock on his door. He started up.

"Who's there? What do you want?" he called.

There was no reply. He fell asleep again, only to be reawakened by the sound of tramping feet and voices in the hall. There was also a roaring noise from outside. In his semiconscious state he took it to be the rumble of wheels on the wooden pavement below. He listened for a few minutes, thinking morning must be near, and tried without success to fall asleep. He found himself gradually possessed by a nameless dread.

He jumped up and opened the blinds. He was confronted by a sheet of flame towering a hundred feet into the sky.

Chapin had the presence of mind to pack his valise, and even remembered to remove his watch from under the pillow. Then he dressed and went into the hall. Fellow guests were rushing through the corridors half-dressed, dragging trunks and carrying carpetbags and other luggage. Many people who had never moved their own baggage before discovered that night it could be done. Chapin walked downstairs and found the cloakroom closed. He decided not to waste time trying to find someone to open it, but went into the warm night coatless and walked west, away from the fire.

When it became apparent that the Sherman would be destroyed, John Hickie, the night clerk, collected what important papers he could, and had every guest notified. The unescorted women were taken to the Lake shore and placed under the protection of the police. Four of the ailing ones were brought downstairs and removed to safety in hansom cabs. Then Hickie realized one was missing.

He and two other employees went back upstairs. The woman failed to answer the knock and they broke down the door. She was still in bed, and helpless. They doused her dress and cloak with water, soaked a quilt to wrap her in, and helped her from the building. Two of the rescuers had their clothing scorched, and the other burned his hand. The walls of the Sherman House fell in moments after they emerged.

Chapin made his way to the Washington Street tunnel, which was still open. He was, by either luck or design, heading in the one safe direction. He helped an old lady carry some belongings, and aided a mother who held an infant and was trying to keep track of six other youngsters as well. He glanced back after reaching the West Side, and as far to the east as he could see there was a wall of fire, 100 to 200 feet high, moving very fast. Chapin was wet with perspiration, and shivered from the sudden chill of the West Side air. Someone

directed him to a boardinghouse on West Washington, where he changed his clothes.

He walked a block north to the Randolph Street Bridge. There he found a vantage point and began to sketch the burning city. There were flames and smoke along a broad arc for two miles to his right. The Nelson elevator, on the riverbank in the West Division, was a burning pillar, sending smoke and fire high into the night. The Nevada Hotel, a seven-story brick building which was home to many minor newspaper and theatrical people, was circled by flames but stood defiant at the southwest corner of Washington and Franklin.

Then a wisp of smoke went twisting up from one corner, followed by a dart of fire, and in a few minutes the 100-foot-square hotel, owned by William Bross of the *Tribune,* came down. The Briggs House, where Lincoln's first campaign headquarters had been, and Peter Schuttler's Wagon Works, whose owner made a fortune selling to the Union Army during the war, were burning at the same time. The fire, as Chapin put it, "was devouring the most stately and massive buildings as though they had been the cardboard playthings of a child. . . . One after another they dissolved, like snow on a mountain."

From this spot Chapin had virtually a panoramic view of the entire West and South Division fires, though buildings on his left shut out the scene on the North Side. Immediately to the right were block after block of burning buildings, stretching down to what now were the ashes of the O'Leary barn. In the light of the flickering blaze—and of the moon which emerged fitfully through the smoke clouds—the river could be seen glittering in an arc before him. Some of its bridges were aflame and

swinging free; others had already burned. Hordes of refugees poured across the Randolph and Lake Street Bridges.

The noises blended into a nightmarish cacophony: the crash of falling walls, the roar of flames, the shrieking of the wind, the shouts of men and the weeping of women and children, and the shrill whistles of the tugs working to move ships out of danger.

The streets were thronged with wagons and carts, many of them pulled by hand, and wheelbarrows, trucks, and handcarts. A man was pushing a three-wheeled store truck, loaded with desks, chairs, cushions, and other office furniture. The load fell off as he tried to ease his cart over the horsecar tracks. It was smashed to bits under the wheels of a speeding express wagon.

Much of Randolph became covered with flames, and barrels of oil at Heath and Milligan's began exploding like the crackle of muskets. The Garden City House, on the east side of Market, burned like a toy build-

ing, its iron pillars melting as if they were butter. Randolph Street Bridge was a scene of Dantesque confusion, as vehicles of every style and shape tried to force a passage together. There were constant collisions, but when wagons broke down, as they frequently did, crowds of men dragged them by hand to the west bank.

Harlots from various houses crossed in groups, seated in wagons. A string of youths, each carrying a coffin on his head, went toward the west, followed by an undertaker driving a dray on which was a large casket. The span swung open from time to time, while pedestrians cursed, to permit some tug with vessel in tow to pass through. And the captain of a brig anchored nearby kept calling in vain for one of the passing tugs to throw him a line.

Other observers during this same period, when the South Side fire was reaching a crest of fury, described how it swept down alleyways, then "burst through the rear of buildings on either side, swept through them, and dashing through the fronts united in one solid, writhing, twisting column of fire, which would shoot up into the air a hundred feet, and then, seized by the wind, leap to roofs in the next block and fire them."

The wind played other tricks. Some saw it seize flames from the fronts of large blocks, "detach it entirely and hurl it in every direction . . . leaving the building as if it had been untouched, for an instant only, however, for fresh gusts would once more wrap it in sheets of fire." This phenomenon was accompanied by a sound "like the flapping of sails" which could be heard even above the bluster of the wind.

The river, long considered a barrier to the spread of fire, was at this time a scene of furious activity.

A PRE-FIRE LOOK WEST ALONG THE RIVER FROM RUSH STREET BRIDGE. SHIP RIGGING IS CLUSTERED IN THE DISTANCE. (CHICAGO HISTORICAL SOCIETY)

When the fire broke out, there were perhaps two hundred vessels of varying tonnage moored up and down the stream. All of these were of wood, and most of them were propelled by sail, and depended on tugs to get them in and out of the narrow channels.

As the fire moved up the east and west banks of the South Branch, everything on the river was imperiled. The bridges to the West Side were in danger from the time the fire jumped to the South Division. The Adams and Van Buren Street Bridges had been the first to go, and the Polk Street Bridge was set afire separately somewhat later. Good fortune and Bridgetender Boyer's courage saved the Madison Street Bridge, but it had to be kept swung out so much of the time that it was all but useless

opened often, hindered and terrified those who sought to escape.

One onlooker saw the tarred ends of rigging blazing above the South Branch "like a queer sort of Irish pennants." After the *Fontinella* caught fire, other ships found themselves in immediate danger. Some of the vessels, threatened with destruction before a tow could be arranged, were abandoned by their crews, who leaped into the water, and swam or used pieces of floating debris to reach safety.

As the tugs got their efforts coordinated, a long procession could be seen gliding slowly up the South Branch and main stream, silhouetted against the South Side fire—"long lines of gaunt, bare masts, lit up with the glare of the flames, moving along the river on their way to the lake."

Charles Noble, first mate of a vessel out of Buffalo, ordered all sails tightly furled and kept soaked with water when he found he couldn't have the ship towed out of the river. Crew members stood by with long poles to fend off burning derelicts as they approached. The clothes of the crew were riddled with sparks, but the ship suffered only minor damage. Finally the fire went on to easier victims. When the ship was safe at last, most of the men volunteered for patrol duty ashore.

Joseph Chamberlin, the young reporter for the *Post* who had been reporting the West Side fire, tried to reach his office on the south side of Madison, between Clark and Dearborn, after the courthouse tower fell. He started south down Dearborn from Lake Street, but the blazing blizzard forced him into an abandoned store. He found a blanket lying on the floor and wrapped it around him. He came out again and doggedly turned south, but walked only as

to refugees. The Washington Street tunnel was open when Chapin passed through, but drafts of heat sucked through it made it impassable shortly after. Only the Randolph Street and Lake Street Bridges were then open. This pocket was bypassed by the main line of fire moving directly toward the courthouse, and was not threatened until most of the business area was destroyed.

The shipping had begun burning early, but only a small percentage was actually destroyed. Most of the ships were saved by the labors of the tugs, the main stream of the river to the Lake, or up into the far reaches of the North Branch. This rescue operation, for which the bridges had to be

far as Washington before giving up the attempt and running back north to Lake, then west five blocks to the river.

He paused for a time on the Randolph Street Bridge, probably within hailing distance of Chapin. From a perch on the railing he too saw the Briggs, Metropolitan, and Nevada hotels, Schuttler's Wagon Works, and Heath and Milligan's all burning at once. At last he grew weary of the spectacle, and wandered across to Canal Street, where he lay down on a lumber pile in Avery's yard. Half a dozen men were there, and a friendly argument sprang up—while the town burned—concerning the weight of one of the group, "a fat fellow called Fred." The object of controversy admitted at last that he weighed 206 pounds.

He asked that it not be noised abroad.

Meanwhile the fire was driving east in the lower end of the South Division and into the Grand Pacific Hotel, whose unfinished magnificence covered the entire block bordered by Quincy, Jackson, Clark, and La Salle. It was convenient to the Michigan Southern railroad depot, across Jackson Street to the south. The Grand Pacific, six stories of olive-tinted Ohio sandstone, was being built with an initial stock subscription of $600,000. It was virtually completed, but not yet open for business.

This ultramodern hotel boasted a carriage court covered with a glass dome, where a dozen omnibuses could discharge passengers at once. There were shops in the office rotunda, which had a stained-glass roof. A marble staircase led to the upper floors, its landing windows surveying the carriage court. Steam-driven "vertical railways," the last word in splendor, were prepared to carry residents of the Grand Pacific

"as lightly and as smoothly as a cloud rises in the summer air," according to the modest prospectus.

There were 100 private parlors, the smallest fourteen-by-twenty feet, with baths attached, and 450 single rooms. The basement of this self-contained establishment held a bakery and a laundry. Tanks under the roof could hold 12,000 gallons of water and flood any part of the building at a moment's notice. These might have been useful in this crisis—except that they were empty.

By the time the *Long John* arrived from the ruins of the gasworks, the Grand Pacific had yielded to the importunities of a visitor that wouldn't take no for an answer. This brawling guest had taken over the whole hotel and was busily wrecking the place.

The mammoth Grand Pacific burned with tremendous speed, starting so far above the street that the *Long John*'s stream

couldn't reach it against the wind. Stones began falling from the stricken hotel, thudding into the roadway and making it perilous for the firemen to remain at their posts.

Schank, who had come down State Street after the courthouse was hopelessly ablaze, was directing this one-sided fight. Now, with the building disintegrating, he ordered the *Long John* to move for the fourth or fifth time since it had come over from the West Side. As Foreman McMonagle directed the uncoupling of the hose, a plunging stone struck the engine, shearing a bolt and three rivets off the boiler. When the driver went after the horses, they had mysteriously disappeared. The engine had to be pulled away by hand.

The *Long John,* battered but still serviceable, moved east along Jackson Street, to oppose the wave of flame that had carried off the hotel. Schank meanwhile went south to see what the fire was up to below Jackson.

Another hostelry several blocks north reluctantly admitted a similar visitor about the same hour. The Tremont House was a five-story hotel built in 1850 by James and Ira Couch. It had been known then as "Couch's Folly," because few citizens believed Chicago could provide enough guests to keep it running. Two smaller Tremont Houses, previously on the same site, had been destroyed by fire. The new one, which cost $75,000, was the first large building in town to be lighted with gas.

Lincoln and Douglas spoke from the Tremont's iron-railed balcony on successive evenings in 1858, three years before the Little Giant died in his Tremont House room. Ralph Waldo Emerson was a guest during an 1858 lecture tour.

The Tremont was without rival among Western hotels until the Sherman was built. It stood at the southeast corner of Dearborn and Lake, within easy walking distance of the great Union depot.

Around 3 A.M. the roof of the Tremont caught fire. All was confusion inside. The elevators were no longer working, and hysterical women were crying for absent husbands. A man, obviously searching for someone, went from floor to floor looking in all the rooms with open or unlocked doors and calmly kicking in those which were fastened. From the small-paned windows with flowered lace curtains, the fire could be seen advancing from several points.

Smoke began to curl down the stairways in quiet eddies. Men who had been fighting the flames on the tin-covered roof ran silently past the escaping guests, as if pursued by a phantom enemy. Some guests, in their haste to descend the crowded stairs, leaped the banisters and limped off with sprained ankles. On one of the lower floors a man was dragging to the stairs the limp form of a large woman in a striped satin dress and a profusion of jewels. A stranger helped carry her to the lobby. She suddenly regained consciousness and ran out in a panic, her husband at her heels.

Through the main entrance, buildings on the west side of Dearborn could be seen burning.

Lake Street swarmed with people and buzzed with a babel of voices. A man had been stacking a store truck with goods stolen from J. B. Shay and Company's dry goods store, ignoring with maddening insolence the protests of loyal employees. Just as he finished loading, an employee came to the door with a revolver and threatened to shoot. The thief was unmoved.

"Fire and be damned!" he cried, then drove away.

The clerk put the revolver back into his pocket.

John B. Drake, who had risen from steward of the Tremont to sole owner since joining the staff in 1855, left when the fire checked in. He saved nothing but some money from the safe and a few pillowcases filled with silverware.

An hour before the Tremont finally went, a druggist from the hotel, named Wilson, had run across the street and pounded on the door of the building occupied by John Ashleman's jewelry store. Ashleman, who was sleeping soundly, lived in the two upper floors, because he often worked nights and wanted to be near home. Wilson beat the door until it shook and shouted:

"For God's sake, John, get up!"

The noise aroused Mrs. Ashleman, who opened the curtain to see a blinding glare outside. The family arose at once. After taking what they could from home and store, the family of four went out. Ashleman carefully locked the front door with a great, old-fashioned key, which he put into his pocket. The key, some money, and a few books were the only things saved, except for some diamonds later recovered from his otherwise useless safes.

The family hurried toward State Street, their house already burning behind them. The jeweler paused long enough to hand up a pail of water at the request of a man in a store on Lake Street.

As the party crossed State Street Bridge, Mrs. Ashleman's cloak twice caught fire, and one girl's hat was blown into the gleaming water. The other daughter was pinned against a girder by the force of the

wind and had to be aided by her father before she could go on. The Ashleman's English bulldog trotted along behind.

The *Chicago Times* building was on the west side of Dearborn Street, two-and-a-half blocks south of the Tremont. It was a five-story stone-front structure with its press in the basement, offices and library on the first floor, and composing room on the fifth. The floors between were occupied by reporters and editorial staff. All were working on a special fire edition. By 2 A.M. an editorial had been written, suggesting that

TREMONT HOUSE, THE CITY'S MOST HISTORIC HOTEL, WAS BUILT IN 1850 ON THE SITE OF TWO SMALLER TREMONT HOUSES, BOTH OF WHICH BURNED DOWN. THE NEW TREMONT WAS BUILT BY TWO BROTHERS, JAMES AND IRA COUCH, AT A COST OF $75,000 AND WAS KNOWN LOCALLY AS "COUCH'S FOLLY" BECAUSE IT WAS CONSIDERED TO BE A POOR INVESTMENT. BY 3 A.M. ON OCTOBER 9, 1871, THE FIRE BEGAN NIBBLING AT THE ROOF, AND VERY SOON, THE TREMONT WENT DOWN. (LESLIE'S ILLUSTRATED WEEKLY, OCTOBER 28, 1871)

THE SHERMAN HOUSE, ACROSS THE
AVENUE FROM COURTHOUSE SQUARE, WAS
ONE OF THE LARGEST AND FINEST HOTELS
IN THE MIDWEST. BUILT IN 1861, IT GAVE
ITS GUESTS A SUPERB VIEW OF THE CITY
FROM ITS RAILED OBSERVATION TOWER ON
THE ROOF SIX STORIES ABOVE THE STREET.
(SHEAHAN/UPTON)

the stricken town would need help from her sister cities.

Employees were watching the progress of the fire from the upper-story windows. As the flames drew nearer, those printers with families to worry about began disappearing, until only half the regular staff of thirty was left. It was suddenly decided to go to press at once. The final bulletin was written:

"THE VERY LATEST—The entire business portion of the city is burning up, and the TIMES building is doomed."

The fire leaped easily over Madison, and all hopes of issuing a paper vanished. The building caught fire about 3 A.M. and was gone half an hour later. Departing employees paused long enough to break into the vault and save a few of the files. As the last of the printers fled, the spiral staircase was starting to burn.

The post office and customhouse, a block south of the *Times* building on Dearborn, were outranked in volume of business only by New York and Philadelphia. Their building was threatened not

long after midnight, but didn't actually catch fire until half an hour or so after the *Times.*

Henry H. Nash, cashier of the United States Depository in the post office, came with his nephew, Frederick Blount, and placed various valuables, including $50,000 in currency and some of his wife's silver spoons, in the vault. The two then helped the watchman and a janitor close all the iron shutters. When the building had been repaired in the spring, the shutters on the first floor and basement windows had been removed at the request of employees who wanted more light.

Alonzo Hannis, a postal clerk, had gone to bed in his home on the West Side after distributing outgoing mail for the West Division railroads. He was awakened by cries of fire, and helped fight the blaze near Van Buren for a time, until he began worrying about the post office. He tried several bridges and finally found the one at Randolph open to traffic. The courthouse was burning as he dashed by, and men were tearing flaming awnings from the Sherman House. He saw several men he knew and asked why they were doing nothing to save their property. They assured him the fire soon would be stopped.

At the post office, he rang the night bell and was admitted by Wells, the night watchman, and David Green, night superintendent of mails, who had been at work since 7 P.M. Hannis, believing the post office was sure to go, asked permission from Green to begin packing letters for removal. Green was unconcerned and very official:

"If you touch any letters without orders from headquarters you will get your discharge!"

Hannis protested that the gasworks had

burned, and that there would soon be no light to work by. Green left to check the progress of the fire, and Hannis began at once—without orders—to pack letters to be put into bags. Green returned shortly, observed what Hannis was doing, but did not protest. At 1 A.M. he sent a clerk to the home of Charles Walsh, a contractor who carried the mails. Green asked Walsh to come, and to send a messenger to C. S. Squire, assistant postmaster, to tell him of the emergency.

At 1:45 teams were brought to the building to stand by. At 2 A.M. it was decided to move the mails at once. Hannis and another clerk soon had the western mail in sacks and thrown downstairs. By now there were numerous other employees on hand. At 2:30, Colonel George W. Wood, assistant superintendent of the railway mail service, came in from his home on South Wabash.

Ignoring the protests of a customs official, he told the clerks to save everything possible. Wagons were loaded with all the mail on hand. Only a small batch which had arrived over the Fort Wayne railroad four hours before was overlooked. Registry books and the furniture from one office were also carried out. When the customs man objected, Wood replied:

"You may wait for an act of Congress if you like. I'm going to save what I can."

Hannis and Bliss went into the delivery cases and took all the letters, leaving the newspapers and circulars to burn. The gas went out at 2:45. The offices were dark, except for three flickering candles and the glare from outside. Green left with a large amount of mail, which he dragged to State and Monroe and guarded, waiting for the wagons to return.

The building at the northwest corner caught about 3:30. Green had returned, but was refused admittance by a suspicious policeman guarding the door. Inside, other clerks and carriers still worked with feverish haste. The order to clear the building was given at 4:15. Bliss and Hannis were the last two out, Hannis refusing to leave until he had put the remaining letters into bags, locked them, and thrown them into the lobby for removal. He was working by the light from the Lombard and Reynolds buildings, in the same block, which seemed ready to collapse against the post office.

Hannis finally left on the run, stumbling over a large Number One leather mailbag as he fled. He grabbed the strap and pulled the bag into the street and down to Michigan Avenue. He stood guard over it for a time, along with a wagonload of fine cutlery from a Lake Street wholesale house. Then he became fearful that the fire might cut off his escape. He went south on Michigan, still dragging the mail.

When he reached the park across from Peck Court, he saw a woman sitting on a pile of household goods. He decided she had an "honest look" and asked whether she would mind watching the mail while he found a wagon. She arose, spread her silk dress over the bag, and sat down again, saying:

"If anyone attempts to take the mail, I will shoot him on the spot!"

Hannis never discovered whether she could have made good her threat. He found a wagon and took the mail to safety.

The post office fell easy prey to the flames through the absence of the ground-floor shutters. Fire swept in from the new Lombard block, about thirty feet to the west. The large wooden letter cases on the main floor burned with such heat that they warped the iron beams supporting the floor above. These bent and fell, and the upper floors slid into the basement. With them fell two brick vaults containing about two million dollars, a total loss.

Next door to the post office, in rooms in the post-office block, lived a Mrs. Ackley and her son Jesse. As the fire approached Dearborn, she and the boy packed some of their belongings in trunks and carried them a block east to State Street. She left Jesse to guard them and started back home.

On her way, a passing stranger warned her that some stables were burning nearby and advised her to leave at once. She ran into the building to pass the warning on.

She went to the apartment of John E. Donovan, a former Wisconsin sheriff, who had lived several years in Chicago. He had already sent his wife and daughter to State Street, and was picking up some papers in his room.

He and Mrs. Ackley looked out and saw no sign of immediate danger. They wrote off the stranger as an alarmist, and Mrs. Ackley returned to her rooms.

A few moments later her son rushed in, almost incoherent from excitement.

"Mother," he cried, "you will be burned alive!"

The two ran at once down the Monroe Street stairway, forgetting in their panic to warn Donovan. Smoke blanketed Monroe Street, and it was almost impossible to breathe. Jesse said he had seen no one on the street or in the building during the trip back.

"We cannot go to the trunks," he added. "We must go down Dearborn Street!"

They dashed to the east side of

Dearborn and ran up to the *Tribune* building, a block north. As Jesse glanced back he thought he saw the post office burning. They decided to try to go west to the Madison Street bridge—a nightmarish journey over six burned blocks.

The street on both sides was still afire in many places. The wind drove smoke and cinders into their eyes. They passed a few men whose faces were paper-white in the unearthly light. A man following the same route helped Mrs. Ackley across piles of hot bricks and through tangles of telegraph wires, which caught at her feet. She and her son saved nothing but the clothes on their backs.

Donovan disappeared. His wife and daughter never saw him again, and for many weeks no one knew what had happened to him.

Many blocks to the south, a new drama was now taking place which was to have important consequences for much of the South Division.

Shortly after the fire triumphed over the courthouse, it launched a new attack across the river from the West Side. The last pockets of resistance were being cleaned out along the west bank of the river, and the Polk Street Bridge was crowded with refugees. The fire on the South Side did not extend far below Van Buren Street.

Someone shouted a warning that the end of Polk Street Bridge was on fire. Pedestrians started to run. Two heavy wagons on the bridge swayed and rumbled as their horses were whipped into a gallop. The bridge oscillated so wildly that some of those crossing it had to leap to reach the sidewalk at the east end. Flames then gnawed the structure until it tumbled into the river.

Those who reached shore safely had to

keep going. The destruction of the bridge heralded a new beachhead of fire on the South Side. The flames worked their way swiftly east around Polk Street, fanning out as they came.

At two o'clock that Monday morning, Isaac Milliken, another of the town's seemingly innumerable former mayors, had been awakened in his home at 123 Third Avenue, two doors south of Harrison Street, by the sound of conversation outside. It was so light, he thought at first that morning had come. Then he saw scarlet skies to the west and dressed at once.

He headed west toward the fire. When he reached the Michigan Southern depot, which was at the foot of La Salle below Van Buren and a couple of blocks north of his

home, the fire had not yet reached it. But lumber piles along the tracks were ablaze, and the Bridewell prison nearby was gone. Milliken saw no one except some people gazing stolidly at the fire. The cornices of a building at Griswold and Harrison began smoking, and were about to burst into flame.

Milliken opened the front door of this building and found himself in a saloon with a group of men who had no interest other than the bottles in front of them. But he persuaded one man and a boy to carry water up on the roof to try to save the building.

Milliken then managed to recruit some other men in the neighborhood in order to move the freight cars standing in the direct path of the flames. At this point Marshal Schank arrived from the remains of the Grand Pacific Hotel.

Schank and Milliken, by a combination of luck and hard work, then waged a successful battle against an important sector of the spreading flames. It was the first time any of the firefighting forces had succeeded in even so much as slowing them down.

Schank agreed with Milliken that if the freight cars were not moved from the yards, the fire might leap to them and continue east right across the South Side to the Lake. Schank sent an urgent appeal to the West Side for help, and the crew of volunteers began the laborious process of pushing the cars south by hand. After a hundred or so had been moved, a couple of switch engines appeared from down the tracks and magnanimously moved the last two.

The steamer *Rice,* which had been working on the far flank of the West Side fire, arrived in response to Schank's plea for aid, and the *Economy* moved into the same area, after almost being trapped and destroyed at the Clark Street Bridge. Despite the efforts of the two engines, the huge stone depot between Jackson and Harrison Streets, whose central roof sheltered five tracks, finally caught fire, and the walls and roof caved in. The freight depots on the west side of the tracks south of Harrison also were destroyed but those on the east, of brick with slate roofs and no side windows, presented an impassable barrier to the flames.

Schank and the men with him were nearing collapse, but worked doggedly on. The water failed and the hoses of the two steamers went slack. Schank did not then know why. He ordered the men to draw water from the river, and they resumed pumping in time to stop the flames from leaping the track and continuing east above the freight depot.

This fight along the railroad took several hours. But through the foresight and determination of Milliken and Schank, the fire never moved east of the tracks below Harrison.

CHAPTER 9

Everyone about me likened the awful scene to his fancy of the Judgment Day.

—Joseph Medill

A S THE fire moved relentlessly through the heart of the South Division, it seemed as if the whole city were on the move with it. Not only were the streets and bridges jammed with refugees, but many other people—out of simple curiosity, or the desire to save something of their property, or even to take advantage of unprecedented opportunities for looting and theft—came pouring into the business section, only to be driven out with the inhabitants as the fire came bearing down upon them.

The danger, the excitement, the destruction, and the spectacle of the holocaust provoked a broad range of reactions. The scene was one of violent contrasts in emotion and experience, a panorama of human behavior more varied and more dramatic than the show the fire itself provided. Avarice and self-sacrifice, reason and panic, sorrow and gaiety, courage and cowardice appeared in close juxtaposition; sudden good luck in the midst of calamity, and sudden misfortune on the verge of safety, were equally common.

In the path of the flames and around the fringes of the doomed area every street was packed with jostling refugees, on foot and in every sort of conveyance. At intersections, and on the remaining bridges, the press and confusion were particularly severe. Wagons and buggies were brought almost to a standstill in the seething masses of pedestrians, while the latter ran the risk of being trampled by terrified horses, or of falling beneath the wheels. Lost children wandered crying through the throngs. The sick and helpless were often carried on chairs or improvised litters, or in others' arms to safety. Occasionally processions of mourners passed through the streets—carrying coffins or even inert bundles wrapped in sheets—attempting to save from the devouring flames the bodies of their yet unburied dead.

A horde of people moved west over the Lake Street Bridge. One of its guard rails was broken away. A man carrying a load of clothing stumbled and fell into the river. No one tried to save him, although there were numerous small boats, laden with salvage, nearby.

On the approach to Clark Street Bridge was seen the body of a ragged youngster, crushed by a marble slab apparently thrown from a window. The dead boy wore white kid gloves, and gold cuff links spilled from his pockets.

At Randolph and Wabash, two men were struck by bolts of cloth thrown from upper windows. One of them failed to get up.

Saloons were broken into and their shelves looted. Others opened the doors or rolled barrels into the street, and held impromptu parties. Drunken men, according to one spectator, "staggered through the crowds, apparently possessed of the idea that the whole affair was a grand municipal spree, in which they were taking part as a duty that should be discharged by all good citizens."

Wabash Avenue was almost solid with people, wagons, and abandoned possessions, including oil paintings, books, musical instruments, toys, mirrors, and bedding, many of which were trampled to bits underfoot. A woman of obvious wealth was seen forcing her way awkwardly through the throng; some of the less-favored snatched at her jewels as she passed. A drunken man standing on a piano apostrophized the fire as "the friend of the poor man," and urged everyone to help himself to the best liquor he could find. He was felled by a thrown bottle.

All the space between Michigan Avenue and the Lake, south from the river for almost a mile, was filled with furniture and other salvage. This was a grassy area, seventy-five to a hundred feet wide, where tidy neighborhood housewives customarily had their carpets carried out to be beaten.

The avenue itself was crammed with wagons, some loaded and some empty, until at last the police blocked it off. Even then many of the teamsters simply swore at the policemen and drove past, shouting that they had valuable cargo aboard. Others tried to turn in obedience to orders, and had their wheels smashed for their trouble.

On the Illinois Central tracks, running on a trestle just offshore, locomotives, pulling strings of cars toward the south, went puffing by, their whistles making mournful music across the narrow inlet where Chicagoans boated in the summer and ice-skated in the winter.

A barefooted little girl walked down Michigan Avenue, tenderly carrying a box of four puppies. She was wiser than many of her elders. One man carried a length of stovepipe, another an empty box, another a feather duster. Two wheeled away a wooden Indian.

A Negro woman trudged by, a washbasket full of clothes on her shoulder, a frying pan and some muffin rings in the other hand. An ember dropped into the basket, and the clothes flared up and were dumped into the street. A rooster rode haughtily past on its owner's shoulder. A cigar dealer, loaded with boxes, stumbled and fell, precipitating a scramble for the stogies scattered in the street.

Some put a higher price on whatever particular business they had in hand than they did on their lives. On Adams Street, a woman was forcibly removed from her burning home three times, and on each occasion ran back inside, finally to be consumed. Another man ignored horrified shouts as he ran toward a doomed building on Market Street. He was swallowed by a puff of flame before he reached the door.

Owners of express vehicles, drays, and other conveyances charged outrageous prices for their desperately needed services.

Ten thousand dollars' worth of electrotype plates and books burned at the curb in front of a downtown publishing house because clerks who had carried them from the building lacked money to pay the $100 fee demanded in advance for their removal. Other drivers refused to take loads at any price, preferring to cruise the streets and pick up whatever of value they found. It was common for a load to be paid for and taken on, then dumped a few blocks away so the driver could find a new victim.

At the St. James Hotel, a man with an invalid wife had just hired a hack for $60 when a jeweler, not knowing it was engaged, ran up and offered $500 for its use. The hackman gave speedy assent to the better offer, slammed his door, and was about to pull away. But two bystanders grabbed him and pulled him off the box. A third member of the contract-enforcement group opened the door and helped the lady in, then drove husband and wife to safety.

Not all vehicle owners were trying to get rich at the expense of their fellows. A few offered service at the normal rate, or for nothing. The Brinks Express Company loaned wagons free of charge, and Young's horsecar line on Wabash carried refugees and their belongings without fee—although a rival line, Zipp's, asked high prices. Rudolph Geiser, proprietor of a bird store at Randolph Street Bridge, turned down offers of $25 for his wagon and hauled numerous loads for free. He then had to hire another conveyance to carry his own effects.

Behind the fleeing masses, in the blocks immediately menaced by the fire, a curious lull often prevailed. The buildings and streets were largely abandoned. A few firemen and engines might be found, fighting a desperate rear-guard action before being forced on once more. Occasionally wagons careered by, carrying salvaged goods to safety. A few citizens remained in the area, engaged in last-minute errands, both legitimate and otherwise.

Attorney George Payson, who awakened in his home in the North Division about 2 A.M., left a fine description of the scene in the business district. He went to his office at 39 South Clark, a block below the burning courthouse, and by that time found the streets virtually deserted:

"A few persons . . . came and went like specters. They either had nothing to tell, or no time to tell it in. The wind was bewildering, for it seemed to come from every quarter and with a fury I had hardly ever seen before. Showers of sparks rained all around me, and blew along the pavement, threatening to start a fresh fire at every turn."

He thought the empty thoroughfares oddly frightening. He saw no engines, no firemen, no spectators. "The great city was left to burn alone, without any attempt to save it."

Payson ran to his office, brought out a couple of books and a volume of briefs, and went north again through the tunnel. The lights were out, and people feeling their way in the blackness were guided by shouts of: "Keep to the right! Keep to the right!"

A great number of businessmen made such visits to their downtown offices, attempting to save money, papers, or books—not only their own property, but that of other people for which they felt responsible. These missions were often accomplished at great personal risk, especially since many of these men lived outside the area, and were unable to reach their offices until they were in imminent danger of being destroyed. The cash, securities, and official papers rescued by such men were of incalculable value in the aftermath of the disaster.

The experiences of George and William

Sturges and John De Koven, officers of the North Western Bank in the Chamber of Commerce building, behind the courthouse on Washington Street, were typical of this group.

When William came to his brother's North Side house to warn him that the bank was in danger, neither George nor De Koven, who was staying overnight, had been convinced. Nevertheless they walked down to the South Side to have a look. When they reached Washington and State, three blocks from the bank, they realized only a miracle could save the South Side.

They broke into a run. The fire was rapidly approaching the courthouse. De Koven momentarily lost his nerve.

"We shall only risk our lives if we go on!" he shouted.

"We will try and go in!" George Sturges yelled back.

De Koven thought it possible that the roof would fall in after they had opened the bank vault, not only costing them their lives but also destroying the vault's contents. The Sturgeses, on the other hand, did not trust the vault to be fireproof, and wanted to remove what they could. It was a nice point, but there was not time to argue it. The building was already surrounded by fire when they burst inside.

They were met by Owen Reese, the watchman, who had his revolver drawn against the possibility of attack by thieves. A private policeman, who had seen them go in, entered also and offered to help.

The five men went at once to the vault. No one spoke. George fumbled with the combination of the outer door, set for the letters O-A-T-S. "If my horse were here," he commented wryly, "he could find OATS faster than I can."

The outer door swung open at last, and De Koven, who knew the combination to the inner vault, walked inside. "Keep cool, old fellow," he muttered to himself. "You must not make a mistake in the combination."

He opened the inner door on the first try, threw it back, and handed all the large bills to William and the securities to George. He took out the safe-deposit box belonging to Judge U. T. Dickey, and also his own, figuring that since he was risking his life he was entitled to save his own valuables as well as those of the bank.

At this point Eben Matthews, a young clerk in an office of commission merchants in the building, ran in asking if he could store the books of the firm in the vault.

Matthews was one of a surprising number of employees, throughout the business section, whose loyalty to their employers—accompanied perhaps by dreams of promotion—caused them to risk the flames in defense of other people's property. Matthews, all by himself, had been trying to save the whole building, beating out sparks in the attic as they drifted through the ventilating slits under the tin roof, but finally gave up the job as hopeless.

"I don't think our vault is worth a damn," said William Sturges in answer in his request, "but you're welcome to put the books there."

Matthews did so, and returned to his empty office. A moment later a fireman knocked out the window and told him to run.

Meanwhile De Koven was handing out the tellers' boxes when the watchman rushed in, shouting to them to flee. The two doors were shut and locked, and everyone ran for the street. The air was filled with firebrands. Washington Street was clear on the east, and they took off running. De Koven, his hat pulled down over his eyes to protect his face, carried in each hand a box whose contents were worth hundreds of thousands of dollars.

A hack was standing at the corner of Dearborn. The bankers told the driver they wanted to hire it. He said it was not available.

"One hundred dollars to take us to Twentieth Street," George Sturges cried. The hackman yielded, and the money was carried south to safety.

Solomon Witkowsky, who lived on Third Avenue between Van Buren and Harrison and owned a clothing store near the courthouse, did not face the disaster so coolly. He first saw the fire heading dead east along Polk Street. It was still several blocks away, but Witkowsky became somewhat rattled.

He began to pull down his crystal chandeliers. Then suddenly he ran upstairs, took out a revolver, and fired it from the window at the approaching flames. His wife, Dorchen, managed to remain more calm. She suggested saving the family sewing machine in preference to the chandeliers. Meanwhile a son, Edward, twenty-one, took the pistol from his father and went out to put it to better use. He returned shortly with a horse, wagon, and protesting driver, corralled at gunpoint.

The family loaded a sofa, some chairs, the sewing machine, and other goods, and called their pet spaniel, Fanny. The dog was under the front sidewalk, where she had recently given birth to a litter of pups. Fanny ran out and leaped eagerly into the wagon, then realized she was being asked to leave her puppies, which were too far under the sidewalk for the Witkowskys to reach. She jumped down and rejoined her little family in their wait for death. The Witkowskys had to leave her.

Witkowsky, now more self-possessed, went north to the Randolph Street store with his eighteen-year-old daughter Hannah. The rest of the family accompanied the loaded wagon south to the home of a married daughter. There they unloaded their goods, paid the driver $50, and dismissed him.

Father and daughter, meanwhile, had reached the clothing store and removed $300 and papers from the safe. They were still in the shop when the courthouse tower fell. A rush of flames fired the front of the building. They managed to escape through a rear door just in time. Hannah's long curls were partly burned off, but she was otherwise unharmed.

Another notable salvage feat was performed by John G. Shortall of the firm of Shortall and Hoard, one of the Garden City's most prominent real-estate firms.

Shortall had come from his home on the far South Side to watch the fire, and began to fear that his offices on the corner of Washington and Clark, across from the courthouse, would soon catch fire. He tried to cut down burning awnings from the building, and from the one next door, and rolled up those he couldn't remove. The fire was still a few blocks off.

As minutes went by, his apprehension increased. He stopped a number of trucks and express wagons, and hired six or seven, telling them he wished to save some valuable books. All promised to return after dumping their loads. None did. Shortall hailed a friend named Nye and told him his need for a wagon was urgent. Neither man could find one. The cupola of the courthouse began to burn. Shortall set a deadline of five minutes, after which he thought all chance of salvage would be gone. He stood on Washington Street, and Nye on Clark, each prepared to halt the first wagon which appeared.

A wagon came down Clark Street. Nye drew a revolver from his pocket and grabbed the horses' reins. The driver cursed luridly, but pulled up to the sidewalk. Nye handed the reins and revolver to Shortall and ran upstairs to help some of the firm's employees carry down the scores of volumes containing abstracts and deed records. These were vital not only to the company, but to the city as well, since all deeds and titles in the official archives were at that

economically as he could. The courthouse tower fell, and someone warned that Smith and Nixon's, on the southwest corner of Clark and Washington, was about to be blown up.

Blazing embers rained down, and people hurried by on their way to the Lake. The nervous driver began edging his horses away, but Shortall stopped the team seven or eight times, meanwhile throwing burning bits of debris off the books. The loading continued as the wagon moved slowly toward Dearborn. When it finally drew away, the courthouse was flaming from end to end, and the office building was beginning to burn.

Other persons were less lucky. One milliner filled a wagon with her choicest merchandise. Lacking a horse, she got between the thills herself and started pulling it away. Within a short distance, when she was forced to stop and rest, she discovered that thieves had picked the wagon clean as she was drawing it along.

One of the most well-intended deeds during those dark hours was performed by Elias R. Bowen, owner of a Lake Street store which sold military and lodge regalia. Bowen was among a crowd of spectators on South Franklin Street. Nearby, a span of superb horses was tied to a corner of the Frank Parmelee stables. The horses were rearing and plunging in terror. A man opened the sliding door of the stable.

"For God's sake," he shouted, "unhitch those horses!"

Bowen ran up, despite the blistering heat and the danger of being trampled, jerked the slipknot, and loosened the pair. He hastily led them away from the fire down South Franklin. He tried to turn down Van Buren Street, but a blazing mat-

moment going up in smoke across the street.

The wagon was brought to the Washington Street entrance. A quarter of the volumes from the office filled it. Just then a two-horse truck pulled up, with a passenger so covered with dirt and soot that Shortall did not at first recognize his friend Joseph Stockton, agent for the Empire Freight Line.

"I think, John," said Stockton, "this is just the thing you want!"

The wagon was hastily unloaded, and its irate driver dismissed with a five-dollar tip. The flames steadily drew nearer. Half a dozen clerks ran downstairs with the precious volumes, which Shortall packed as

tress, dropped or thrown from a wagon, fired other discarded articles in the street and blocked the way. Bowen and the horses turned back and found Franklin impassable.

He and his charges managed to escape through a stoneyard. They finally reached the Field and Leiter stables, but their stalls were full. Several other stables also had no vacancies. There was room in a government stable, but not for strange horses; petty bureaucracy is not a modern development. By this time, Bowen could see the fire approaching his place of business at the corner of Lake and Clark Streets. A more callous man would have turned the horses loose and rushed to save his own property. Bowen could not bring himself to abandon them.

Finally he found room at a stable, but the woman in charge said the only key was in the possession of a man who had gone to the fire and would return soon. Bowen told her the animals belonged to Frank Parmelee, tied them to a post, and started away. The horses began trying to break free. Bowen, afraid they might hurt themselves or someone else, turned back. Again he untied them, and headed north, the horses trotting behind.

After trying several other places in vain, Bowen at last found a stable between Michigan and Wabash Avenues, near Adams Street, in an area which seemed out of danger. The albatross was removed from his neck. He then dashed to his store, arriving in time to save only a few books, maps, and papers. At least $15,000 worth of uninsured goods went up in smoke.

Bowen returned to his home on the North Side, still uneasy about the horses. After breakfast the next morning, he and his son traveled a roundabout route by buggy to the South Division. They helped

some friends move, then went to the stable where the horses were. Bowen found the stable owner and his family placidly eating breakfast. They were unconvinced by his assertion that their place would burn within the hour. Bowen again took the horses into protective custody. This time he took no chances. He led the horses home and put them in a neighbor's barn, then sent them to safety in the suburbs.

Some days later, he advertised for their owner and found that they were not Parmelee's, as he had thought, but belonged to the steamer *Long John*. He had taken them while the engine was working nearby at the Grand Pacific Hotel. After that, the firemen had been forced to move the *John* by hand.

It is not recorded what sort of thanks Bowen received for his services.

As a general rule, during the migration from the South Division—and in the other parts of town struck by fire—the plight of animals was far worse than that of the human refugees.

Lost dogs trotted through the streets, barking and whimpering, searching often for masters they might never see again. Many pets were run over in the confusion, or were trapped at home as their owners, made thoughtless by fright, ran off without them. Abandoned horses galloped in terror through the crowds, or stood trembling in the midst of a tormenting shower of sparks. Even less lucky ones perished in their blazing stables. Cats were seen leaping fences or racing across rooftops pursued by flames, but many chose to die rather than desert their homes.

Underfoot, brown rats came out of their secret places and were kicked as they scurried along, or trampled in the street.

Others retreated to the basements of doomed buildings and were burned or crushed to death. Overhead, pigeons wheeled through the flame and smoke. The wind and treacherous convection currents often seized them and flung them into the fire. Even in the business section, the inevitable livestock appeared. A woman trying to lead a pig turned it loose when it refused to follow. A goat, whose owner carried a feather bed under one arm, wandered out of line at the end of its tether, and was killed by a speeding wagon. A few bewildered cows, lowing disconsolately, rambled through the streets.

A pet store opposite Farwell Hall, near Clark and Madison, burned with all its inhabitants: parrots, macaws, mockingbirds, sparrows, canaries, several monkeys, and an assortment of choice poultry. It was said that as the fire approached, the trapped animals set up a hideous cry of anguish, just before a blast of superheated air struck the building and silenced them forever.

At least two animals survived the South Division fire in extraordinary circumstances. One was the post office cat, a white and brindle female, which was discovered some hours after the building burned in a half-filled pail of water between two ruined walls. The other was a huge Saint Bernard, which served as guard inside the fireproof vaults of the Fidelity Safe Deposit Insurance Company, next to the Sherman House, and which was found alive when the vaults were opened after the fire.

CHAPTER 10

The sight went to my heart. Something human seemed to touch the thing we had used so long. I stopped for a moment to pat it on the shoulder..

—THE REVEREND ROBERT COLLYER

FROM MIDNIGHT on, sleep was fleeting and troubled for the residents of the North Division. Some awakened suddenly without knowing why. Others were summoned from their dreams by the courthouse bell, a dancing glare against their chamber windows, the worried barking of a family dog, or the peremptory knock of a neighbor.

The North Division, like the South, was essentially a peninsula. The northern branch of the river divided it from the West Division, and the main stream separated it from the South. To the east was the Lake. In the northeast section, along the Lake front, lay Lincoln Park and the old German cemetery. The northern boundary of the division, and of the city, was Fullerton Avenue, about two miles from the river.

The North Side was primarily residential—unquestionably the most imposing residential section of the city. There was a narrow industrial belt directly north of the river, which included several grain elevators, the McCormick reaper works, the Chicago and North Western depot, and the wholesale meat market. There were some stores along Chicago Avenue, and at the foot of that street stood the waterworks and several breweries. Otherwise the division was largely occupied by the homes of the oldest and wealthiest families of the city, including many impressive and expensive structures of brick and stone. Intermingled with these were more modest buildings, usually frame. Most of the streets were lined with trees. Few of them were paved. Despite its size the North Side had the air of a country town.

Seventy-four thousand, four hundred and fifty people lived in the division. The wealthier residents were mainly of Anglo-Saxon extraction and could often claim American birth for several generations of ancestors. Several had come to Chicago in its early days and had prospered with the city. Much of the rest of the population was of German, Irish, or Bohemian ancestry. As in the rest of the rapidly growing city, many were immigrants.

Although the houses in the North Side were not so close to each other as those in the other divisions, there was plenty of kindling available to feed and spread any fire. The streets were edged with the familiar wooden sidewalks, and wooden fences were common. Also, many of the yards were covered with fallen leaves, which tended to blow into convenient piles next to house walls and fences.

While the courthouse was crumbling under the battering of the flames, a continuing barrage of fiery debris soared high above the river into the eastern region of the North Side. Even as early as 1:30 Monday morning, a carpentry and paint shop at Lill's Brewery began burning. This stood on pilings near the Lake shore just south of Chicago Avenue and the waterworks. It was, fortunately, so isolated that the flames did not immediately spread.

About an hour after the carpentry shop caught, the fire also struck other points in the division, nearer the river. A car of kerosene on the North Western tracks, Wright's stables just east of the State Street Bridge, the bridge itself, and a wooden trestle just above it caught within minutes of each other. Some of the houses to the northeast then started burning.

The fire drove through the blocks of this quiet residential section like a giant wedge. It made a narrow path stretching in an almost straight line from its first point of attack at Wright's stables toward the water tower. The inhabitants of houses in the way had very little warning of their danger, so swift was the progress of the flames, and were simply shoved aside to the east and west as the blaze roared by. As usual, its speed was increased by the flight of sparks and embers, which set off fresh blazes ahead of the main line of destruction. Having crossed the river a few minutes after the courthouse tower collapsed, it traveled eleven blocks north in less than an hour.

The first residents of the North Side to be endangered were, paradoxically, completely surrounded by water. John Tolland, stationed at the Crib, two miles from shore, fought a lonely battle for five hours, with the lives of his wife and himself at stake.

The Crib, a five-sided caisson made of huge timbers, reinforced with iron and caulked with tar, had been towed to its resting place in 1865, and gates were opened to let the bottom fill with water. The Crib sank to the Lake bed, thirty feet below, and was anchored securely to the opening of the Lake tunnel. It was covered to provide shelter for the keeper and his wife. A fog bell and lights also were installed. Forty feet high and with a diameter of ninety feet, it contained fifteen water-tight compartments. The city's water passed through its sluices and thence, via the Lake tunnel, to the waterworks.

The fire storm began to grow thick around eleven o'clock that night. Tolland, a thoughtful husband, sent his wife to bed because he didn't want her to become alarmed. A heavy sea was running. He knew he would have trouble launching a boat if they had to leave.

The brands kept settling on the south side of the shingle-covered Crib. Tolland, using a broom and six buckets, which he

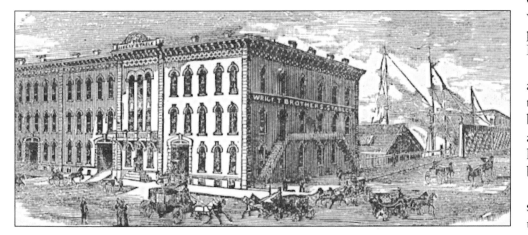

AT 2:30 A.M. MONDAY, THE WIND-DRIVEN CONFLAGRATION SAILED EASILY OVER THE RIVER TO THE NORTH SIDE AND TOOK OVER THE STATE STREET BRIDGE AND WRIGHT'S LIVERY STABLES NEARBY (SHOWN HERE). THE FIRE'S NEXT MAJOR OBJECTIVE WAS THE WATER TOWER AT CHICAGO AVENUE AND PINE STREET (LATER MICHIGAN AVENUE). IT WAS REACHED QUICKLY, AND MOMENTS LATER THE ROOF OF THE WATER-WORKS ACROSS PINE BEGAN BLAZING AND FELL IN, CUTTING OFF WATER FOR THE FIREFIGHTERS. (ANDREAS)

kept dipping into the Lake, swept potential death into the tossing waters until four o'clock that morning. Between two and three o'clock the embers fell in such furious profusion that Tolland "would have sold out my chances for a dollar to any man that came along." None did.

One of the first North Side residents to lose his home was the famous evangelist, Dwight L. Moody, who lived at 132 North State Street, not far above Wright's stables. He had conducted a meeting for 3,000 of the devout in Farwell Hall Sunday evening. The well-known gospel singer Ira Sankey was in the middle of a hymn when the alarm was heard and engines began clattering by. Moody prudently closed the meeting early, and proceeded homeward with his wife. Soon it became evident that the fire would pursue them to their house. A friend took their two children to safety westward, and the Moodys had time only to pack a baby carriage with household goods.

But Mrs. Moody had to ask a passing stranger to take down from the wall a Healy portrait of her husband. Moody himself flatly refused to do so. He had what seemed to him an excellent reason.

"Take down my picture?" he said. "Well, that would be a joke. Suppose I meet some friends in the same trouble as ourselves and they say: 'Hullo, Moody, glad you have escaped; what's that you have saved and cling to so affectionately?' Wouldn't it sound well to reply: 'Oh, I've got my own portrait.'"

Shortly after the Moodys abandoned their home, the fire struck at Ohio Street, a couple of blocks north, between State and Cass Streets.

Another minister, the Reverend David Swing, thirty-five-year-old pastor of the Fourth Presbyterian Church, lived at 288 Ohio in the direct line of the onrushing fire. He was on his roof after midnight, viewing the shower of sparks overhead. He suddenly decided the city was doomed, and went down to have a look, going as far as the courthouse before turning to join the steady stream of people heading north. As he returned, the bridge he crossed was in flames. On the way to his house he saw withered leaves and dry grass burning, and wooden fences, porches, and stables caught as he watched. He noted also that flames occasionally would chase the twisting ivy as it wound around porch pillars.

All over the neighborhood, he saw people "attempting to put the house into a trunk." The streets were crowded with wagons and pedestrians.

Swing found his own trunks on the walk in front of his house. There was no means of transport so they had to be left behind. The family went on foot. Mrs. Swing carried her favorite marble clock. One daughter clutched a pet cat and the other a caged canary. The Reverend Mr. Swing's only burden was a handbag containing his sermons and other manuscripts. A theological student met the clergyman and offered to take the sermons, promising to guard them carefully. He soon forgot his promise and abandoned them to help a pretty girl carry some dresses. The pretty girl later married a lawyer, so the sermons were lost in vain.

The Swings went north on State. The violence of the wind made walking difficult. At times it whistled high overhead. Then it would dip and send a whirling, tumbling mass of smoke, fire, and dust around the refugees—much like the draft of a speeding train.

They had gone only a short distance when they found flame on three sides of them and only a very narrow passage open through the inferno. Then, for a sudden terrifying moment, the fire closed the street ahead with a shimmering crimson curtain.

"Perhaps," thought Swing, "this is death!"

No one spoke. Before they could give way to panic, the wind shifted and the flames receded, leaving the street open again. The party ran on until the danger point was passed.

As the Swings passed ahead of the fire, they saw many of the finest homes in the North Division left abandoned and open to any caller. Many still held virtually all their furnishings, fine paintings, well-bound books, pianos, silverware, and clothing. It was a debatable point whether anyone rushing into a house, certain to be destroyed with its contents inside of an hour or so, could be termed a thief for taking whatever struck his fancy.

"There were," as Swing later pointed out, "not enough thieves in the North Division to meet the demands of the night."

For the most part, the fleeing crowds were too busy escaping to burden themselves with valuables. The streets and walks were cluttered with baskets filled with dishes. Bookcases and books, for which no wagons could be found, waited for the fire beside loaded trunks, carpets, musical instruments, and works of art. Here and there a piano burned. Open trunks caught fire and silk dresses and more intimate garments went blowing in flames down the dusty streets.

The Swings reached the home of Gurdon Hubbard, at La Salle and White, about 4 A.M., where they were given coffee and biscuits. Swing was much amused by the sight of beautiful women holding teacups in coal-black hands, and hearing polite and proper words emerge from faces "which looked as though dirt had been flung into them with a shovel."

Swing himself provided amusement for his hostess, Mrs. Ann Hubbard, who was one of his parishioners. She watched him approach down the street, hands clasped behind his back and face tilted toward the sky, and later saw him seated at the kitchen table and "munching food as if he had the day before him and nothing to do but enjoy his meal."

Later that day, a friend met the Swing family, still walking. The minister held the baby by one hand, and with the other pulled a small wagon containing some table silver.

"Hello, Donald," Swing said cheerfully. "These are all I have left. Gold,"—pointing to his wife and children—"silver, and hope!"

Some near neighbors of Swing's to the west had by no means such an easy time of it. The fire came upon them so unexpectedly that their family group was split in two, and several of them nearly lost their lives in the process.

Circuit Judge Lambert Tree lived on the south side of Ohio Street, directly opposite the home of his wife's parents, the Haines Magies. He returned from a hurried trip to his office to find bonfires of dead leaves under the Ohio Street sidewalks and flames already spurting up through the cracks. When he reached the house he told his wife, his eight-year-old son Arthur, his elderly father, his sister Ellen, and the servants, to get dressed as quickly as they could. From the rear windows he could see Wright's stables ablaze four blocks south.

Ten minutes later a small cottage just west of Tree's two-story brick-and-stone residence was burning. Tree went to his roof and had the servants pass water up, but soon realized the hopelessness of the situation. A blazing piece of matted hay, as large as a bed pillow, flew over his head, and other burning objects began dropping onto nearby roofs.

The neighborhood was a fury of activity. People fled carrying bundles or dragging trunks and boxes. Neighbors were burying prized possessions in the spacious garden of the Magie house, which stood isolated in the middle of the block. Two of Tree's servants left in panic, bumping their trunks downstairs and disappearing into the crowd. The cottage next door was wrapped in red, and Tree's barn caught. About 3 A.M. the judge ordered everyone to run to his father-in-law's.

Tree lingered to cut a portrait of Arthur from its frame on the parlor wall and fill a trunk with the family silver. In the middle of the street he paused for a farewell look at his home, still ablaze with gaslights and awaiting the onslaught.

Just as he entered his father-in-law's house he saw the Magie stable, on Ontario, in flames. He found the Magies and his own household gathered in the parlor, along with the mother of Sylvester S. Bliss,

SOME OF THE FIRE'S VICTIMS STACKED THEIR POSSESSIONS AT A LAGER BIER SALOON. (CHICAGO PUBLIC LIBRARY)

a neighbor of the Trees, who had become separated from her own family. Tree glanced from the window and saw that the covered wooden porch, which ran the width of the house, was on fire. He urged immediate flight, and went out the back door with his wife and son. His father, Mrs. Bliss, and Tree's French maid followed. As they stepped into the yard they were almost overcome by the smoke and the heat.

Tree grabbed his wife with one hand and Arthur with the other. They ran around the corner to the west. The property was entirely fenced in, and the only way out was by either of two gates, both on Ohio. But the heat struck with terrible impact the moment they passed the corner of the building. The women's bonnets were torn off, as were the hats of Arthur and his grandfather. Flying embers burned their faces, hands, and clothing. Instinctively they wheeled and ran to the northeast corner of the yard, their faces turned away from the scouring heat.

The fence was burning in many places, as were the sidewalks and many of the trees and shrubs. Mrs. Tree and her sister-in-law each gave indications of an imminent fainting spell, and Tree and the faithful French maid supported Mrs. Tree between them. There was no opening ahead in the six-foot fence, but they had no choice but to move in that direction. They seemed caught in a fiery trap.

Then suddenly, as they were only a few feet from the fence, some twenty feet of it collapsed, providing a passageway over the blazing sidewalk. As they leaped across, Mrs. Tree's skirt caught fire. Tree ripped it off, throwing it into the roadway. They paused for a quick roll call and found neither Mr. nor Mrs. Magie present. It was impossible to return to search for them.

Several of the party were slightly burned, including Arthur and old Mrs. Bliss. They went quickly east, and joined a growing community of refugees at a barren stretch of Lake front called the Sands.

The Magies, both nearing seventy, had left the house behind the others, and run to the northwest corner of the yard. There they tried to hide under a giant elm. As they were about to abandon all hope of survival, a small hole was burned in the bottom of the fence near them. The two old people managed to crawl through, although both were burned severely around the face and hands. They then escaped in the opposite direction, northwest. They were not able to make contact with the rest of the group for many hours.

Attorney Daniel C. Goodwin returned to town Sunday afternoon from his country place in Lake View, some distance north of the city limits. He planned to transfer the insurance Monday from his country home to the one at 291 Ontario Street.

Just before going to bed at 9 P.M. Goodwin stepped into the basement to see that the family cat and dog were all right. He saw some clothes soaking in the tub, ready for the Monday wash. As he climbed the stairs he favored his back, which he had wrenched when he fell off a wagon while helping move the family stove.

The Goodwins were routed out about midnight by Thorne Clarkson, who lived one door west. They dressed, and from an attic window could see the swarming sparks and a bright light from the direction of the courthouse. Goodwin took a hose and began wetting down the walks and porch. Then James L. Stark, another neighbor, ran up to warn him he must leave at once or he and his family might be trapped by the flames.

Goodwin's carriage was three blocks away in a stable on Indiana Street. There was no time to get it, and Stark took command:

"My carriage will be at your door in five minutes," offered Stark, "and I want you to put your wife and children in with mine and drive out to your country place. I will follow you with the servants."

Goodwin hurried his wife, Agnes, a son, Goertner, nine, and daughter, Lulu, seven, into the carriage. The dog and cat were forgotten in the excitement, and left behind to die. Firebrands were showering down as they left, and the horses were near-ly unmanageable from fright. Goodwin drove at high speed up Cass Street to Chicago Avenue, and thence to Lake View. On the way a bundle of clothing, hastily packed by his wife, fell into the road. Goodwin did not stop.

Kitty Tucker, one of four sisters, lived with her family on Huron Street near Cass, a block northeast of the Goodwins. There was barely time to salvage a few necessities as the flames came vaulting up from the southwest. Others in the family were helping their ninety-year-old grandfather into a wagon, when two pillowcases full of valuables caught fire on the sidewalk. They decided that it was high time to leave. Kitty was missing. One of her sisters ran into the house, calling her name. Kitty answered from upstairs.

"What are you doing?" cried her sister.

Kitty shouted back that she was looking for something.

"Come!" her sister ordered peremptorily.

Kitty came at last, grumbling.

"What will I do tomorrow morning," she demanded, "without a buttonhook?"

One of the pleasant houses in the North Division was that of Julian Rumsey, forty-eight-year-old commission merchant and another ex-mayor. It had been built in 1850 in a wooded area occasionally frequented by Indians. Twenty-one years later it stood facing south at the northeast corner of Huron and Cass. The house had been enlarged three years before.

A large lot surrounded the residence, and a portion of the yard was flooded for wintertime skating. One of the town's first billiard tables was in a small building at one corner, while a barn, containing cows and horses, stood behind the house. Near it was a fountain stocked with brook trout. The garden was circled by a gravel path, around which the children once rode in a tiny carriage drawn by four miniature ponies owned by Gen. Tom Thumb.

RUINS OF THE GEORGE RUMSEY MANSION AFTER THE FIRE. (ANDREAS)

The home of George Rumsey, brother of Julian, was immediately to the east and also occupied a quarter of a block. St. James's Church, one of the city's "most elegant," was directly across the street.

Rumsey's wife and six daughters had awakened in the night to see the fire leaping up in the South Division. Rumsey had gone downtown to his office.

As brands came flying over the house, Christian Larson, the family coachman, brought out the hose and began wetting down the house and grounds, a task of which the girls soon relieved him. Larson then harnessed the two black ponies to the phaeton.

While the courthouse bell was tolling its last, Rumsey returned exhausted, and black from smoke and cinders. He gave Larson a tin box containing insurance receipts which later proved to be worth some $60,000. The other four servants had gone. Rumsey found his wife seated in the library with one of the girls on her lap, wrapped in a blanket. She had already packed a clothesbasket and put it in the back yard. The family silver, six portraits, a brass clock, linen, an Italian porcelain, and an onyx box for writing paper (a gift from her husband) were out in the driveway to be loaded by Larson. Someone stood on the the sofa to take down one of the paintings, and Mrs. Rumsey scolded him for "soiling the upholstery." An hour or so later the sofa, soil and all, sifted into oblivion.

Before he made his escape northwest, Rumsey snatched a picture of Deerfield off the wall—the first "luxury" purchase he and his wife had made after their marriage. As he went down the front walk he saw a passing stranger and offered him half of what he had in his pocket, twenty-five dollars, to save the painting. The man took it and went on. Later he returned it.

Rumsey left his watch under a pillow. It was found in the ruins, the hands pointing at 3:30.

Attorney Chalkley Hambleton and his family left their home at Rush and Huron Streets about 3 A.M. His wife's sister, Francis Lander, was wearing two silk dresses Mrs. Hambleton had bought in Paris, and a white hat adorned with pink roses. Over the dresses she wore a mackintosh, its pockets filled with silver spoons, opera glasses, and other small objects. Mrs. Hambleton, still shaken from having believed an hour or so earlier that her two-year-old son, Lannie, was lost, refused to do anything but cling to the child.

The fire was ahead of them in places as they walked along Rush Street, Hambleton pushing a baby buggy filled with his clothes. As they went through the throng, a man snatched the lawyer's overcoat from the buggy and disappeared. Hambleton's hat blew off and soared away on the wind. They passed a woman carrying a dead baby and a group bearing the corpse of a man in its winding sheet. Frances, who was wearing a percale wrapper with a train under the two silk dresses—a garment designed for private practice in walking with a train—was troubled by people who kept stepping on the unexpected appendage.

When they had gone north as far as Chicago Avenue they met Dr. Robert Collyer, their pastor, who told them to go to Unity Church and give their names, and they would be admitted. They did so. The interior of the church was hushed, in restful contrast to the hurly-burly outside. But they could see flames against the sky and catch the muted clamor of the crowds beyond the stained-glass windows.

Dr. Collyer was one of the Garden City's most famous clergymen. He began working in a factory at the age of eight, became a blacksmith, and finally a Methodist minister. In 1859, ten years after coming to the United States at the age of twenty-six, he became a Unitarian, and organized the Unity Church in Chicago. He had been an Abolitionist, and during the Civil War had been a camp inspector for the Sanitary Commission. His parishioners still remembered the Sunday he notified them he was planning to don a uniform. He walked in carrying a flag, draped it over the pulpit, and announced:

"This place is closed. I'm going to the war."

The Collyer residence was on Chicago Avenue. It was near the water tower, and a few blocks southeast of Unity Church, which stood on Dearborn diagonally across from the elegant Mahlon Ogden home.

Collyer had preached two sermons that day and retired early, despite the West Side fire, since he was worn out. Mrs. Collyer remained on watch and aroused her husband just after midnight to warn that the flames seemed about to cross to the North Division.

They awakened the children, and Collyer asked a passing policeman to alert the rest of the neighborhood. The preacher then took his youngsters to the South Side for a quick look at the fire, despite his wife's protests, but soon returned after find-ing the courthouse blazing and the wind rising every moment. The Collyers took what they could carry and started for the church.

A landscape which Collyer prized highly was hung over his youngest son's neck. The wire holding it was too long, and the picture banged against the boy's shins as he walked. He began crying quietly but reached his destination with the picture since, as his father observed with pride, "he takes after his mother."

The oldest daughter, arms loaded with books, and face dirty and tear-streaked, was approached by a young man as she walked along.

"Miss Collyer," he said politely, "may I wipe your face?"

"If you please, sir," the young lady replied.

He did so, she thanked him, and he left. As far as she knew, she never saw him before nor after.

Collyer hired a wagon to take most of his cherished collection of books to the home of a woman who thought her house would not burn since the wind was blowing away from it. Less than an hour later her residence and his books had vanished together. After accompanying his family to the church, Collyer returned home, where he remained until the front of the house was in flames. He walked from room to room, picking up what might have seemed worthless trifles to anyone else. Then he left by the back door, pausing to pat the teakettle in farewell.

CHAPTER 11

I do not think it could have been stopped unless you picked it up and threw it into the lake.

—**Michael W. Conway, Pipeman, steamer <u>Chicago</u>**

THE WATERWORKS, and its attendant water tower, supplied the mains of the whole city. On them depended what forlorn hope there was of saving any significant portion of the North Side.

Both were built of cream-colored stone. Bristling with battlements and turrets, they gave a comforting impression of being invulnerable to any sort of attack. Specifically, the waterworks was considered fireproof. The shingle roof had been replaced by slate—although Georgia pine lay beneath the fireproof covering—and the building was in a somewhat isolated location. There was a broad roadway on three sides, and the Lake lay on the fourth.

Despite tin-covered wooden cornices, wooden window frames and doors, and some coal piles nearby, it seemed likely that sparks or firebrands could get only temporary lodging on these buildings. As a routine precaution, when the fall of flying embers began, men were sent to the roof, and stationed between the roof and the lath-and-plaster ceiling with buckets of water. A line of hose was run in from a nearby plug.

The fire rapidly worked its way through the intervening blocks. Shortly after 3 A.M., D. W. Fuller, a city employee who was standing just north of the waterworks, saw a flaming piece of timber about twelve feet long, sailing in on the wind. It just missed the water tower and struck a projection on the northeast corner of the waterworks roof. The projectile dropped onto the roof, and its flames could not be put out. By this time, the fire had already reached other parts of the neighborhood. Lill's Brewery was soon ablaze. The fire ate its way inside the waterworks, and began devouring the wooden underroof, the ceilings, and the floors.

Possibly the defenders were lulled into overconfidence within their stone castle. Or perhaps the enormous flying firebrand broke through the slate and dumped its cargo of flame inside before they could rally their forces to drive out the invader at their battlements. At any event, although the building was allegedly fireproof, although all the water anyone would ever want was near at hand, and although a force alerted to the danger was on its toes, the fire attacked and conquered its most formidable enemy in less than an hour.

The assistant engineer, Francis Trautman, was on duty with the regular night crew. They stayed at their posts until a por-

IN 1867, CHICAGO BUILT FOR $2.5 MIL-
LION A NEW WATER TOWER AND PUMPING
STATION (THIS PAGE) ON OPPOSITE SIDES
OF PINE STREET (LATER MICHIGAN
AVENUE). WATER CAME THROUGH A TWO-
MILE TUNNEL FROM LAKE MICHIGAN AND
THEN WENT THROUGH 154 MILES OF PIPE
THROUGHOUT THE CITY. BEFORE THIS WAS
BUILT, IT HAD NOT BEEN UNUSUAL FOR LIT-
TLE FISH TO COME WRIGGLING THROUGH
KITCHEN TAPS. IN THE FIRE, THE WATER
TOWER (OPPOSITE), WAS VIRTUALLY
UNDAMAGED, BUT THE PUMPING STATION
SUFFERED A DEATH BLOW. (CHICAGO
PUBLIC LIBRARY)

tion of the roof fell in, shortly before four
o'clock. Then the pumps were stopped, the
fires pulled out of the boilers, and the safety
valves tied open with rope. The rope quickly burned through, and the heated boilers
were in danger of exploding. But, as the gas
pipes had done at the South Side works, the
eighteen-inch pipes melted, and the steam
hissed harmlessly away.

The engineer and his aides fled about
3:50, most of them running behind the
water tower to seek refuge from the heat.
Probably because of its isolation, the tower
remained essentially undamaged.

One of the workmen, James Blenkinsop, brought some new engine designs by
D. C. Cregier, the waterworks engineer,
from the waterworks to the tower. When
he returned with a second armload, a thief
was just climbing from one of the windows,
designs in hand.

Blenkinsop drew a five-shooter. The
looter simply snapped the rubber band
which held the papers together, permitting
the labor of weeks to blow away on the
southwest gale, and ran off.

Lorens Walter, the assistant marshal
responsible for the North Side, was crossing
the State Street Bridge shortly before that
span vanished. He noted that Wright's stables
were already burning. At the same time he
saw the *Coventry,* returning with a new taper.
He stopped the steamer and put her to work
at the corner of State and Kinzie Streets. But
the crew, soon driven away by the flames,
had to move the engine a block north.
Walter then heard that the waterworks was
going. He sent the *John Huck* hose cart,
whose house was only a few blocks west, to
the waterworks. He told the crew to start
throwing water from a nearby plug until a
steamer could get there to help them. But
before the *Coventry* could uncouple and start
for this vital point, the *Huck* was back with
word that the waterworks was gone.

Marshal Williams, still very much in
motion, had gone from the Sherman House
to the West Side in search of additional
engines and found only the *Illinois,* which
was busily throwing a stream of river water
on the Pittsburgh and Fort Wayne freighthouse. He left it there and returned to the
South Division, to be met with the chilling
news that the flames had soared north across
the river and the waterworks was burning.

Williams, after this new report, decided there was little chance of saving much of anything. Nevertheless, he hurried to the North Side, took a confirming look at the waterworks, then came south once more. The steamer *Williams* was playing on the corner of Lake and Wells, and the *Chicago* was at Franklin and Washington, both in the northwest section of the South Side. The marshal sent the *Chicago* to Schuttler's corner, at Randolph and Franklin, where the fire was roaring through Gale and Blocki's drugstore. This was only about 150 feet east of where Williams himself lived.

Soon the flames smashed out the front of the drugstore and seized three or four other buildings nearby. Williams decided the time had come for him to save his wife and a few of their belongings. He ran to his home and upstairs. There he found that Police Captain Miller and several other men, including Andrew Coffey of the *Long John,* had already evacuated his wife and taken out some of the furniture. The marshal asked Coffey, who had been told the *John* was burned up, to carry his piano into the street.

Williams began unscrewing the legs, thinking that after the piano was out he would save the carpet. Then the window-panes started cracking from the heat. The marshal quickly tumbled his new forty-six-dollar stove on its side, to release the carpet, and took the carpet downstairs. Someone relieved him of it as he reached the front door. He turned to go back. Halfway up the stairs the heat nearly overwhelmed him. He turned and ran, leaving everything else to burn.

It is small wonder that the fire was afterward often spoken of as if it had been directed by some conscious evil force. Expert

saboteurs could not have devised a better scheme for destroying the city by fire: to start from an obscure and inflammable working-class neighborhood, and to proceed swiftly and directly to the pumping station—destroying the courthouse and much of the central business district on the way.

The halting of the water pumps meant an end to the use of Lake Michigan as a reservoir. The only water available from the fireplugs was what was left in the mains. When this was exhausted—as the firemen in all three divisions found to their dismay—the streams dwindled and died. After that there was no way of fighting on, except where the engines could draw directly from the river or Lake.

During the period when the water supply was running out, the engines were widely scattered. Five were still in the West Division—including the buried *Gund*. The *Illinois* was defending the Pittsburgh and Fort Wayne freighthouse, working from underneath the Madison Street Bridge, and the *Little Giant, Rehm,* and *Waubansia* were at the Chicago Dock Company warehouse, on the west bank of the river several blocks south.

The fight was simply a delaying action on the South Side, where four engines still battled along the southern flank of the fire between the South Branch and the Lake. The *Brown* and the *Long John* worked between Jackson Street and Harrison Street in various locations, while the *Economy* and the *Rice* fought under Schank's direction in the Michigan Southern freight yards farther south.

The *Titsworth* found itself alone at State and Washington Streets, where she lost her stream about 4:30. The *Sherman* was on the Goodrich docks, at Michigan Avenue where it ended at the river. Two other engines, the *Williams* and the *Chicago,* were making a fight to save a small portion of the northwest corner of the business area. The *Coventry* and the *Winnebago* were working just the other side of the river, in the North Division.

When the water stopped and the situation looked bleak, many of the firemen simply quit and went home. Williams, however, returned wearily to continue directing the equally weary remnants of his force.

He sent the *Chicago* to Randolph and the river, where the Lind block still stood in sturdy defiance. The Lind block, on the west side of Market between Randolph and Lake, was saved mainly through the courageous and well-planned efforts of a volunteer corps formed by Attorney I. C. Richberg and Alderman James Walsh. All awnings and exposed signs were torn down, and the sides of the five-story brick building drenched with water. A plentiful supply of water also was kept on each floor.

The building's outer walls were too hot to touch at the peak of the fire in that area. But all volunteers remained at their posts until ordered to retreat by a sentinel, whose duty it was to warn all hands if the building caught fire. They withdrew after each of three false alarms, but returned quickly when it was discovered that the supposed flames were only the reflection on the windows of blazing buildings nearby. The Lind block still stood when the fire had gone past.

At one period during the morning, the South Side fire threatened to jump back across the Madison Street Bridge and gain a new start in the West Division. No engines were at hand, except the already busy *Illinois,* which was standing beneath the span. The five-story brick Oriental Flouring Mills, with a two-story cupola on top, standing at the west end of the bridge, looked like an easy victim.

But a crew headed by William Canfield, the mill superintendent, and including Charles Munger, Robert Whitley, and Jesse Hollenbeck, manned a powerful force pump, attached to the mill machinery, which threw a stream of water high above the roof. This ended the threat, and quite probably saved the still-unburned portion of the West Side.

The *Illinois,* standing in the shelter of the bridge and drawing water from the river, waged a long but successful fight to save the Pittsburgh and Fort Wayne railroad freighthouse. The six-man crew worked without food for twenty-four hours. When the men in the freighthouse offered them brandy Foreman Mullen refused:

"I haven't had anything to eat for a few days now, and I do not think I will take any of that. It is too heavy."

"I'll bring you a bottle of wine," said one of the railroad men.

"I do not think that will hurt me any," replied Mullen after brief consideration. Wine and cider were brought for the weary firemen.

Dennis Swenie, unhorsed foreman of the lamented *Gund,* had been working with several companies on the South Side when word came that the fire had crossed the river. Swenie headed north with a hose cart. He had found the *Coventry* idle soon after he got there, and took it over temporarily from Foreman Walsh. Walsh and some of his men took a few lengths of hose and tried to defend their own house, on Michigan Street, while Swenie took the *Coventry* farther west. He tried, unsuccessfully, to save the Revere House, at Clark and Kinzie. As the water was giving out he went over to the river near the forks. There the *Winnebago* was trying to take water from the river, and pour it on two enormous grain elevators at the foot of Wells Street. The *Chicago* soon joined them, as did Walsh and his men when the *Coventry* house was swept away.

The wind shifted a little, and flames struck the roof of the eastern elevator. There were men on the roof trying to stamp out the sparks. Swenie yelled for them to lower a rope so he could send up a hose. They did so, but when the hose was hauled almost to the top, the west elevator also caught.

Swenie called the men to fasten the rope and slide down the north side of the elevator, away from the heat and wind. They made the rope secure, threw it down, and began to descend. Swenie then told the crews of the *Winnebago, Chicago,* and *Coventry* to get their horses and pull the steamers out.

SOMETHING OF THE FRENZIED ACTION DURING THE FIRE IS SHOWN IN THIS SCENE ON THE WEST SIDE: THE GALLOPING HORSES, A FIREMAN RUNNING WITH A HOSE, ANOTHER SHOUTING DIRECTIONS TO HIS COMRADES THROUGH A HORN, AND A THIRD CLAMBERING UP A LADDER. (CHICAGO HISTORICAL SOCIETY)

ALL OF CHICAGO'S FIREFIGHTING EQUIP-
MENT WAS HORSE-DRAWN, AS IS ILLUS-
TRATED IN THIS PICTURE OF HOSE CART
NO. 6 HEADING FOR ACTION. (CHICAGO
PUBLIC LIBRARY)

The first two emerged in good shape, but the *Coventry,* its driver blinded by billowing black smoke, collided with the west elevator. Swenie crawled almost to the engine and screamed to the driver to come toward his voice. The driver backed the *Coventry* off, lashed the two horses, and came out safely in response to Swenie's guiding shouts.

All three companies had abandoned their hose, a vital commodity which was becoming more and more scarce. The fearless Swenie went back once more between the flaming elevators. With the aid of some of the others he pulled out seven lengths. He then asked Lawrence Walsh, the *Coventry* foreman, what he thought should be done. Walsh said he didn't think there was much use doing anything and that he was "used up."

Walsh left to get something to ease the pain in his eyes, and Swenie kept command of the *Coventry.* He tried to save the Meeker building at 7 North Market. A crowd of about three hundred men, many of them drunk, kept interfering with the *Coventry* and her crew. The exasperated Swenie finally ordered the hose turned on the mob. Although he feared this might bring an attack in reprisal, someone had the wisdom or good nature to laugh as the water soaked him. Instead of becoming belligerent the crowd broke up in good humor.

During this period Swenie saw a man hurrying away from the fire, carrying a cast-iron frying pan.

"If he had saved the city," Swenie said later, "he couldn't have borne a look of greater triumph."

George Leady of the *Sherman* was on the Goodrich dock when the water supply was cut off. There was no one left with the engine but Leady and Johnny Reis. Finally they had their fill of smoke and fumes, and managed to harness the four frightened horses. As they were about to leave, Leady tried to persuade a drunken stevedore to come along. The man cursed and swung at Leady.

"Throw him in the river," shouted Reis from the driver's seat.

"He'll go in by himself when it gets hot enough," Leady replied.

Leady then jumped aboard and the *Sherman* rolled away.

At the approach to Rush Street Bridge the two firemen found a pie woman, loudly mourning her lost wares. Leady dismounted and pushed her across to the north side of the river.

CHAPTER 12

From that moment the flames ran in our direction, coming faster than a man could run. The rapidity was almost incredible.

—MRS. AURELIA KING

WHILE THE water-works was burning, the flames suddenly lunged east in the streets south of Chicago Avenue and began gobbling up houses missed in their first diagonal thrust through the North Division.

Although the wind still drove the flames before it, as it had done for approximately six hours, the fire now showed an alarming skill at working back in the face of the gale to attack areas believed immune. Because of the comparative absence of heavier construction, and the almost complete lack of opposition, the flames also moved faster than they had below the river.

While people fleeing the South Division often had a choice of escape routes, no such choice existed in the North Division. Persons to the east usually had little chance of crossing the corridor cut by the flames during the onslaught on the waterworks, so they headed toward the Lake. Those to the west or north usually could not go east. No one could go south, even if an open bridge could have been found. The south was an inferno.

Cyrus Hall McCormick, the sixty-two-year-old reaper king, who had been living in New York City for the past four years, was in town and stopping at the Sherman House. Around midnight he arrived at the home of his brother, Leander James McCormick, at the corner of Rush and Ohio, to warn him that the flames were spreading. Cyrus added that he didn't believe the fire would cross the river to the north.

About 1 A.M., however, a neighbor banged at the door with word that the McCormick stable was burning. The household also included Robert Hall McCormick and his bride, who had returned home from a European honeymoon a week before, and fourteen-year-old Henrietta, Robert's sister. They packed quickly, and several vans were brought from the reaper works near Rush Street Bridge, which was missed by the fire in its first leap northward. Henrietta, in cleaning out her closets, carefully overlooked two dresses she didn't like.

The newlyweds left with Henrietta about 3 A.M. before the escape route west was closed. The child's long hair was tucked beneath her coat to reduce the chance of a stray ember's setting it afire. As the three drove north to reach an open avenue to the West Side, Nettie—as Henrietta was

called—stared back at the house. It was a blaze of lights and the front doors were open. She thought it looked as though a gay party were in progress.

After taking his bride and sister to the home of an aunt, young McCormick returned to help his parents. Among the items saved were a number of portraits by the perennial favorite Healy. Leander McCormick objected to the way in which his son was jerking the paintings from their moorings.

"Hall," he said sternly, "be careful! You will ruin the walls!"

The elder McCormick would undoubtedly have been horrified had he witnessed an incident on Cass Street, where a fourteen-year-old boy was being driven from home with shotgun in hand. This young fellow, seized by an obscure but powerful impulse, lingered behind his parents long enough to blast with buckshot a pair of magnificent French mirrors in the family parlor.

The McCormicks left together. The gas had gone off, and the house was in darkness. Robert Hall McCormick locked the front door as they departed. But some time after four o'clock the flames found numerous ways to break into the two-story brick house, with its square cupola and overhanging eaves.

A short distance east on the same street, the wife of Miller, the jeweler, faced a formidable task while he was at his store downtown. She was in charge of a household consisting of her father, mother, two servants, her four-year-old son, and a four-week-old baby. To add to her problems, her father was in bed with a badly injured back; he had been thrown from a carriage during a runaway two weeks before.

Mrs. Miller's mother filled every container in the house with water, and the two women and the maid took them to the housetop, stuffed the drains with rags, and poured water over the entire roof. It was so hot that steam arose. The coachman, aroused from his quarters in the barn, hitched the carriage, and drove Mrs. Miller's father to his office at the corner of Michigan Street and Wells, where he believed himself safe.

The four-year-old was dressed, and stood gazing from the south window of the house. Suddenly he cried out:

"Mama, the glass is so hot it will burn me!"

Mrs. Miller touched the French plate glass and found it too warm for comfort, although the flames were still below the river, some seven blocks distant. Then a woodshed to the west began burning and the family decided to leave for the Lake. They took along a French clock, bronze busts of Shakespeare, Rubens, and Rembrandt, and the contents of a drawer of Mrs. Miller's bureau, which had been dumped into a bedspread and tossed into the carriage. This bundle soon began to smoke and was thrown into the street.

At the Lake, Mrs. Miller's mother, wearing six of her favorite dresses, stood holding the baby, ready to wade into the water if necessary. She expressed regret that a feather bed, slept on by four generations of her family, had been left behind. Miller and his wife walked back to the house for the feather bed, also bringing along a small white-cherry table of similar sentimental value. The sidewalk was burning as they made the return journey, and Mrs. Miller's wrapper caught fire and had to be beaten out. The family spent the rest of the night on the Sands.

The residence of Isaac Arnold, fifty-five-year-old lawyer, author, former congressman, and member of the honor guard which brought Lincoln's body home to Illinois, was surrounded by a wide yard at Erie and Pine Streets. Arnold realized the danger about 1:30 that Monday morning. He thought it probable the broad lawn and gardens would make it possible for him to save his home. So with the aid of the servants and his three children, Kitty, Florence, and Arthur, he began a determined fight to outwit the flames, instead of running away at once as so many of his friends were forced to do.

When the barn caught, the cows and horses were led into the yard. But after 3 A.M. the fire attacked the dry leaves, the grass, the barn, and the porch on so large a scale that resistance became futile. Arthur Arnold, thirteen, shouted:

"The barn and hay are on fire!"

"The leaves are on fire on the east side!" called the gardener.

"The front piazza is in a blaze!" a second servant cried.

"The front greenhouse is in flames and the roof on fire!" was the warning from a third.

Some minutes later came the most disheartening information of all:

"The water has stopped!"

Arnold quickly sounded the retreat, and began to cut some of his favorite paintings from their frames—landscapes by Kensett and Mignot. But there was no time to save them. He grabbed an armful of papers and fled with the children, the servants, and the animals. They went toward the Lake, where they joined the thousands of earlier refugees on the Sands.

Samuel Greeley, the city surveyor, lived at the northwest corner of Erie and St. Clair on the edge of the Sands. This was marginal land, occupied by a few industrial buildings and some shanties. The tract extended from the piers at the mouth of the river to Lill's Brewery, a few blocks north. It had been a notorious red-light district until it was burned out a few years before at the order of Mayor John Wentworth. The largest buildings on it were a frame bathhouse at the foot of Erie, a varnish factory and oil refinery, and a long row of sheds containing tar and pitch.

The Greeley home was one of a block of a dozen new three-story brick houses in a neighborhood of wooden dwellings and barns. The family consisted of Greeley, his wife, three sons, and a daughter.

Greeley awakened about 11 P.M., and, as was his custom, arose "to see how the weather was and how the night was passing." It wasn't passing very quietly. Flaming masses were scudding overhead, and he could hear cinders dropping on the roof and sidewalk. He roused his wife, who began dressing the two younger children.

Greeley himself hurried to the roof with a bucket of water and began shouting, "FIRE! FIRE!" This brought angry cries of protest from nearby windows until the sleepers realized their danger. Greeley also sent Frederick, fifteen, up and down the street ringing doorbells, and the whole neighborhood quickly became wide awake.

A resounding crash to the southwest and a quick, harsh burst of fire signaled the collapse of the courthouse dome. Greeley soon after saw flames between him and the masts in the river and knew the fire was in

"THE SANDS" WAS AN OPEN AREA CLOSE TO THE LAKE WHERE MANY REFUGEES SOUGHT A HAVEN. SOME WADED INTO THE WATER WHEN THE HEAT BECAME INTENSE. (CHICAGO PUBLIC LIBRARY)

the North Division. He heard his name called and peered over the edge of the roof to see Matthew Higgins, an odd-job man.

"What can I do to help you?" Higgins yelled.

"Not much," Greeley called back. "But you might turn the horses out of the barn and give them a chance for their lives."

Higgins pointed out that Greeley might need the horses soon, a thought which had not occurred to him. Finally most of the family left in the rockaway, driven by a friend, while Greeley and Frederick stayed to save what they could.

The two found the gas turned off. They made their farewell trip through the waiting house by the light of a succession of matches. The books and papers Greeley and his wife had been reading a few hours before still lay where they had been tossed on the parlor table, and a snowy-white cloth in the dining room awaited the serving of breakfast. Greeley took the family silver from the iron safe in the basement and tossed it into the buggy with a tray valued at $1,000, which had been brought to the house by his brother-in-law, Joseph Ryerson.

Greeley and his son drove off. As they left, Greeley noticed with a twinge of remorse that the cage containing the canary still hung in an upper window. He believed there was no time to return.

The flames were approaching from the west on Erie. The Greeleys went north on St. Clair, and finally managed to thread their way west to the residence of William H. Clarke on Dearborn near Burton Place, where the rest of the family awaited them.

Mrs. Clarke busily prepared food for this unexpected influx of guests, and politely refused offers to help her pack for flight. She explained that the house was a mile and a half north of the river and should be safe. Some of the women lay down in bedrooms. The men catnapped in chairs or walked restlessly outside, watching the progress of the fire.

Greeley, who had left his horses harnessed and the buggy loaded, went out— wearing a shabby dressing gown over his nightshirt—to stand guard at the hitching posts where the horses were tied. He fell asleep sitting on the curb. When he awoke he was wearing a new overcoat. He thought Ryerson had probably slipped it around his shoulders as he slumbered.

Edward Ilsley Tinkham, fifty-two-year-old cashier of the Second National Bank, lived across the street from Isaac Arnold. Mr. and Mrs. Tinkham had been up ever since someone pounded on the door with the false report that one of their chimneys was on fire. Tinkham had hurried to the bank as soon as he recognized the scope of the fire. Mrs. Tinkham sent a son, Julian, to fetch Jimmy Rowe, their handyman, who lived a block east on Erie, to watch their house. No account tells who watched Rowe's home while he watched Tinkham's.

Tinkham returned about 2 A.M. with a trunk containing $600,000 in greenbacks, which he had taken from a vault, along with more than one million dollars' worth of negotiable securities. A policeman and Perry H. Smith, vice-president of the North Western railroad, helped him bring the treasure home. Tinkham told his womenfolk to dress, and to tie anything they wished to save in sheets, in case they had to leave in a hurry. The chance of the fire's reaching them still seemed remote. Then his daughter, Annie, looked from her third-floor window and saw a building flaming at the end of Lill's pier.

Young Julian Tinkham placed close at hand his small iron box filled with foreign coins, and Grandmother Tinkham prepared to save her silk remnants for making patchwork quilts. About 3 A.M. the heavy-eyed Julian went into his mother's room and lay down, weary from a running battle with burning leaves. He was comforted by the quiet way his mother moved, "as though nothing momentous were happening outside." He felt very safe.

The women left in a little while, Mrs. Tinkham carrying nothing but an armful of umbrellas. Tinkham and Julian remained, the banker trying frantically to hire a vehicle to carry the precious trunk. That was another scene Julian never was to forget:

"In vain he stood out in Pine Street hailing teams as they tore by going north—many of them empty. I see him still as he stood there, offering as high as $1,000 to anyone that would stop for him, but none did."

Tinkham went to Greeley's home in the same block, seeking assistance. Greeley had already gone. He then hastened to a nearby livery stable and offered the owner $1,000 to take the trunk to safety. The man was loading some of his own property and refused, saying his own family came first. But he told the banker he would let him take a buggy with a Negro driver. Tinkham accepted the offer.

The trunk was put on and the two Tinkhams got into the buggy and started for the Lake. As they drove away, the brownstone mansion of Mrs. Walter Newberry, diagonally across the street, was blazing, and Arnold's stables were afire. Burning sidewalks and fences added to the horror of the scene. Tinkham's brick house still stood undisturbed, although smoke and embers swirled around its marble front.

Julian, wearing his grandmother's night cap as a protection against the sparks, released his pet fox squirrel before departing, watching as it leaped into a tree. But there was nothing he could do to save his foot-long alligator, his goldfish, his white mice, or his rabbits. Milo, the family dog, trotted along behind the buggy.

Just at dawn Tinkham and his son stood on the Sands and watched their house go down. Some time later they found the other members of the family resting in a small bathhouse at the foot of Erie Street. They also met the Arnolds.

There too was Mrs. Mary Wishmeyer, a stout florid woman, who had driven east in one of the family wagons loaded with furniture. She saw another neighbor, a man named Calhoun, who had recently bought the house next to Tinkham's. She asked him in great excitement:

"Is this the Day of Judgment?"

Calhoun gave the matter brief thought.

"Can't say," was his placid reply. "No time for conundrums."

Superior Court Judge Joseph Easton Gary, who lived in a brick house on the north side of Ontario, a few doors east of Pine, preserved a judicial calm. He learned of the fire about 1:30 Monday morning, when a neighbor, John Borden, roused the household. The fifty-year-old jurist considered the evidence briefly, and ruled that the fire could never jump the river. He then sat at his window and watched the throngs of refugees stream past.

His wife, Elizabeth, was worried, and told her daughters—Mary Louise, twenty-one, and the younger ones, Fanny and Charlotte—to go upstairs and empty the contents of drawers and closets into pillowcases. This vexed their father, who enjoined

the girls to remain downstairs. But as soon as he turned his back they ran up and resumed packing.

Several minor fires were put out on the roof of the Gary home. At last the water-works caught fire, the water stopped, and the windowsills began burning from the intense heat. Judge Gary then reversed his decision and decided to move. The loaded pillowcases were piled on two chairs equipped with casters. Judge Gary, his wife, and the maid pushed them down to the Sands, since by this time they could go neither north nor west.

The company on the Sands now com-prised thousands of disconsolate humans and hundreds of frightened animals, all encircled by fire and the lashing waters of the Lake.

Children slept with heads on their mothers' laps. A girl protecting a caged canary with her shawl burst into tears as the bird fell dead in the heat and smoke. Drunken men and women wandered through the throng, without either purpose or destination. A number of thieves, taking advantage of the confusion, broke into trunks and boxes and boldly took whatever struck their fancy. One woman died on the Sands in the midst of strangers.

WHEN THE FIRE PLAYED ITSELF OUT, LINCOLN PARK BECAME THE CAMPING GROUND FOR THOUSANDS OF HOMELESS PERSONS. SOME GROCERS HAD DOUBLED THEIR PRICES ON SCARCE COMMODITIES, AND BREAD, CHEESE, AND MILK WERE IN SHORT SUPPLY. BUT FOOD SUPPLIES POURED IN FROM MANY PLACES OUTSIDE OF CHICAGO AND ILLINOIS. (CHICAGO PUBLIC LIBRARY)

Piles of household goods began to burn. Feather beds and hair mattresses smoldered and burst into flame, giving off a dreadful odor which was to remain in the memories of those who smelled it. Shortly before dawn, some stacks of lumber to the south flared up, and clouds of acrid smoke threatened to suffocate the throng. There was a wild rush for the water, in which the animals joined.

Some men dug holes in the sand and buried their wives and children, leaving only air holes to breathe through. They then poured water on the sand to cool it. Others, including A. T. Willett, the cartage man, drove wagons into the Lake as far as the horses would go, and sat on the wagons with their feet in the water. Hundreds more waded out until the waves were up to their knees, and stood with backs hunched to the wind, splashing water on their clothes to quench the sparks.

Among the waders that bleak dawn was black-haired Charles Kelow, thirteen, holding a prize Seth Thomas clock which had been given to his mother as a wedding present. He and his parents had fled their North Side home several hours earlier, when a man on horseback came along their street shouting: "Run for your lives! The fire has jumped the river!"

CHAPTER 13

*Rude Boreas whistled his windy lays, and finding that
failed to charm the multitude, he seized upon the burning
debris and threw it at them in great anger.*

—CHICAGO TIMES

IT TOOK a little over
four hours for the
South Side fire to
sweep through the
western half of the division. By 4 A.M.
Monday, the area destroyed or still burning
stretched south beyond Polk Street, and
north as far as the river.

In the far southern portion of this mile-
long strip, the fire was stopped from pro-
ceeding any farther east than the Michigan
Southern yards, on a line with La Salle
Street. North of Harrison the flames were
attacking irregularly toward Dearborn
Street. Above Monroe Street the fire
extended in a line along the west side of
Dearborn as far as Randolph, and had made
scattered forays east above that street.

Burning or already gone were the
Michigan Southern depot, the Lombard
and Reynolds blocks, the post office, the
courthouse, the Chamber of Commerce
building, the Sherman House, and the
Briggs, Metropolitan, Nevada, St. James,
Tremont, and Grand Pacific hotels.

Most of the theaters were gone: Woods'
Museum, which held Lincoln's catafalque,
Dr. Florenz Ziegfeld's Chicago Academy of
Music, Farwell Hall, and Hooley and

Aiken's Opera House. The catalogue of
destruction also included most of the town's
major newspapers, including the *Times,
Republican, Post, Staats Zeitung, Volks
Zeitung, Mail,* and *Journal.*

The State, Clark, and Wells Street
Bridges to the North Side were destroyed,
as were the Adams, Van Buren, and Polk
Street Bridges to the west. Washington
Street and La Salle Street tunnels were
impassable. By a fluke, a small portion of
the northwest corner of the division was
spared, including the bridges to the west at
Lake and Randolph Streets. The Madison
Street Bridge also was saved.

The only place where the fire had
crossed Dearborn Street was at the northern
end, between Randolph Street and the
river. It had seized the Tremont Hotel on
the east side of Dearborn, but for a while
showed no inclination to devour the rest of
the block. It had reached east as far as the
State Street Bridge, on its way to the North
Side, but the rest of State Street seemed
safe.

Below Randolph, it was believed that
the southeast part of the South Division
would escape. This district was out of the
direct line of the wind, and the flames

THE HOTTEST TICKETS IN TOWN WERE AT
CROSBY'S OPERA HOUSE, WHICH HAD BEEN
CLOSED FOR THE SUMMER FOR EXTENSIVE
RENOVATIONS. NEW CARPETS, BRONZES,
AND ORNATE MIRRORS WERE INSTALLED
AND A GRAND REOPENING WAS SCHEDULED
FOR MONDAY, OCTOBER 9 — THE DAY IT
BURNED. (HARPER'S WEEKLY, OCTOBER
28, 1871)

appeared to have passed it by. Since the water had given out, however, the fate of this area depended simply upon luck to survive.

From four o'clock until dawn—about an hour later—the fire south of Monroe Street down to Harrison moved eastward gradually, from the flaming ruins of the Michigan Southern depot and the Grand Pacific Hotel toward the Dearborn Street line.

In the blocks running along the east side of Dearborn, Crosby's Opera House, the Shepard block, the *Tribune* building, and the Academy of Design stood like expectant sentinels.

Along Wabash Avenue, two blocks to

the east, throngs of refugees were gathered "like a routed army," according to a *Tribune* reporter, watching the progress of the fire from the intersections. Many of the women held children in their arms. Carts and wagons stood here and there. Between the shafts of some of them stood men who in their haste to escape had not been able to find horses. The wind was blowing hard to the northeast. Most of this crowd was silent in the grim dawn.

At about 5 A.M. the hope that the destruction had been stopped was carried away in furious waves of flames. The fire burst out east of Dearborn in two attacks, one at the northern end heading for Crosby's Opera House, and the other surging across a broad area between Adams and Jackson.

Crosby's Opera House faced Washington Street, with an entrance on State. It had been considered the finest public building in the Middle West when it was erected in 1865. It seated 2,500 people.

Its opening had been delayed for three days because of the assassination of President Lincoln. During the past summer and fall it had been closed for redecorating—at a cost of $80,000. Carpets and upholstery were made to order in France, and new bronze statuary alone cost $5,000. It looked as if the reopening would proceed on schedule Monday night.

Sunday evening Albert Crosby had met with Melville Stone on the stage of the theater, to discuss the setting up of a thousand folding iron seats from Stone's foundry. Crosby wanted them in place Monday morning, so they would not disturb the rehearsal of the Theodore Thomas orchestra. With them was George Upton, the *Tribune*'s music critic, scouting the premises.

One of the visitors mentioned that the stage carpenter had been burned out of his house in the Saturday night fire, and commented that it would be terrible if the Opera House burned.

"Oh, it will not," said Crosby, laughing. "I have studied the statistics of theater fires, and they occur on an average of once in five years. We had a fire two years ago, so we are immune for three more."

Albert Crosby's estimate was wrong. The imposing theater proved as much of a pushover as any wooden shanty. It was tapped for destruction about 5 A.M.—just eight hours after Crosby's remark.

Tickets for the ten-day series of concerts by the Theodore Thomas orchestra had been selling extremely well, and a capacity crowd was assured for the opening. Thomas and his musicians were notified in spectacular fashion that their engagement was canceled. Their train pulled into the 22d Street station while the main part of the downtown section was being engulfed by fire. They went on to St. Louis.

At dawn the posters outside the Opera House, advertising the evening attraction, were being erased in efficient if overly dramatic style, and the music stores of Root and Cady and Bauer and Company took turns receiving a customer whose wants were simple—the entire stock.

The Opera House restaurant, where a short while before one of the firemen from the *Little Giant* had bathed his aching head in whisky and declared—wrongly—that the entire department was giving up, the offices on the second and third floors, the luxurious opera hall and smaller music hall, all disappeared as Crosby's was reduced to rubble.

A music teacher, C. W. Perkins, was

ALMOST NOTHING WAS LEFT OF THE NEWLY REFURBISHED OPERA HOUSE. (CHICAGO FIRE DEPARTMENT)

trapped on the third floor and jumped. He struck a telegraph wire as he hurtled down, but escaped with a broken arm.

The First National Bank building, at the southwest corner of State and Washington, caught fire about the same time as Crosby's. The First National, in theory one of the town's fireproof structures, survived the ordeal better than almost any other building in the business district. Only the Lind block and the unfinished Nixon block, at La Salle and Monroe, which as yet had no wood at all in it, suffered less damage.

The outer walls of First National were left virtually unscathed. But the heat was so

MARSHALL FIELD (TOP) AND LEVI Z. LEITER (BOTTOM) FORMED A PARTNERSHIP AND BOUGHT OUT THE DRY GOODS FIRM OF POTTER PALMER IN JANUARY 1863. THREE YEARS LATER, THEY MOVED INTO THE HUGE NEW BUILDING ON NORTH STATE STREET KNOWN AS "PALMER'S MARBLE PALACE." EVENTUALLY, THE FIRM BECAME MARSHALL FIELD AND COMPANY. (FIELD ARCHIVES)

great that girders inside were bent, and the iron ceilings bowed and made useless. All woodwork and furniture were of course completely consumed.

Some time before the building ignited, Melville Stone, balked in efforts to reach his foundry on Illinois Street in the North Division, sat down wearily on the bank steps. Soon he was joined by another man, who busily shredded a number of sheets of postage stamps with a pair of scissors and tossed the resulting confetti to the winds.

"It seemed," said Stone after the fire, "a perfectly natural thing to do."

Field and Leiter's, the town's finest store, standing in marble magnificence on State Street across the street from Crosby's, was the scene of a bitter fight for survival. Both Marshall Field and Levi Leiter reached their store early and left desperately late.

Even before they arrived, Harlow Higinbotham, thirty-two-year-old head of the accounting and insurance department, had been to the company barns and ordered out teams and wagons. These were lined up in the alley behind the building.

Meanwhile H. B. Parker, one of the salesmen, was sent to the basement to start a packing-box fire in the furnace, so there would be steam for the elevators. The finest silks and laces were taken first, and piled under guard a short distance away. The wagons returned for further loads. After considerable stock had been saved, the store itself, for which Potter Palmer was paid an annual rental of $50,000, was threatened.

The gas had gone out and work went on by candlelight and the brightening glare outside. Field called for volunteers, and nine men went to the top of the building. Some poured water from three storage tanks onto the mansard roof. Others turned

hoses down the pillared outside walls. Soaking blankets were hung at the windows to keep them from cracking. A lone fire engine, the *Titsworth,* threw a feeble stream of "dead" water from a plug on Dearborn Street, until the stream died completely away.

It was a lost cause. Blazing bits of debris lit on the roof. The windows cracked and splintered, and firebrands sailed through. Fires began springing up on several floors at once. The stricken building was quickly emptied of its defenders. But their work was unfinished.

They trooped to the Lake shore, piled some $600,000 worth of fine merchandise back into wagons and buggies and took it all to the far South Side. Included in the goods saved were $20,000 worth of silks and velvets, which one enterprising clerk placed in a State Street horsecar and drove to safety. Some of the salvage was placed in Leiter's home. Other items went into carbarns at State and 20th, and a church at 32d Street and South Park.

But $2.5 million worth of stock and furnishings burned to ashes. The gleaming pillars cracked and crumbled. The iron girders sagged and gave way, and the six-story "palace" was transformed into a jumble of ruins fit only to be shoveled up and used to extend the Lake Michigan shore line a few more feet.

The walls of Field and Leiter fell with deadly abruptness, killing Samuel Shaw-cross, a tailor, who was hurrying through the alley on the way to his store on Washington.

Andrew MacLeish, a partner in Carson, Pirie and Company's store, on the west side of State Street about 100 feet north of Madison, had been routed from bed at

2 A.M. by his brother-in-law, James Chalmers. MacLeish drove from his home in the West Division to pick up George Schott, who lived near Union Park, still farther west.

The two then tried to cross every bridge from Madison to Kinzie, where they learned the fire had reached the North Division. They had to drive all the way down to Twelfth Street to reach the store. By then it was too late. Efforts to hire express wagons or trucks proved futile, and little could be saved.

Farther to the south, the people had begun to relax. H. W. S. Cleveland, a landscape architect, had come from his home on Indiana Avenue in the middle of the night to see whether his office in the Shepard building, at the southeast corner of Dearborn and Monroe, was threatened. His wife and sister-in-law accompanied him as he strolled north on Wabash, the streets almost as bright as day. Pedestrians were visible several blocks away, even though it was still several hours before dawn.

When he reached the Shepard building, he found the flames already at La Salle. With the help of John Newman, clerk for Samuel Greeley, who had the office adjoining his, he managed to take away many of his possessions. The wind was howling through the streets, and dust was everywhere. The two men stacked the rescued goods at Wabash and Monroe, and Newman left to get an express wagon.

A woman sat near where Cleveland waited, a sleeping baby in her arms. A quartet of roughs came along, and one broke the neck of a whisky bottle against the wall, offering the contents to his companions. Some of the liquor spilled on the sleeping child, and this drew a vigorous protest from the woman. Cleveland expected trouble but the men simply cursed and lurched on.

A few moments later a runaway horse dashed by, dragging a wrecked buggy behind it through the crowd. Miraculously, no one was hurt. Cleveland waited an hour and a half, and a friend of Newman's came. He was smiling broadly and said the Shepard building was out of danger. This seemed so patently absurd to Cleveland that at first he thought the other man was joking, and when the other insisted, he set him down for a fool. But Newman showed up shortly after and confirmed the story. He and Cleveland returned to their offices.

Cleveland surveyed the situation and found it hopeful. The post office, diagonally across on the opposite corner, was gone, as were the Bigelow House and the two Honore blocks, on the west side of Dearborn. It was about 7 A.M. and Cleveland headed for home, going by way of the *Tribune* building, a block north, which he found untouched. He left behind both his son, Ralph, who had come to

THE SHEPARD BUILDING ON THE CORNER OF DEARBORN AND MONROE SEEMED TO LEAD A CHARMED EXISTENCE BECAUSE ITS NEIGHBORS SUCH AS THE POST OFFICE, THE BIGELOW HOUSE, AND THE HONORE BLOCK SUCCUMBED FIRST TO THE FIRE. BUT THE SWIRLING WINDS EVENTUALLY CAUSED THE SHEPARD BUILDING TO JOIN THE FLAMING PARADE. (SHEAHAN/UPTON)

help, and Newman. Cleveland walked down Wabash to his home and ate a light-hearted breakfast.

Artists with studios in the Academy of Design, on Adams Street near the Palmer House, had begun gathering as early as 1 A.M. The current attraction at the gallery was Peter Rothermel's *Battle of Gettysburg,* a canvas distinguished in size, if nothing else. It measured sixteen by thirty-three feet, and had been bought by the State of Pennsylvania but not yet delivered. The gallery held about three hundred other paintings as well.

Some time after four o'clock some of the artists ventured west, seeking a better view of the Honore blocks on the other side of Dearborn Street. They were driven back by the merciless heat. The upper three stories of the Honore blocks were twisted off balance by the flames and came crashing into Adams Street with an earthshaking impact. A gigantic fountain of fire shot up from the ruins, lighting the Palmer House and the Academy of Design in unearthly fashion. But within half an hour the flames had dwindled, and the artists took heart once more.

Then the Bigelow block began burning. Only a five-story brick building and some wooden tenements lay between it and the Academy. Two Negroes, armed with a hose and tremendous courage, stood steadfast against the advancing inferno, keeping it at bay for a time by pouring water onto the intervening structures. The Bigelow House itself, four stories of Athens marble and pressed brick, stood at the southwest corner of Adams and Dearborn.

It had just been completed at a cost of $500,000. Dozens of roses waited on the gleaming black-walnut tables for the formal opening that morning. But soon the Bigelow was a glowing furnace. Red and white flames poured from the windows and archways and leaped nearly across the street.

The artists at the Academy began removing some of the smaller paintings about 6 A.M. The fire also appeared to be advancing down Jackson Street. Rothermel's monumental painting was taken from the frame and carried away by a group including the Academy janitor, artistically christened Don Pedro Carlo von Stoeckel.

Shortly after 7 A.M.—about the time the relieved Cleveland started for home—the dream that the southeast part of the business section might escape vanished. A whirlpool of wind plucked embers from the ruins of the Bigelow House and tossed them into some wooden buildings near the Shepard block. These caught at once, and the flames resumed their journey to the north and east.

Cleveland tried to return to the Shepard building after his meal, and found Harrison Street between State and Wabash blocked by flames. He went south to Polk Street and walked west of the flames to Fourth Avenue. He hastened north on this street, on which the buildings on both sides had burned to the ground. The smoke and lingering heat were very painful.

When he reached Van Buren Street he cut east to Third, since Fourth was an inferno beyond that point. The wooden pavement on Van Buren was burned to a depth of half an inch or so in places, but was still passable.

At length Cleveland reached Adams and Dearborn Streets. He stopped and stared in horrified disbelief. The Shepard building was in ruins. He retraced his steps and met two men on Third, near Harrison, the only living creatures he had seen in the burned district.

Worry over Ralph and Newman ended, when the former finally reached home. The two had been watching from the south windows of the Shepard building for wind-borne embers, when the fire ambushed them from the north. The first they knew of their danger was when flames burst in through the windows on Monroe Street. The two took a trunk between them, dashed down the stairs to Dearborn Street, and raced across to find shelter behind what remained of the post office.

They were trapped there for almost two hours, part of the time with an alarming fellow refugee—a large dog which foamed at the mouth. It fortunately ran off at last without harming them. The two men

IT APPEARS AS IF RECONSTRUCTION IS UNDERWAY AT THE FIRST NATIONAL BANK BUILDING AT STATE AND WASHINGTON IN THIS PICTURE TAKEN BY NOTED CHICAGO PHOTOGRAPHERS LOVEJOY & FOSTER FOR A STEREOPTICON SLIDE. DAMAGE TO THE BANK WAS ESTIMATED AT $160,000, BUT NO MONEY OR VALUABLE PAPERS WERE LOST. THE BANK REOPENED ON JANUARY 1, 1872. (JACK LEVIN COLLECTION)

finally escaped by dashing through the burned district on Monroe to Clark Street, covering their faces to keep from breathing in the superheated air and fumes. They returned some hours later and recovered the trunk unharmed.

The same misplaced optimism displayed by Cleveland prevailed during breakfast time at the Palmer House. This imposing hotel, eight stories high with 225 rooms, stood facing State Street at the corner of Quincy, just southeast of the Academy of Design. The building had been open only about a year, and one of its modern features was the installation of fire hoses on every floor.

The calm of the early morning was in sharp contrast to the near panic of the night before.

Among the guests of the Palmer House was The Reverend William James Leonard, visiting from Plainfield, Illinois. The Reverend Mr. Leonard had been uneasy all Sunday evening, for no reason he could pin down. As he was preparing for bed, he saw a letter he had written lying on the desk. He had a sudden fear that the letter might fall into alien hands before morning. Although he knew his premonition was childish, he took the letter off the desk and put it in his pocket.

At 1 A.M. his slumbers were broken by pounding on the door. A voice warned that the fire was very close. Leonard put on his clothes and went down to have a look. He got no more sleep that night.

He went to Courthouse Square just before two o'clock, and witnessed the collapse of the courthouse tower, the great bell clanging to the last "like a funeral knell." Then suddenly he remembered that the trunk containing his sermons was stored in the Michigan Southern depot. He retrieved it shortly before the station was destroyed, and wheeled it on its convenient rollers back to the Palmer House.

At the hotel the guests were in a state of panic. Hotel employees scoffed at their fears, reminding them of the fire hoses. Leonard decided to take no chances, and packed his manuscripts into valises and took them to a friend's house well to the south. He made a second trip with his best clothes. Dawn was breaking, and the hotel was still safe. The minister then took another sightseeing tour, to the North Side, to see the waterworks ruins.

He returned about five o'clock. As he passed the Field and Leiter building and Bookseller's Row, he believed that both would escape. Strolling down State Street— a casual onlooker wandering along the outskirts of Avernus—he saw a thief caught by a policeman after stealing a new pair of boots, and another knocked down by an officer whose badge he tried to take. He also overheard a pair of rascals debating the best way to get to the North Side with some stolen goods.

He passed the *Tribune,* where an optimistic sign on the front door read: "Open at 2 P.M." Employees were urging some firemen to go down with Babcock extinguishers through the coalhole on Dearborn into a basement under the sidewalk where there was a minor blaze.

When the pastor reached the Palmer House again he found it still untouched. The guests in the lobby were relaxed, since danger seemed to have swept beyond them. They were talking of breakfast, and some who had moved out their baggage were beginning to bring it back. Leonard sat in a quiet corner to rest, and a few minutes later

hotel employees began to form a bucket brigade. Leonard, who had seen the water-works in ruins, wondered where they planned to fill their pails.

At about eight in the morning the fire was speeding toward the hotel along State Street from both the north and south. The bucket brigade fled, and the guests after them.

Leonard wheeled his now-lightened trunk across the marble lobby to the State Street entrance, and went south and east to Jackson Street and Wabash Avenue, where he sat on his luggage and watched. He could see the tall shape of the Palmer House towering over the intervening roofs. The building next to it on the west caught and burned, then the Palmer House itself.

Soon the hotel was bathed in flames from the sidewalk to the three-story mansard roof. The walls swayed and came down as runners of flame leaped to the Academy of Design, twenty feet to the north, and entered that building through the skylight and windows. Among the mas-terpieces destroyed there was Reed's *The Land of the Assassins,* which depicted that part of hell supposedly occupied by John Wilkes Booth.

The new Palmer House at State and Monroe was being constructed under the supervision of John Mills Van Osdel, who had become the Garden City's first architect in 1841. It was heavily damaged, shortly afterward, as the fire swept up State Street. The temperature was so high that it warped the heavy iron streetcar rails in the center of the street, pulling the bolts loose and curv-ing the metal two feet in the air.

Van Osdel, when the fire neared the unfinished building, buried some books and construction plans in a pit in the basement. He covered them with two feet of wet sand and clay, which were baked by the fire and served not only to preserve the objects beneath, but also led to the idea of using clay tile for fireproofing.

CHAPTER 14

And the wind raging, and the fire burning, and London and Paris and Portland outdone, and no Milton and no Dante on earth to put the words together.

—CHICAGO TRIBUNE (BURNED BEFORE DISTRIBUTION)

THE NEW stone building of the *Tribune* stood at the southeast corner of Dearborn and Madison Streets. Its main entrance was conveniently placed at an oblique angle facing the intersection, with a marble plaque proclaiming its name in sturdy block letters over the door. The building was four stories high, plus a basement occupied by the heavy steam-driven presses. It had been built two years before at a cost of a quarter of a million dollars and was reputedly fireproof.

The prosperity of the *Tribune* was a sign of the times. Published by Joseph Medill, the paper had grown in importance and popularity through the Civil War and after; now it was the most influential newspaper in the city.

Throughout Sunday night and into Monday morning, the *Tribune* put up a resistance to the fire as staunch as the Republicanism on its editorial pages. The flames from the area of Crosby's beat their way south toward Madison, while the fire around the Shepard block threatened from Monroe. For some time the *Tribune* stood in lonely defiance on Dearborn Street, the last remnant of the line that had held until sunup.

When Elias Colbert, commercial editor of the *Tribune,* had seen the gasworks catch fire at midnight, his first thought was that there would soon be no light to work by. So he went to the McKindley wholesale grocery store on Water Street, where he bought a box of candles from the night porter for $1.25. He then returned to the office, where City Editor Sam Medill dispatched him to the roof to start working on the story. Reporters English, Lewis Meacham, and Tod Cowles, the paper's baseball writer, were sent along. Medill told English, whose knowledge of the town was extensive, to help Colbert identify as many buildings as possible.

A short while later someone came up to say their services were no longer needed. The chief engineer had become alarmed and blown the steam from the boilers, making it impossible to run the presses.

English, exhausted after reporting two fires in a row with no sleep between, retired to Sam Medill's office and fell asleep over a desk.

Colbert's telescope, which he used to observe sunspots, was mounted on a wooden stand on the roof. This was torn down, and the timbers thrown from the roof to eliminate a possible ally of the flames. Colbert decided to insure the safety of the valuable telescope before helping further with the defense of the *Tribune*. He took the six-foot instrument over his shoulder, tucked his scientific notebook under an arm, and left the building, heading for his home at 90 South Green Street in the West Division. Burdened though he was, Colbert gallantly took the time to help a girl who

was struggling with a heavy trunk. He dragged her trunk a couple of blocks, while she carried his notebook.

Samuel Medill's brother, Joseph Medill, forty-eight-year-old publisher of the *Tribune,* arrived at the paper about 1 A.M. He found things well organized by his brother. The building itself seemed safe. The flames had bypassed it and were heading north. Someone had taken the precaution to remove a caldron of tar left by roofers in front of McVicker's Theater,

which stood next door on Madison Street, and to sweep up the trash in the alley.

But at three o'clock the fire was beating its way down Clark against the wind.

Seeing this, Medill grew alarmed for the safety of the building and organized a defense squadron. Several of his staff had left for their homes. But there were plenty of water tanks on the top floor, and buckets and shovels in the pressroom. Although the "fireproof" cement material which covered the roof was warranted by its Cincinnati makers to withstand temperatures up to 250 or 300 degrees, Medill had noticed during the summer that it grew quite soft in the sun. He considered the roof one of the danger points.

He called for volunteers among the remaining printers and editorial staff. He and fifteen or twenty men took shovels, flat pieces of wood, and buckets to the top of the building. They began beating out and drowning thousands of sparks and pieces of burning debris, which fired the roof mater-

ial many times. The flames were moving north and east, buffeted by the wind. All the buildings on Dearborn north to the river were gone. The atmosphere was so stifling that the roof gang sought shelter every few moments behind the half-dozen chimneys. The men stood with backs pressed against the chimneys, sucking in cooler air from the east as they tried to clear the smoke from their aching lungs.

George Upton, who had come to the office from his preview of Crosby's Opera House, thought that the *Tribune* would not burn. He saw Sam Medill napping at 3:30 in someone else's office. Men in the pressroom were working by candlelight, and thoughtful employees in the counting room placed a bunch of matches in the safe lest they catch and fire the building. Upton went home, not even bothering to take valuable notes and manuscripts with him.

Meanwhile the others continued their fight on the roof. In the eerie light they could see thousands of people in the North

Division, streaming up Dearborn Street toward the old cemetery or running in panic toward the Lake.

The spreading fire sounded like a giant waterfall. The thunder of falling walls was heard intermittently as the brick and stone of the business section surrendered to the assault. The flames leaped high against the heavens, in many-colored and fantastic shapes, rolling and pitching like a seascape painted by a madman.

Joseph Medill left the roof periodically to check the rooms on the west side of the building, where other men worked with equal desperation. Some of the offices were so hot that the window glass cracked, and varnish on the desks and chairs melted and began to smoke. These were doused with water or covered with wet cloth. The iron shutters on the south and east, the latter facing McVicker's Theater across the narrow alley, were closed and fastened.

William Bross, fifty-eight-year-old former lieutenant governor of Illinois, who was part owner of the *Tribune,* had awakened at 2 A.M. in his home in Terrace Row, on Michigan Avenue near Congress Street. He was alarmed by the glare and went out to see how far the fire had spread. He returned to his family with word that it still was west and south of them. He told the womenfolk not to pack, adding:

"The results of this night's work will be awful. At least 10,000 people will want breakfast in the morning. You prepare for one hundred."

The women started preparations for this mammoth meal, but became frightened and resumed packing when Bross left for the *Tribune.*

He thought the paper safe enough, and remained only twenty minutes or so before

going to check on his Nevada Hotel. He got home about 5 A.M. Monday after watching the Nevada burn. Daylight was fighting for recognition with the glow of the fire.

Bross found his carriage team harnessed and a riding horse under saddle in the stables behind Terrace Row. Friends were helping his family pack, and sandwiches and coffee were being given anyone asking for refreshment. Bross mounted the horse and rode north through the smoke-filled streets to the *Tribune* again. The buildings near it were gone but the only damage he could see to the *Tribune* building was some cracked plate-glass windows.

There was a fire in the basement barbershop, which had caught from under the sidewalk. This worried no one, since everyone knew the building was flameproof. Bross helped put it out. He told Conrad Kahler, who ran the pressroom, to try to get out an edition as soon as a graph showing the extent of the city's losses was ready. Then he rode off to scout the fire again.

He found the flames almost to State and running before the wind. He met some friends and urged that buildings south of the Palmer House be blown up, but they could get no powder. He went into Church's hardware store and grabbed about a dozen heavy axes, which he handed out, suggesting that it might be wise to chop down some buildings in an effort to slow the fire. While he was trying to stir bystanders from their indifference, he saw that the buildings west of the Palmer House were burning and knew that the *Tribune* was sure to go.

About 7 A.M. English awakened in Sam Medill's office and looked out the window across Madison. He saw a crowd in a vacant lot, staring up at the rear of the Speed

block, a row of four-story brick buildings with stone fronts. It was on fire at the corner. A man appeared in one of the windows and peered down to the ground. Some in the throng shouted to him to jump. Others found a long plank and shoved it up against the building so he could slide down it to the ground.

English came out and went across the street. A second man was trapped on the fourth floor of a building next door to the Speed block, whose interior was on fire. The man looked from the window, disappeared for a moment, then returned and threw a mattress and bedclothes out. It was a drop of about fifty feet. He came out of the window backward, and clung to the sill as he cautiously lowered himself against the side of the building.

Miraculously, he managed to drop to the third-floor sill. The crowd cheered. He went into the building but seemingly found no other escape route. He reappeared and tried to swing from the sill across to the building from which the first man had been rescued. He was unable to make it. He hung for a few agonizing moments, then plunged into space. He was lifted from the ground and carried to Buck and Rayner's drugstore on State Street, where he died, his head resting on a makeshift pillow provided by a compositor from the *Tribune*.

English, bone-weary and with no place to print the story if he got it, didn't even find out the victim's name. He went to the Lake front, then south to Cottage Grove, where he stopped at the police station. The desk sergeant, startled by his grimy appear-

HARPER'S WEEKLY PRINTED THIS GRAPHIC PICTURE ON NOVEMBER 2, 1871. THE FIRE WAS OVER, BUT SOME OF THE BURNING COAL PILES SMOLDERED FOR DAYS.

ance and obvious fatigue, asked if he was in trouble.

"I've been burned out."

"Got any money?"

"Thirty-five cents."

"Here's ten dollars," said the sergeant. "Put it in your pocket and pay me when you can."

At about the time English left the *Tribune,* a worried pressman found Joseph Medill on the roof and told him there was so much smoke in the basement the men could not remain. He added that the rollers on the presses had melted, and even if there were some way of using them, there was only water enough to get steam up for a short run, and no way of replenishing the supply. Medill abandoned all thought of getting out a paper, but clung to the hope of saving the building.

An hour later some employees told Medill the fire had crossed Dearborn, near Adams, and was moving east toward Michigan Avenue, south toward Van Buren, and north toward the beleaguered *Tribune.* Medill ran downstairs and out into the lurid morning to verify the report. He turned down the alley between McVicker's and the *Tribune* and moved close to the flames, which were rioting through a dozen or so frame buildings in the rear of some brick ones fronting on State Street.

A column of fire was marching toward the Lake, and also north on a line which soon would bring it behind McVicker's and to Mackin's building, which stood nearby on State Street. Medill was too experienced a campaigner not to recognize defeat. He returned to the roof and informed the exhausted fighters—their faces black with soot, hair and beards singed, eyes red and swollen, clothing and shoes eaten by

sparks—that the battle was lost. There was nothing for them to do now but think of their own safety.

Shortly before the building was abandoned, the fire in the basement broke out again, near the boiler used for heating water for the barbershop under the sidewalk. Benjamin Bullwinkle and some of his men from the insurance patrol had come by and were using Babcocks to extinguish this blaze, when the fire came in from behind and took McVicker's Theater. Bullwinkle left a couple of men, and went off to try to save some of the merchandise from nearby stores. In certain shops there were so many looters that they barred the patrol from entry.

McVicker came down the alley and into his theater from a side door. He was driven out by flames and found that he couldn't stand in the alley in the face of a blast of heat and embers. He crawled on hands and knees to Monroe Street and finally staggered through the streets to safety, but his eyes were so inflamed that his sight was impaired for a week.

The beaten men on the *Tribune* roof took a last look at the approaching enemy and trooped downstairs. On the way out they searched each floor to be certain everyone was evacuated. In the rooms to the east they found some of their exhausted comrades sleeping as though drugged, Sam Medill among them. There was no time for gentle awakenings. The slumberers were abruptly jerked to their feet and told to run for it.

At the last moment, the Medill brothers thought of trying to save the files by putting them away in the vault. They searched out William H. Christian, a counting-room employee, who kept the keys. But Christian, who had been roused out of bed in the middle of the night, had dressed hurriedly and left the keys behind. The men in the counting room had slammed the vault door shut, and it could not be opened. When the safe was opened after the fire, its contents were found unharmed—including the box of matches.

Colbert, who had returned, suggested to George Woodwell that they simply carry out some of the files. On the way downstairs they met Thomas Sullivan, the composing-room foreman, and James Hutchins, his assistant. Each of the four took one of the half-yearly volumes down a back stairway and into the alley. Hutchins carefully locked the door and pocketed the key, a futile, force-of-habit gesture which many men all over town performed. Colbert then went to seek an empty wagon, only to meet the flames coming down State Street. He dashed back, shouting:

"Boys, run for your lives!"

The others abandoned the files and dashed toward State Street, finding fire near the Madison corner blocking their way to the Lake. They detoured through a stable, whose mangers were burning, running at top speed for the door at the far end. Colbert, the last one through, turned to see the wooden stable erupt like a volcano seconds after they were outside.

Joseph Medill, who had a set of recent *Tribune*s in his home, told each man to take whatever he could carry of the bound volumes prior to 1860. All were abandoned in the street when it became apparent the paper would ignite before it had been carried half a block. Some of the men then fled west into the burned area on Madison, escaping with the aid of Providence. Others crossed Madison Street and took refuge

behind a pile of bricks left when the Dearborn school was torn down a short while before. They soon saw flames leap from McVicker's and set the side of the *Tribune* ablaze.

Conrad Kahler left the pressroom during this final retreat. On the street he met John McDevitt, the former billiards champion, starting up the alley toward Tom Foley's billiard room at 153 Dearborn. Kahler grabbed his arm and warned him of the danger.

"Oh, the hell with you," McDevitt growled. He broke away and was never seen alive again.

Kahler started east on Madison, but couldn't get across State. He returned to the *Tribune* building, where he saw a large man, wearing a wide-brimmed hat, sleeping in a drunken stupor on the steps leading down to the Madison-Dearborn entrance. Kahler

MEN WORKING ON THE RUINED PRESSES OF THE CHICAGO TRIBUNE (JACK LEVIN COLLECTION)

shook him awake and told him he'd be burned to death if he stayed where was.

"That's none of *your* damn business," the big man said.

Kahler left him sitting there.

It was growing unbearably hot. Kahler looked west and saw two men on Clark Street. He ran toward them and reached Clark only after the flames had singed his hair, beard, and mustache. Kahler caught his breath at Clark, then dashed for Fifth Avenue. He tried to reach the West Side through the Washington Street tunnel, but it was too smoke-filled to be passable. He finally found a bridge intact and made his escape.

Meanwhile the two Medills and several other *Tribune* men headed east on Madison. They held their breath as they ran down the middle of the horsecar tracks, with buildings on fire on both sides of the street. At last they reached the haven of the Lake shore. The two Medills went south along the water, since Michigan Avenue was jammed with refugees and wagons. Once home, Joseph Medill drank a cup of strong coffee, threw himself on his bed, and was asleep at once.

John R. Clarke, one of the proof-readers, went to his Wabash Avenue home, packed a trunk, and started dragging it through the streets. He saw his colleague Lewis Meacham seated on a load of goods in a wagon, and was invited to toss the trunk aboard. After their possessions were disposed of, the two sat in a grassy yard and had an early morning feast of crackers and canned lobster, which Meacham pulled triumphantly from his pocket.

Six weeks later, workmen digging in the ruins of the *Tribune* found two bodies. They had been crushed beneath the sidewalk when a segment of the north wall fell during the height of the fire. One of the dead men was Joseph P. Stubbs, who had come from Canada shortly before to become a reporter on the Chicago *Republican*.

The other was identified as the missing John Donovan, who had disappeared when the post-office block burned. His broken watch was stopped at eighteen minutes to ten. What he had been doing during the seven hours between the destruction of his home and the time the *Tribune* burned was never known. But his reason for taking refuge at the *Tribune* was more easily explained.

Donovan had often been heard to say the building was so safe from the danger of fire that it needed no insurance.

CHAPTER 15

As I went out . . . and saw the vine-covered walls and the windows filled with flowers all shining so peacefully in the moonlight, it seemed impossible to realize that in a few moments the smoke and flame I saw all around me would seize that too and that I was looking on my home for the last time.

—MRS. GEORGE HIGGINSON

WHILE THE fire was sweeping away the eastern remainder of the business section, an odd and even more disastrous phenomenon was taking place on the North Side. When the flames had reached the Lake just beyond the water-works, they had started to burn across the wind, devouring the rest of the division to the northwest. These two main arcs of fire, one on the South Side, one on the North, were like two arms of an enormous flaming pinwheel, pivoting slowly counterclock-wise, with its center at the sunken ruins of the State Street Bridge.

Since the North Side was so predominantly residential, an even larger number of refugees was driven from it than from the other divisions. It was said that if the fire walked through the South Side, it *ran* through the North, and thousands of families were scattered before it willy-nilly.

Few dawdled over dressing, although one man was observed, in the middle of the night, wearing a dressing gown and calmly shaving. One young man wore a woman's dress over a long linen duster. A girl in a man's trousers had a shoe on one foot and a slipper on the other.

Near Dearborn and Ohio Streets, a man with a beautifully bound set of Shake-speare's works offered an expressman fifty dollars to carry it to safety. The expressman refused, saying that he had his own things to care for. He was then asked if he would take the books as a gift. He agreed to this bargain. The bibliophile wept as he loaded his treasures into the stranger's wagon.

A frightened man ran up Dearborn Street with a window blind tucked under an arm, as the onrushing flames crossed Kinzie.

The noise was so great that people a few feet from one another had to shout to be heard. Those who looked back saw three blocks below Indiana Street burst simulta-neously into flame, including sidewalks, wooden paving, and buildings made of brick.

On Clark Street, near Ohio, a dis-traught storekeeper ran in and out of his upstairs apartment to keep track of both the fire and his wife—who was giving birth to a son. Mother and baby were carried away on a stretcher when the flames were only a few doors distant.

A store owner offered free hats to all, but no one stopped.

In the same neighborhood a bewildered woman, clad only in a nightgown, was lifted into a buggy by her husband, who then had to pull the vehicle away by hand. An elderly man wept for a lost dog. He told passers-by his family was missing as well, but explained that they could look after themselves while the dog could not. Two boys, carrying a case of candy, went sobbing through the throng of refugees in quest of their parents.

Even as they were being burned out, a few of the residents of the Garden City managed to find something funny in the disaster.

One, who lost both store and home, was seen carrying a marble mantel as the fire still raged. He laughed and said:

"That's all there is now, but I'm going to see if I can't find another and build a house to fit."

Another helped load his household goods on a wagon, then followed behind in his buggy as they were driven away. Suddenly he saw his goods burst into flame, and the spectacle of a bonfire being driven along by the unsuspecting driver sent him into convulsions of mirth.

Postmaster F. A. Eastman tried to rent a hack to carry his trunks from his Erie Street residence, but found the tariff too high. He then dragged the trunks to safety with the aid of the family maid, while his wife carried the baby. They reached "safety" four times.

Frank Loesch, the young Western Union employee, typified the reaction of a great majority of people that night. After a frantic effort to save some of his belongings and carrying them out of his boarding-house, he left them in the street and simply walked away, feeling fortunate to be alive.

William Corkran, a young Easterner, was secretary and librarian of the Chicago Historical Society, on Dearborn and Ontario Streets. He had helped fight the Saturday night fire by throwing lumber into the river until about 3 A.M. As a result he was so weary that he ignored the alarm bells that sounded as he came home from church Sunday night. But when they continued to ring he arose and went sightseeing on the South Side until he was driven away.

The brick-and-stone neoclassic Historical Society building had been described at its dedication three years before as "spacious and perfectly fireproof." Corkran found the cellar door pushed open from the outside and several residents of the neighborhood displaying their trust in the building's immunity to fire by stacking their belongings inside. Corkran shared this faith, and encouraged the flow of valuables into the cellar.

The building, the first wing of a proposed $200,000 structure, housed 18,000 books and 150,000 pamphlets. Several paintings by the ubiquitous Healy were on display—among them *Benjamin Franklin at the Court of Louis XVI* (which won a gold medal at the 1856 Paris Exposition) and *Daniel Webster Addressing the House in Reply to Hayne*. President Lincoln's walking stick, a pike which had belonged to the late John Brown, and the original of the Emancipation Proclamation were among the Society's most prized possessions.

The building included large reading and lecture rooms, and a reception room where daily papers were available to the public. The grounds were surrounded with a low picket fence.

Col. Samuel Stone, the seventy-two-year-old assistant librarian, had worked at the Society since 1858. He arrived about three o'clock from his home several blocks north. The fire was close, but had bypassed the building in its first northern onslaught.

Stone suggested to Corkran that it might be unwise to accept any more goods for storage, especially bundles of clothes. He himself closed the basement door. Some object wedged at the bottom prevented him from locking it, so he stood with his back against it, ignoring abuse shouted at him from outside.

The janitor showed up, and he and Corkran filled all the buckets they could find, for use if the wooden sidewalk caught fire. Corkran also offered the janitor and two other men fifty dollars apiece to go to the top of the roof and wet it down thoroughly. They agreed but falling embers burned their hands and prevented them from completing the ascent.

Houses across the street were blazing and the sidewalks started to smoke. Corkran and the janitor, an elderly man, began pouring water on the boards, but some of the men who had been aiding them took off on the run, shouting back to Corkran to flee. He nevertheless called to Stone to let the janitor into the basement for a couple of buckets of water. Meanwhile he threw several wheelbarrowfuls of dirt on the walks.

A woman dashed from the burning E. W. Griffin house across the street. "With a loud voice through the roaring wind," she identified herself to Colonel Stone and asked him to take care of a small box, which she handed to him. Others told him there was great danger and he must leave at once.

He shoved a trunk against the door, to hold it shut, and went to the north end of the cellar. Climbing to the top shelf of newspapers, he lay on his back in the narrow space, to shut the northwest window. The yard and sky seemed alive with flying sparks.

Colonel Stone climbed down and ran upstairs faster than a man of seventy-two should move. The wind shrieked down Ontario Street, whipping fire and smoke before it. The casements of the front windows were burning as the stalwart old man rushed into the reception room for the record book and the priceless Proclamation. He couldn't find the record book, nor break the frame to remove the Proclamation. Flaming bits of debris were striking the windows, and from somewhere overhead came a "chinking" sound, as though pellets of fire were falling inside the building.

The colonel decided it was time to sound a retreat. He ran to the basement, stamped out a couple of smoking bundles, and ripped open another, grabbing a shawl to wrap around his head. Then he toppled the trunk, flung open the door, and ran out.

The sidewalk, a cottage next door, and all the buildings to the south, as far as he could see, were burning furiously. Stone did not look for the gate. He managed to get across the fence, and leaped over onto Dearborn Street.

The heat hit with such power that he dropped the shawl and ran up the middle of the street to Erie, followed by a bellowing cow whose back had been scorched. As Colonel Stone fell to his knees to avoid being bowled over by the fiery wind, the harried animal was forced to the east by another withering gust and disappeared in the smoke.

There were three brick buildings behind the Society, facing south on Erie Street. The panting colonel climbed the steps of one of them to take a final look at his beloved building and "the destruction of our fifteen years of labor." The front, roof, and sides of the Historical Society building were flame-covered and the heat was almost overpowering. Stone, thinking himself alone in an abandoned neighborhood, started west.

Suddenly he saw a woman, out of her mind from fright or grief, or perhaps bent on some hopeless errand, running directly east into the fire. There was no way he could interfere. A woman's body was later found in the vicinity.

At the same moment a wandering mass of flame, many feet above the ground, passed overhead and was driven against the top of the Holy Name spire. As Stone watched in unbelieving fascination, some of the buildings nearby seemed to "melt down" in less than five minutes.

Corkran, meanwhile, had gone into the building with the janitor to see what could be saved. They carried Volk's bust of Lincoln from its pedestal and placed it in a corner just as a group of frightened women came in seeking refuge. Corkran told them they were welcome to remain, but he couldn't promise that the building would survive.

He and the janitor unlocked the Emancipation Proclamation from its case and carried it upstairs. There Corkran tore some battle flags from their standards and wrapped the Proclamation in them. He also obtained Lincoln's walking stick and took down one of Healy's smaller paintings from the wall.

But the two men abandoned their efforts and fled empty-handed when the women ran upstairs crying that the rooms below were on fire. Explosions shook the building and the skylight fell in, as Corkran and his companion leaped down the stairs, dashed through the blazing lecture room, and went out a window into a neighboring garden.

Everything around them was on fire. Corkran escaped to his boardinghouse, although his coat, trousers, and vest were burned so badly they had to be thrown away.

The janitor, possibly not so nimble, was certainly less fortunate. His body was found nearby a few days later.

Arthur Kinzie had recently brought his family to Chicago and was living with his uncle opposite the Historical Society. He had gone down to the river to look at the South Side fire and, certain that the flames would remain there, returned home. He sat down to read but, peering from the window, saw that the fire had crossed the river after all. His wife was not home and he began to dress the children. She soon returned and, shortly after, a boy pounded at the door, pumped the bell, and shouted:

"Mr. Kinzie, your house is on fire!"

Kinzie dashed upstairs and looked out from a back window to find the information quite accurate. He took one child, and his wife the other, and they headed north on Dearborn. They passed the Mahlon Ogden home, a large frame house standing

THE COL. ROBERT A. KINZIE HOME AT
RUSH AND MICHIGAN (LATER HUBBARD)
STREETS WAS ONE OF THE MANY ELEGANT
RESIDENCES THAT BURNED ON THE NORTH
SIDE. THE PEOPLE IN THE PICTURE ARE
MOST LIKELY FRIENDS AND RELATIVES OF
DR. SIDNEY SAWYER, WHO WAS LIVING IN
THE HOME WHEN THIS PHOTOGRAPH WAS
TAKEN IN THE 1860S. (CHICAGO
HISTORICAL SOCIETY)

on an ample lot just north of Washington Square Park. Mrs. Kinzie suggested that they stop. Kinzie assured her it was no safer than his uncle's place, and they hurried on.

They stopped briefly at the home of Obadiah Jackson on Dearborn to ask for water. There was none, but Mrs. Jackson brought out some ale. They were enjoying the brief respite from their flight when the lights went out. The Kinzies walked slowly on, stopping each block or so to rest on the sidewalk until the flames drew near again. Although people and vehicles of every description crowded the streets, scarcely anyone spoke, and there was no shouting.

In the crowd they saw a man carrying a rubber tube and the broken base of a drop light. Another wheeled a cookstove on a barrow. A woman passed with a live hen in her arms.

Their friend Dr. Tolman Wheeler went by, pulling a trunk by a strap. He was trudging determinedly *toward* the fire. Kinzie gently turned him around.

At Clark and North Avenue, just after daybreak, they met John Wentworth, the former mayor, accompanied by a Tremont House bellboy carrying his black leather bag. Wentworth urged them to go west, but Kinzie continued north.

The fire soon swept on past the Historical Society, continuing up Dearborn to

Chicago Avenue. It had some difficulty negotiating the 100-foot barrier at that point, but, once across, the flames moved as freely as before. They soon engulfed the vine-covered home of George Higginson, 150 feet beyond.

Higginson sat up reading Sunday night after his family had gone to bed. At 10:30 he made his nightly round, before retiring, and through the dining room window saw a reddish glow to the southwest. He climbed through a trap door to the roof for a better look, but found the view obscured by smoke.

A little later he looked onto Dearborn Street. Embers were falling thickly, and the scene was lighted by an unearthly glare. He took off his coat and boots and lay down. It was about midnight, and the rest of the household was asleep.

The flickering light outside disturbed him, and he rolled over with his back to it. The windows were closed but the wind came moaning through the cracks until the blinds began chattering. He got up, looked out, and lay down again. At last he fell into reluctant slumber, but awakened half an hour later and saw his wife at the window, her figure silhouetted against the brightening sky. She told him she heard the noise of falling walls.

Higginson put on his coat and boots and left for his office downtown, meeting a number of policemen with some hand-cuffed prisoners as he went through the La Salle Street tunnel. After picking up a few things he returned home, where he had trouble persuading his wife the fire would reach them. She finally started packing.

Higginson went to his bedroom and anxiously peered out. The streets were black with people going north. Some had wagons, carriages, handcarts, or wheelbarrows. Others carried their belongings on their backs.

He saw a small fire near the Lake and a greater one in the neighborhood of Wright's stables. About 4 A.M. there was an eruption of flame from the direction of the waterworks. A little later he tried the faucets and found only a trickle, then nothing.

The Higginsons packed some of their possessions and sent them to the home of William Clarke, near the Catholic cemetery at the south end of Lincoln Park. Another load of clothing, linens, and oil paintings was taken to Mahlon Ogden's house. Higginson and his wife went to the home of another neighbor to the northwest, Gurdon Hubbard.

Higginson came back to his home about 7 A.M. It was daylight, and the fire was still lapping at Chicago Avenue. The flames were in control of the North Division from Wells Street and the river east to the shattered waterworks, and they roared unchecked through the South Division. An unending stream of people was still passing the house.

He greeted a number of his friends as they went by. They replied in what seemed to him the most ordinary manner imaginable. No one watching would have believed they were leaving their burning homes behind them.

At last Higginson made a farewell trip through the house he had bought from Cyrus McCormick three years before. He found nothing more he cared to take away with him. The house went about 7:30, and Higginson reached Clarke's about 8:30.

One of Clarke's other guests needed a prescription filled and Higginson took it to a drugstore half a mile north on Clark Street.

He found the druggist, a young man, talking with three or four other people and apparently unperturbed. He began making up the medicine in leisurely fashion, and Higginson avoided mentioning the fire for fear of causing him to make a mistake. But after getting the prescription and paying for it, he asked the druggist if he didn't feel strange performing his ordinary tasks, and if he didn't think the fire soon would be at his doorstep.

The young man remained splendidly aloof.

"Perhaps so," he said. "I don't know." And he began tidying up the shelves. It was a job with no future.

Having passed Chicago Avenue at Dearborn Street, the fire also fanned out directly west. Henry E. Hamilton, who lived on Chicago at La Salle Street, had left home earlier that evening on a business trip to a coal mine he owned. The wind was rising, and it looked like rain when he left. He stood on the rear platform of a Pullman car as the train rumbled through town, idly watching a fire burning somewhere in the West Division. Then he went inside and forgot it.

At home, the maid had quit that day. Mrs. Hamilton was alone in the house with the three children. She awoke several times, as the wind began rattling the blinds with growing insistence. The fire bells rang, but she ignored their warning in drowsy comfort.

Then there were hasty footsteps and other unfamiliar noises outside. She jumped from the bed to look.

A string of wagons and carriages was going by, heading north with loads of furniture, trunks, and refugees. The startled young matron, suddenly wide-awake, leaned out far enough to see past the branches of the elm trees in the yard. Down La Salle Street, the whole city seemed to be in flames.

Her neighbors the Barclays were fully dressed and sitting on their front steps. Mrs. Barclay wore her fur coat. Mrs. Hamilton called down to ask if there was any danger. Barclay said the flames had crossed to the South Side, and he thought they would keep coming.

Mrs. Hamilton banged the window shut and awakened her ten-year-old son Harry, telling him to put on his best suit. She looked into the back yard and saw large pieces of blazing wood sailing by. Pigeons flew up from the roof. Some were caught by a sort of aerial undertow and dragged down to die. The worried mother sent Harry to the home of his uncle, Gurdon Hubbard, two blocks north, to ask what to do.

Harriet, eight years old, who had been sleeping with her mother, was awake and in tears.

"I can't leave my new wax dolly to burn," she sobbed.

Mrs. Hamilton dressed Harriet and her youngest child, five-year-old Richard. She heard one or two loud explosions, and the lights flickered and died. The glow outdoors made it bright enough to see.

Hubbard soon returned with Harry. He told her to pack whatever she wanted most and he would send someone to pick up the trunks and bring them to his place. He thought it would not burn, since it was a brick house, set well away from any other buildings.

"We have a cistern full of water," he added, "and are going to dip the carpets in that and spread them over the roof and cornices."

Mrs. Hamilton, a conscientious house-keeper, had carried a basket of silver upstairs when she went to bed—a normal precau-tion against thieves. Hubbard saw it and emptied the basket into a pillowcase. He then left for his own home with the impro-vised bag over his shoulder. Mrs. Hamilton packed swiftly, and a man came from Hubbard's for Richard and the trunks.

Harry and his good companion, Alex Barclay, wandered down to the corner of La Salle and Chestnut and cheered like honest youngsters when they saw the cornice of the Ogden School catch fire.

A friend of the family appeared to see if he could be of service. Dr. Williams, a brother-in-law who knew Hamilton was out of town, also showed up. Some neigh-bors offered the use of a team and wagon and Mrs. Hamilton managed to hire an expressman. The piano and some of the smaller furniture were loaded on one wagon and sent off to Dr. Williams's home, the doctor going along to show the way.

The other household furnishings, including the stove, were carried across the street and left next to the Grace Methodist Church. The wagon did not return in time, however. The church wall fell and smashed the stove. The rest of the things burned.

As the furniture was being loaded, little Harriet came out of the house clutching her hat with both hands to foil the wind and said sternly:

"I want my breakfast!"

A jug of spring water was the only drinking supply; water in the cookstove reservoir was used for washing purposes. Promptly at 7 A.M. the washwoman appeared to start the day's work and was

told to begin packing. She put fruit preserves in baskets, boilers, and washtubs with such care that not a single jar was broken. Mrs. Hamilton couldn't help noticing the contrast between her washwoman's efforts and those of the man helping move the piano, when she saw him slip some silver fruit knives and other small articles into his pocket. She said nothing. The loss seemed trivial under the circumstances.

The fire was driving swiftly from the south and east. Mrs. Hamilton made a last inspection of the house and discovered the blinds on the kitchen windows burning. She and Harriet went to the Hubbards'. The house was filled with people, but gave the impression of being empty because so much of the furniture had already been hauled away.

The home of Judge Elliott Anthony of the Superior Court stood a block from the Hamiltons' on the west side of La Salle. Judge Anthony had come to town from New York in 1852 with his bride, a license to practice law, and capital amounting to eight dollars. He had been immediately successful and built a house. He had refused to buy the corner lot because he didn't want to shovel snow from the extra sidewalk. Later, however, he bought some adjoining property in the rear. Now behind the house there was a garden about 150 feet square where peonies and hollyhocks bloomed in summer.

The house itself, which had been enlarged several times, had a large cement-floored basement containing a wine cellar and the usual winter provisions. It was full of barrels containing corned beef, pork, flour, sugar, cider, and apples.

Judge Anthony was a widower, but was far from lonely. The rest of the household included a daughter, Lizzie, eighteen; three sons, Charles, fifteen, Henry, twelve, and George, nine; a cousin, Mattie, from Sterling, Illinois; the coachman, Frenchy, and two Swedish hired girls.

A two-story barn stood at the rear of the lot. It held five horses. Two of them, Boston and Jennie, were a matched pair of white trotters, famed for their speed. The carriage horses, Diamond and Jet, were a matched pair of blacks. Jack, a dark chestnut, was the utility horse. There were two dogs, Dandy and Gypsy. Dandy, a black-and-tan terrier, was an excellent ratter, and Gypsy, a mongrel, was the best fighter in the neighborhood.

Young Charles Anthony first knew of the excitement about 11 P.M., when Frenchy threw a handful of pebbles against his bedroom window. The boy peered out.

"Come on," whispered the coachman.

"There is a terrible fire down about the river."

Charles dressed and tiptoed down the back stairs, thinking he could visit the fire and be back in bed before he was missed. The two went through the barn north into Pearson Street, then west to Wells. They saw Jimmy Davidson, a grocery store proprietor, standing in the doorway of his shop. They asked him about the fire. He said he did not think it would spread, and went inside.

Frenchy and Charles fell in with the crowd and walked across the bridge to Randolph Street, where they suddenly found themselves only a few blocks from a holocaust of frightening proportions.

The two sightseers ran back to Lake Street, then east. As they reached Hunt's hardware, someone shouted to them to go in and help themselves. They walked in, and Frenchy took a rifle and a Colt revolver, handing a double-barreled shotgun to his young companion. The coachman also wanted to enter Chambers's jewelry store at Clark and Lake, which was being stripped by greedy passers-by. The boy wouldn't let him.

They hurried to the La Salle Street tunnel and down the steps to the pedestrian passageway. This was constricted by furniture and other articles piled along the side. Halfway through, something caused the crowd to panic. Charles went down twice, but was jerked to his feet by Frenchy. When they emerged north of the river they had lost the guns.

They walked north on La Salle. Near Kinzie Street a half-dressed woman ran from her home and begged them to rescue a sick woman on the second floor. Frenchy and two other men put the invalid on a mattress and slid her downstairs. They left her lying in front of the house, presumably to be picked up by a wagon.

Never dreaming the flames would reach the Anthony home, the two truants were enjoying themselves once more. They strolled over to Clark and up to Huron, where they saw John Currie standing in front of his bakery. Charles said he was a classmate of Currie's son Frank, and asked where Frank was.

"In bed," said Currie dourly, "where all decent boys should be."

Charles asked for a bag of cookies, and Currie inquired whether he had money to pay for them. The youth said he had none, but as he turned to leave the baker filled a bag and gave it to him. He and Frenchy started munching as they trudged home.

Charles's back began hurting, and he tore off his coat to find sparks had burned through it in many places. His hat also caught fire and his hair and eyebrows were singed. The two became again alarmed and ran west on Chicago Avenue toward the house. As Charles walked in the front door, Judge Anthony ordered him out, saying there had been enough men and boys there already. Then he recognized his son, and tears of relief came to his eyes.

Everyone was up but the two younger boys, whom Judge Anthony awoke about 4:30. A group of neighbors stood in the street in animated discussion. Only one man owned wagons, and he refused to lend them or yield any space. Instead he loaded everything from his house, including the mahogany doors, and took them to his office. They burned there.

Most of the men were members of the Grace Methodist Church, a sturdy stone building on the corner of Chicago and La

Salle, and felt it would not burn. They tore out pews and put their household furnishings inside. These were burned with the church.

Judge Anthony, who had plenty of horses but no wagon, buried virtually everything but his furniture in the garden. Other articles were put into a borrowed phaeton, including a basket loaded with Charles's favorite preserves and a mahogany drawer filled with currant jelly. A rough-looking wagon driver offered to take a load of Anthony's effects for $200, but drove off when the judge said he had no cash.

About 8 A.M. everyone sat down to breakfast. The judge brought some sherry from the cellar. He forbade the children to drink any. He sipped some himself, however, and served it to neighbors who dropped in.

Frenchy hitched Boston and Jennie to the three-seater carriage and tied Jack on behind. Diamond and Jet were hitched to the racing buggy, which was driven to the front of the house. The borrowed phaeton was fastened behind.

Charles released the chickens from their coops, and they promptly began eating what they could find in the vegetable garden. He also turned loose the guinea pigs and most of the rabbits. He took along only one hutch with his two favorite rabbits and a small cage with some Seabright bantam chickens.

Three trunks filled with silverware, table linen, and other treasures were carried up to the Wells and Pearson corner and left, along with the jelly and preserves from the phaeton. There the party split up. Judge Anthony drove off in the carriage, taking with him his two younger sons, Mattie, and the hired girls. Dandy and Gypsy were

under one of the seats. Frenchy drove the blacks, with their double load.

Charles, Lizzie, and Hugh Burch, a clerk from Anthony's law office, remained behind to save the trunks if possible. They had instructions to take no chances, but to run if the fire drew near.

Charles went to the house and—as his father had directed—closed all the shutters, shut the barn door, and covered the second-story barn windows with carriage curtains. Then he went to the front of the house to see how close the fire was.

As he neared the gate a wave of flame from the east side of La Salle swept over his head and broke every window along the west side of the avenue. The youth ran

EVEN THOSE WHO HAVE LIVED IN CHICAGO FOR A LONG TIME WOULD HAVE DIFFICULTY RECOGNIZING THIS VIEW OF THE NORTH-EAST CORNER OF CLARK AND OHIO. (JACK LEVIN COLLECTION)

along a passageway to Pearson Street and down to the trunks, his sister and Burch close behind.

The house had started to burn and the Grace Methodist roof was on fire. The three carried two of the trunks for a block by walking in single file, Burch in the middle holding the end of each trunk, and Charles and his sister holding one end apiece. Then Lizzie sat down to rest while the others made two trips for the third trunk and the preserves.

Charles was extremely thirsty. He entered a corner saloon and asked for a drink of water. The proprietor said there was none, but reached up and took a bottle from the shelf, broke off the neck, and poured a drink of whisky for Charles, the first he had ever tasted. When the youth returned to the trunks, he was walking with an oddly light gait.

They carried the trunks and preserves about six blocks and left them in a vacant lot. An empty wagon rolled by and Burch ran out and grabbed the horses' bridles. The driver leaped down, ready to swing his whip, but Burch offered to hire the wagon. The teamster said he had promised to return for a load for twenty-five dollars but was afraid to go back. Burch offered fifty dollars, the trunks and preserves were put aboard, the the three weary refugees clambered up.

It took them until 6:30 that evening to reach the home of an uncle, Dorwin Harvey, on the far South Side. There Judge Anthony, in a torment of worry over whether he would see his son and daughter again, gladly paid the driver his fee.

Late in the afternoon, it became evident that Dr. Collyer's Unity Church, standing north of Grace Methodist, was almost certain to go. Collyer and many of his parishioners had taken shelter inside when they were driven from their homes farther south and east.

Mahlon Ogden sent word that his cistern was full, and that they could take as much water as they wished. They decided to make a fight for it. Collyer and several of the congregation tore up all the wooden sidewalks and trusted the stone walls to resist the flames.

But their effort proved useless. The fire slipped in between the slats of the spire. The church began burning soon after.

Many of the refugees left. Collyer went up into the pulpit. He took the Bible under his arm and announced that the steeple was on fire. The Collyers then fled with the rest. They paused only to bury the family silver in a nearby celery patch, where it was later recovered.

Mrs. Collyer had to lead her husband. His eyes were swollen shut and he could not open his hands. They found temporary shelter with some friends a few blocks north, until poor Collyer partially recovered.

Mrs. Inga Throlson, whose home was near Chicago Avenue, was a devout Lutheran, who publicly abhorred cosmetics, card playing, and similar instruments of the devil. When the flames reached her neighborhood she dashed back into the house—literally at the risk of her life—and came out carrying a pail of lard in one hand.

In the other, snatched from some secret hiding place, were two treasures: a box of face powder and a deck of playing cards.

CHAPTER 16

Daylight had dawned, but the sun was blotted out by the dense pall of smoke, and hope too was well-nigh obscured.

—H. R. HOBART

THE NORTH Side refugees who had taken shelter on the Sands before dawn found scant comfort there as the sun came up Monday morning. The fire patrolled the riverbanks and the outskirts of that desolate strip of Lake shore. Thousands of refugees huddled there, virtual prisoners.

The lumberyards on the north bank of the river caught fire, along with the reaper works and the Galena Elevator, both near the Rush Street Bridge. This greatly increased the amount of smoke and heat pouring unceasingly into the Sands. On the southern bank of the river, the immense Michigan Central depot, and Elevator A, just east of it, also caught.

Cyrus McCormick himself directed the fight at the twenty-four-year-old reaper factory, many of whose buildings were of wood. Despite the quantities of wood, paint, and oil always on hand, the only previous fires had been small ones. Watchmen guarded the property day and night, and because of frequent sparks from other factory chimneys or passing steamboats, great care was exercised to keep all shavings and other combustible material swept up.

Fireproof doors separated the sections of the factory.

It was company policy to ship all completed machines as quickly as possible, to cut down the chance of a major loss in case of fire. Consequently, some 4,000 reapers were in dealers' showrooms across the country.

About 2,000 machines were destroyed when the factory was leveled, however, and McCormick also lost the McCormick block at Dearborn and Randolph, some State Street stores, the Larmon block on South Clark, and several stores on South Water. His losses totaled more than a million dollars, although he got back about $600,000 in insurance.

When the volume of sparks and fumes grew greater, some of the refugees on the Sands, who had already been forced nearly into the Lake, decided to try to reach the lighthouse pier, which ran into the Lake not far north of the mouth of the river, away from the direct line of fire. Two shorter piers intervened, but the barges moored in those could be used as emergency bridges.

The Tinkham family used this route, leaping down into the barges, walking across, and clambering up again. They finally reached the government pier, which extended well out into the Lake just north of the river mouth. At its end, an iron lighthouse marked the harbor channel. In their haste, however, no one remembered their dog Milo. He was left behind and never seen again.

The last time Tinkham saw the buggy containing the trunk filled with his bank's money, before a curtain of smoke came down, the Negro driver had urged the horses into the Lake as far as he could. He had upended the golden trunk, and was sit-

ting on a $1,600,000 perch, his coat collar turned up and his back to the shore. Two hours later he showed up on foot at the lighthouse pier, the trunk scraping along behind. The pier grew more and more crowded, and some of the arrivals were obviously not accustomed to polite society. Fortunately there was no outside indication of what the trunk contained.

The Arnold party also made its way south along the shore, to W. B. Ogden's pier. This was stone-filled and did not burn, since the wooden planking had not yet been laid on the top. There they hired a rowboat and were taken out to the iron lighthouse. Arnold was gravely worried about his wife. She had left their home before it burned, to find out if she could aid their married daughter who lived near-by, and had never returned.

Tugs passed by steadily, towing ships to the Lake and ferrying refugees to safety. One of them undoubtedly saved the lives of those hovering fearfully near the lighthouse.

Joseph Gilson, twenty-five-year-old captain of the tug *Magnolia,* a hero in two Lake rescues of recent years, had been busy all night on the river and the Lake. During the South Side fire his ship carried several hundred refugees over the river to the North Division, among them Gen. John McArthur, president of the Board of Public Works.

Then the *Magnolia* had towed a couple of vessels from the ships between Elevators A and B on the south bank, just east of the Michigan Central depot. She next took a couple of ships from the river into the Lake, with several hundred refugees aboard. She tried to move the *Navarino,* a new $50,000 propeller-driven ship, which was lying off the Goodrich dock, near Michigan Avenue and South Water Street. But the *Navarino* ran aground under tow on the north side of the channel near Rathbone's Stove Works.

The flames crept closer to the government pier at the harbor mouth. It was feared that the *Navarino* might also catch fire, work loose, and drift down to set the lighthouse dock ablaze. Gilson attempted to pull her free and failed, though he raised the steam pressure on his tug to 150 pounds, sixty above the legal limit, and blew out a safety valve in the process. So a party of volunteers poured water into the beached craft until she sank.

Soon the *Magnolia,* straining her boilers, began pulling another ship, *Sky Lark,* downstream just before the flames reached her. The *Sky Lark* carried important books and papers of the Goodrich Steamship Line, as well as many unscheduled passengers.

Gilson ran the *Magnolia* to the south bank once more and plucked off two stranded policemen. The tug's woodwork caught fire briefly in the process. He got a line on the schooner *Swallow,* whose moorings had burned through after catching fire from a coal yard blaze. The burning *Swallow* was bearing down on some fugitives at the lighthouse slip until the *Magnolia* intervened. Railroad tracks near the shore, on the south side, were curling like burning shavings as the *Magnolia* passed by.

The *Magnolia* made several more trips to carry importunate refugees from shore to the safety of vessels in the Lake, then began nosing slowly upstream. As the tug neared Rush Street, its crew heard cries for help, and rescued a man from a post in the river to which he had been clinging for several hours. He was burned on the arms and head and nearly blind from the smoke.

The Michigan Central depot, standing east of Michigan Avenue near the riverbank, began blazing some time after daylight. The terminal, the largest in the country, had been built in 1853, on filled-in land at the foot of Lake Street. It was shared by the Michigan Central, Illinois Central, and Chicago, Burlington and Quincy roads. The trains ran along the Lake on a trestle protected by a wood-and-stone breakwater.

While the stone walls and iron beams of the depot delayed the inevitable ending, the

flames prevailed at last and there was nothing left on the great South Division passenger station but some fragments of wall.

Central A, one of the two huge grain elevators immediately east of the depot, burned to the ground. But Central B, separated from A by a slip, was saved by a combination of luck and courage.

A man named Walker, agent for Clapp and Jones, manufacturers of steam fire engines, had arrived in Chicago Sunday afternoon with a large new steamer for Racine and a smaller one for Pentwater, Michigan. The two engines were on a flatcar in the Michigan Central yards.

Walker saw the fire and decided to help. When he couldn't get official sanction or interest, he went to the railroad yards, commandeered a locomotive, and told the engineer to pull the car with the two steamers on it north to the elevators. The trip was made between two tracks on which cars were burning. Walker was in despair when the men who had agreed to unload the engines fled.

But some sailors from a Lake boat saw the situation, lifted the engines off, then drew them to the end of the slip, where they could take water from the river. Everything in the neighborhood of Elevator B was on fire—freight cars, coal piles, and sundry buildings. Again the volunteers fled. Then a couple of railroad officials ran up with a gang of employees, took charge of the steamers, and saved Elevator B—and possibly also the lives of a group of frightened people huddled behind it.

The Arnolds, the Tinkhams, and others, including a neighbor, Mary Howe, with her baby, were forced to remain at the lighthouse for several hours.

The lighthouse keeper's wife provided sandwiches, and when food ran out a meeting was held with Judge Grant Goodrich presiding. Arnold suggested the possibility of crossing the river, and going south of the fire to seek provisions. H. E. Barnes and two others volunteered. Arnold, Judge Goodrich, and Tinkham each signed a card guaranteeing whatever amount was demanded for food. Barnes took the card, and the three men rowed to the south bank.

They then made their way down Wabash, through cluttered and smoking streets, to a store near Sixteenth, whose owner honored the card. The foragers brought back the supplies by wheelbarrow to the railroad yards opposite the pier, and were picked up by rowboat. By the time they returned, Arnold and the other signers had gone.

Arnold, about 3 P.M., had explored the possibility of escaping to the north, along the beach past Lill's ruined brewery, and decided it was too hazardous a trip for the women. About this time the tug *Clifford* came down the river and tied up nearby. The captain assured Arnold the return trip could be made, since all the bridges were down and the warehouses, docks, and elevators along both banks were now burning less fiercely.

Arnold was very anxious about his wife and daughter, and wanted news of them. He determined to make the journey, even though the tug's woodwork had blistered on the way down. A hose was prepared for use if the *Clifford* caught fire.

A group of refugees climbed aboard, among them Arnold and his son. Women and children were put in the enclosed pilothouse or below decks, while the men crouched on deck behind the butt works.

As they passed the blackened remains of State Street Bridge, they had to slow down for fear the propeller would become entangled in debris. At the same time the pump supplying cold water quit working.

The paint begin to blister again, and Arnold wet his handkerchief and put it over Arthur's face, ordering him to lie flat on deck as the *Clifford* forced her way through the danger zone. They finally reached an unloading point in a West Side lumberyard near Lake Street. But it was not until the following night that Arnold discovered his wife's whereabouts. She and her daughter had gone north to safety in the suburbs.

Tinkham and his family also were aboard the *Clifford,* with the valuable trunk. They caught a train from the West Side to Milwaukee, where the banker deposited the money, with considerable relief, in a vault.

Although some of the others on the Sands were placed aboard tugs or larger vessels and taken out into the Lake, not all those who escaped went by water. Some decided to essay the difficult walk along the shore.

Judge Gary and his family remained until they were driven north along the water's edge by sparks and firebrands. Mrs. Gary's hair and the clothing of one of the younger girls caught fire. Judge Gary soaked some bedclothes in the Lake and wrapped them around the women. He sent them up to Superior Street to take shelter in a wooden shack filled with women and children. They left when the weight of the throng caused the floor to sag, and the building threatened to collapse.

Judge Gary remained with their belongings at the foot of Ontario Street, hoping to find a wagon. When he failed to rejoin the

others, a relative, Charles Higgins of McNeill and Higgins, wholesale grocers, went to find him and was unable to get through a new onslaught of flames. He returned to say he was afraid Judge Gary had been caught by the fire. Mrs. Gary and the girls took this information with amazing calm, dazed by the procession of events.

There were walls eight or ten feet high on each side of Superior, near the Lake, and the Garys found refuge in an empty carriage behind the north wall with a neighbor, Mrs. Samuel Hamill, and her two children. Mrs. Hamill carried an old wooden box, filled with sugar and crackers, which she shared with the Garys.

Sometime during the afternoon Judge Gary showed up, none the worse for the

GRAIN ELEVATORS BURN AT THE MOUTH OF THE CHICAGO RIVER NEAR THE CENTRAL DEPOT. SHORTLY AFTER DAYLIGHT, THE CENTRAL DEPOT BURNED DOWN AND ELEVATOR A BEGAN BLAZING. ALL EFFORTS TO SAVE IT FAILED, BUT ELEVATOR B, FARTHER EAST ACROSS A SMALL SLIP, WAS SAVED WHEN THE MAN WHO WAS SUPPOSED TO DELIVER STEAM FIRE ENGINES TO PENTWATER, MICHIGAN AND RACINE, WISCONSIN BY RAIL, MANAGED TO DELIVER THEM INSTEAD TO WHERE ELEVATOR B WAS IN IMMEDIATE DANGER AND PROTECTED THE ELEVATOR WITH VOLUNTEER HELP. (HARPER'S WEEKLY)

delay, but forty dollars lighter—the price paid for a two-block ride in an express wagon.

They set up camp next to the wall. Mrs. Gary sat on a chair, the younger girls on quilts spread on the ground. There was a cow close at hand, and Judge Gary got milk enough to fill a small vase, which he presented to his wife. Late in the afternoon they heard someone calling: "Has anyone here seen Judge Gary?" It was the banker George Sturges, a friend of his, in a carriage drawn by two horses. He took the family to the home of other friends on the far North Side.

The Trees and their companions were forced into the water by the heat. They came out several hours later and walked north along the shore. At the foot of Superior Street they found the crowded shanty which had escaped the general fate. Tree went inside to rest his eyes, but it was too jammed, and he left. The burning ruins of Lill's Brewery prevented them from continuing farther. They took refuge behind the north wall of Superior Street, where Mrs. Tree sank wearily to the sand.

Just in time Tree discovered that his wife's clothes were burning. He beat out the flames and decided it was safer for all of them to remain on their feet. It was not until that afternoon that a wagon coming down Superior Street signaled the end of their danger. They hired it—for a bargain price of ten dollars—and left for the West Side.

The horses of Miller the jeweler still stood harnessed to the carriage when he and his wife returned to the Sands from their final trip home, just after dawn. Live coals had burned through the blankets, making the animals plunge in fear and pain.

The carriage wheels also caught fire, and Miller's eyes had begun to cause him great anguish. During the morning the group decided to try to go west, chancing a drive down Huron Street despite the flames. They were forced to bump over a segment of fallen wall at Huron and Rush, where buildings were burning furiously. Finally they reached Dearborn and turned north at a gallop, toward Lincoln Park.

They arrived about 2 P.M. They begged a cup of coffee from the keeper and some tea leaves to make a poultice for Miller's eyes. Mrs. Miller tried to nurse the baby, but found she could give no nourishment. There were no extra baby clothes, so she washed the soiled ones in the little park lake. She pinned the garments to the branches of a tree and found they dried almost at once. But their hopes of having found sanctuary were dashed when the keeper hurried up to tell them the trees were burning and they must move on at once.

Miller could not see, so his wife drove the carriage, heading for the Horatio Spafford home in Lake View. Mrs. Spafford, a former classmate of Mrs. Miller's, was home alone. At first she failed to recognize her callers, blackened as they were with smoke and dust. Mrs. Miller stabled the horses and made a salve for the animals' burned feet. Almost immediately, however, they were forced to move on. The surrounding woods had caught fire.

As Mrs. Miller drove the weary and footsore horses up Graceland Road, the carriage wheels sometimes sank to the hubs in sand. She drove across Clark Street, forded the North Branch of the river, and finally found refuge at a farmhouse—with twenty others.

CHAPTER 17

Sheridan wanted to know if he knew who he was, and Mahoney said he did not care a damn.

—JAMES H. HILDRETH

ON THE South Side the energetic Mr. Hildreth had a busy morning and a busier afternoon. When the South Side fire began to sweep east from Dearborn Street to the Lake, most of the firemen were exhausted. Those still going through the motions of performing their duties were little more than blear-eyed robots. But Hildreth remained indefatigable, dashing up and down the line of fire and offering his unsolicited help whenever the opportunity presented itself.

He was sorely hampered in his pet project, however, during the dawn hours. In his unsuccessful efforts around the courthouse he had used up all his ammunition. Mayor Mason had sent to an outlying area for more. But for some time Hildreth was out of powder.

Just before dawn he and his reluctant assistant, Sergeant Lull, dodged east of the blaze that was about to cross Dearborn Street, providing such service as they could. They awoke a family on Dearborn, just north of the *Titsworth* engine house near Madison. The householders were startled to learn that the city was on fire and their own house in danger of catching. Hildreth

ripped down some burning awnings in the neighborhood, and then went east to State and Randolph Streets, where he and Lull helped carry out some merchandise from a clothing store. At this point the fire began to move across Dearborn in earnest, and Sergeant Lull struck out on his own.

Lull headed south and, as he reached Dearborn and Quincy, after passing the blazing Bigelow House, found firemen trying to save some buildings on the east side of the street. They were short of hose. Lull ran into the Palmer House and came out with some canvas hose.

"Turn on the water," he yelled. But there was no pressure. Nothing was left in the mains but "dead" water.

The *Long John* was at the corner of Jackson and Third, and Lull worked with her for a while. The crew was completely exhausted, and Foreman McMonagle was barely able to move. Buildings were burning on all sides and there was no water south of Jackson and very little hose. Lull started for the Lake front to see if he could find another engine. On the way he sat down on the sidewalk to rest and promptly fell asleep. He awoke a moment later when a team of horses almost trampled him.

Meanwhile, a wagonload of powder,

covered with wet tarpaulins, came up Michigan Avenue for Hildreth.

It nearly did not reach him.

Police Captain Hickey and some of his men had been trying to halt the widespread looting of wholesale stores along Wabash Avenue. They were waging a pitched battle with thieves at the Drake and Farwell building at Washington Street, where they had stored several thousand dollars' worth of merchandise rescued from other stores. One of Mayor Mason's sons told Hickey the powder was coming, and asked him to help Hildreth. Hickey advised that it be stored on the Lake front, away from the sparks, until he got a chance to stop the would-be looters. Soon someone dashed up to tell him there was trouble at the Lake.

A crowd had gathered about the powder wagon. They threatened to hang the frightened young driver from a nearby telegraph pole for bringing a load of powder into their midst. Someone demanded to know where he got it.

"Captain Hickey and the mayor sent it!" was his terrified reply.

"Damn Captain Hickey and the mayor!" someone else cried angrily. Several men were dragging the poor fireman away when Hickey arrived.

"Go about your business," said Hickey, in the crisp voice of one used to being obeyed. "We will try to do some good."

The crowd dispersed.

Hickey found Hildreth, who had decided to blow up some buildings on Wabash Avenue near Washington Street, in the hope of keeping the fire there from working east to the railroad yard. Lull returned from the south and rejoined the demolition crew. He still had reservations about blast-ing, and warned the others that the flames were traveling too fast to be stopped.

Nevertheless, Hildreth pointed out a building, and Lull went into it with a keg of powder. He stayed there waiting for a signal to blow it up, until the heat became so intense he could hardly see. He stumbled out to the street. Hildreth and the others had already blown up several buildings near the Washington corner, as far down as the old "Spotted Church."

This name was derived from the mottled appearance of the stones used in its construction. It was such an eyesore that even its congregation had abandoned it. The fire came along quickly to remedy Hildreth's oversight.

Hildreth's accuracy was improving, but he was still slow on the draw. The fire was beginning to jump the avenue, and to work around him to the south. Hildreth came out of one building to find that the powder wagon had gone on without him, and he headed south, where he imagined he would catch up with it.

Sergeant Lull took this opportunity to break off the explosive partnership, and thereafter devised his own projects.

During the morning, the fire moved eastward to the Lake, carrying off what remained of the business section and leveling the fashionable residential blocks on Michigan Avenue. Along the northern flank, after the flames had swept through Union depot and Elevator A in the early morning, they started working their leisurely way south through the baseball stadium in Dearborn Park.

One of the businessmen who was not caught napping was George M. Pullman, inventor of the Pullman car and president of the firm that made it. While the flames

church remain, even though the fire was already near the rear of the building.

Hildreth and Sheridan inspected the brick walls. They found them impressively thick and decided the church had a good chance to withstand the flames. Onlookers, meanwhile, were loudly arguing whether the building should be blown up.

"Blow her, goddammit, blow her!" one man shouted.

Another—whose opinion Hildreth respected—said: "The church is not any better than any other building. Blow her!"

Benner added his argument against wrecking the church. He went inside and found only a single door leading out of the basement. Benner asked a church member whether this would be guarded, as the most likely entryway for fire. He was told sand and water would be at hand, and a man stationed there. Benner then told Hildreth there was no danger to the church if this promise was kept.

Sheridan finally decided the issue.

"Give her the last hope," he told the reluctant Hildreth, who wanted to blow up the church. "Go on, and I will stay here and inform you if it is necessary to blow it up."

Hildreth then worked his noisy way up the west side of Wabash to Congress and along the north side of Congress to Michigan. During this time Benner suggested that it might be wise to transfer operations to the alley in the rear of Terrace Row, but when the two men looked over the situation Benner changed his mind. The flames already had crossed the alley and were running through the sheds and barns behind the building.

Small fires kept breaking out on the east side of State above Harrison, and Lull sta-tioned men along the block. They obtained water from cisterns and kept the fires down. Lull would go to the top of one building and, when he spotted smoke on a neighboring roof, would shout for a bucketman, who came and put it out.

Hildreth had left his store of powder on Michigan Avenue in the charge of Mahoney, "a very trusty man, a man who would be like the boy that stood on the burning deck, you could not drive him from his post."

Gen. Philip Sheridan, head of the military district whose headquarters were in Chicago, decided he would like to try his hand at blasting. The Terror of the Shenandoah approached this very trusty man and asked for some powder. Mahoney refused.

Sheridan left and returned with another man, but again failed to persuade Mahoney. The fuming little general went off and came back a third time, accompanied by a policeman. Mahoney was unimpressed. He took a revolver from his pocket and told them that if they got any powder it would be after the revolver was emptied—"and I'm just the man that would do it."

While the argument was continuing, someone came with a request from Hildreth for five more kegs of powder. Mahoney told Sheridan that if he wanted to help, he could carry the powder. Sheridan indignantly demanded to know whether Mahoney knew who he was.

"I do not care a damn," retorted Mahoney, and Sheridan did not get his powder.

With practice, Hildreth and his crew grew more proficient and were able to create explosions more quickly. On Harrison, they were setting and blowing charges about five minutes apart, and the men, at first uneasy around the powder, had gone to the other extreme. They were lighting cigars as they sat on loaded kegs. In one building they had to shut the door to keep the flames out of the room they were scattering powder in. Hildreth himself remained so long inside another that his brother started across the street, fearing he might have been suffocated, just as he emerged.

They ran short on fuses, and twice Hildreth manufactured a makeshift one of paper, with powder sprinkled on it. He waited to be sure it was going to carry the flame, then ran.

Residents of the neighborhood took heart as the work progressed, and threw pails of water over the debris to stop it from burning.

The Michigan Avenue Hotel, on the avenue near Congress, below Terrace Row, might have burned if Hildreth had not blown up some of the buildings near it. While it was threatened and presumably doomed, John B. Drake came walking by from the ruins of his Tremont House. Some sudden hunch made him enter and ask the proprietor if he would sell the lease and furniture.

His colleague indicated that Drake must be crazy, since the flames seemed certain to seize the building at any moment. Drake said he would take the risk, and agreed on a price. Drake put $1,000 down and promised to pay the rest in two weeks. The contract was drawn up, signed, and witnessed. As Drake left, the seller pointed out that Terrace Row had caught, and said:

"This building will go next. You have lost your thousand dollars."

As he walked away, Drake had the uneasy feeling he might have made a foolish bargain.

But the work of the *Brown* and the *Rice* made Drake's purchase a good one. They cooperated to bring water from the Lake and play it on some burning lumber near the hotel, and on the hostelry itself. Benner directed the work, until Schank came up and decided to remove the stream from the front and take it to the rear. This move brought another outcry from the officious Wicker.

"That hotel will burn!" he cried.

Schank gave him no more satisfaction than Benner had done.

"It will not burn," Schank said. "I want to play in the rear."

Wicker said this was a foolish idea.

"If you want to take charge," snapped Schank, "you had better take charge!"

He then cooled down the rear of the hotel. When everything was safe he saw Wicker once more.

"How is it now?" Schank asked.

"It is all right now," Wicker sheepishly admitted.

Flames seized the cornice of a brick block at the south side of Harrison Street at Wabash Avenue. Amateur experts clustered around Hildreth like gnats on a summer night. Some advised him to blow up the entire block, others to cross the street and start demolishing buildings there.

Hildreth finally decided to make a gap in the center of the block, and accomplished this with three charges. By this time he had discovered that best results were obtained by putting the powder on the ground floor, preferably in a small closet, where two kegs were as effective as five in a larger space.

Some time after noon the wooden steeple of the Wabash Avenue Methodist Church caught fire. When word was brought to Hildreth, he was most indignant.

"There," he told Benner. "I knew it! If you had only allowed me to blow up that church when I wanted to, we would have stopped the fire from spreading!"

Benner said he still thought there would be no need to blow up the church. He hurried over and found a small tower at the northeast corner in flames. Emory, from the insurance patrol, was inside shoveling the embers away as they dropped onto the sanded floor beneath.

Benner was told that General Sheridan had sent for six pieces of artillery and planned to blow the tower to pieces with gunfire. Someone else told him there was no wood under the tower, and Benner

went back to the Michigan Avenue Hotel.

Aid for the church came from an unexpected source. William Haskell, a former professional gymnast who had served as a Union scout during the war, stepped out of the crowd.

"I think I can put that fire out," he told a friend. "Please hold my coat."

Someone brought a ladder and Haskell climbed to the roof, whose ridge was seventy-five feet above the ground. He carried a rope with him to haul up water, provided by a bucket brigade which formed a double line to the Lake. Haskell soaked himself, and wet down his path across the church roof. Several times he beat sparks

THE WABASH AVENUE METHODIST CHURCH WAS THE MOST FORTUNATE CHURCH IN TOWN. ALDERMAN JAMES HILDRETH, WHO WAS BLOWING UP BUILDINGS TO PROVIDE "DEAD ZONES" AGAINST THE FIRE, MOVED FIVE BARRELS OF POWDER INTO THE BASEMENT BEFORE BEING PERSUADED THAT THE STURDILY BUILT CHURCH HAD A GOOD CHANCE OF SURVIVING. A SHORT WHILE LATER, THE STEEPLE, WHICH ROSE 100 FEET ABOVE THE STREET AND WAS OUT OF REACH, BEGAN BURNING INSIDE. BUT ONLOOKER AND PROFESSIONAL GYMNAST WILLIAM HASKELL MANAGED TO ACCOMPLISH AN ACROBATIC, HOLD-YOUR-BREATH SCRAMBLE UP THE STONE FAÇADE OF THE STEEPLE TO QUENCH THE BLAZE. ADMIRING SPECTATORS PROMPTLY TOOK UP A COLLECTION FOR HASKELL, BUT THE PERSON TAKING THE COLLECTION ESCAPED WITH THE MONEY BEFORE HASKELL SAW ANY OF IT. (CHICAGO SUN TIMES)

out of his clothes. He clambered to the peak and down the north side of the roof to the base of the tower, whose top was 100 feet from the street. He was joined by two other volunteers, one a Negro.

The flames were eating the inside of the tower, and smoke poured from the top. Haskell wrapped cloth around his head and the others soaked it with water. Then he threw water on the rocks of the tower to cool them and began the hazardous climb. When the handholds were insecure, he looped the rope over projecting rocks and used it to pull himself up. His clothes were smoldering. Thousands watching from below held their breath as he pulled water up behind him, then rested for a moment on the rim of the top.

Then Haskell fastened his rope to the top of the tower and descended into the interior. He was gone so long the watchers feared him lost. Finally he reappeared, his hair and clothing nibbled by fire, to get more water. He descended again. After several trips he climbed wearily out, his mission finished.

The crowds hailed him as the savior of the South Side, many feeling that if the church had burned, the flames would have leaped southward into the rest of the division. He was given a tremendous ovation. Someone suggested that a collection be taken up. This was done. The collectors slipped off with the proceeds. Haskell went quietly home, telling no one of his feat.

Hildreth thought the fire was checked in this sector. He was considerably surprised to learn that General Sheridan was directing the wrecking—by hand since he couldn't get powder—of the home of Colonel Hough, a block to the south. Hildreth went to investigate and found the colonel himself on the roof tearing down his own residence. Sheridan was at another corner, swinging lustily with an ax. Scores of men were holding a rope hitched to the southwest corner, ready to pull it down.

Hildreth climbed up and took Hough by the shoulder. He told him the sacrifice was being made in vain, since the fire had been stopped.

The *Long John,* which had departed some time before to clean out its clogged flues, returned. The *Sherman* also came along and Schank put the two in the line from the Lake, supplying water for the smoldering ruins.

Schank sent for the *Titsworth,* which was in the *Economy*'s house on Archer Avenue, and asked why it wasn't working. The men told him they were tired out and their foreman was ill. Schank put them back to work and sent some of the other engines away.

The *Little Giant* and the *Waubansia* remained on Taylor at the river on the West Side until about 3 P.M., when the danger there seemed ended. Dolan of the *Giant* was taken ill about noon, so Foreman Musham told him to rest on a lumber pile until he was needed.

About forty-five minutes later Musham saw the exhausted Dolan lying on a wagon that went by. The stoker, Lagger, had left to help some other engines while the *Giant* was in front of the Michigan Avenue Hotel. At that time the engine had no water and he was not needed. When Dolan collapsed, only Musham and the pipeman were left of the *Little Giant*'s crew.

When the South Side fire seemed under control, Benner left for home. It was not until the next day that he learned the flames had spread to the North Division.

CHAPTER 18

"Oh, Mr. Kelly, do you think that the fire will come here?" "Hell, yes, Madam. We'll all burn up!"

—CONVERSATION ON LA SALLE STREET

WHILE THE firemen still fought to control the South Side fire, the flames in the North Division went on their way north and west with little opposition, and most of that wasted. By noon the fire north of the river had ravaged virtually as much territory as in the South and West Divisions combined.

Where the flames had passed, the destruction was all but complete. Block after block was leveled to the ground, or reduced to gutted walls. Trees were burned down to the trunks, or stripped of their bark and left blackened silhouettes. In many cases, houses would disappear into a litter of ashes and chimney bricks, leaving iron stoves and plumbing fixtures lying on the rubble as the only evidence of past habitation.

Yet the fire could be capricious, and on rare occasions persevering defense could pay off. One house might be swept away, while a nearby neighbor, alike in almost every respect—with effort and luck—might be saved. Such was the case with the homes of Gurdon Hubbard and Mahlon Ogden.

The brick house of Gurdon Saltonstall Hubbard stood at the northwest corner of La Salle and White Streets, and its grounds covered almost one entire block. In addition to the large square house, the property included stables, a greenhouse, and an extensive garden.

Hubbard, who was sixty-nine years old, first visited Fort Dearborn in 1818, when he was sixteen. A native of Vermont, he was at that time a clerk for John Jacob Astor's American Fur Company, having signed a five-year contract with the firm for an annual salary of $125. He returned to Chicago to live in 1833, when it had just been incorporated, and set up in business for himself. By 1871 he was the prosperous proprietor of a packing house.

He was an Episcopalian, and his wife Ann a Presbyterian. Each usually went to his own church on Sunday, and they held differing views on other subjects. Hubbard was very fond of chewing tobacco. His wife slipped camomile blossoms—supposedly a cure for the habit—into his tobacco pouch, but they had no effect on his taste.

The Hubbards were generous and hospitable, God-fearing people in the traditional sense of the word. Their friends and relatives were legion. Their own children had grown up, but two nieces, Alice Tinkham and Mary Clark, were living with them.

When Mrs. Hubbard reached home Sunday night, after attending her third church service that day, she ate a few grapes and began preparing for bed. As she combed out her hair, she looked to the southwest and saw the glare of fire. Scattered embers sailed past on the wind. She awakened her husband in alarm. He was unperturbed.

"It is the old fire of last night, kindled again," he said. "We can do nothing; you had better go to bed."

At last, however, he peered from the window and became as alarmed as she. He ordinarily eschewed strong language, but the situation evidently required something out of the ordinary.

"My God," he cried, "we are all going to be burned up."

He dressed and found that one of the servants had already fled. A neighbor, J. McGregor Adams, had also departed. The doorbell rang, and some relatives of his, the Hebards, arrived from the Palmer House, where they had been staying on a brief visit from their home in Iowa.

The family filled a wash boiler with water from a nearby hydrant and brewed a batch of coffee. Then a nurse showed up, carrying a baby a few weeks old. She explained that she was supposed to take the child to an aunt's house, but had forgotten the address. They were welcomed, and a mixture of cream and water was prepared for the hungry infant.

Refugees who stopped in were served from a buffet with chicken, corned beef, bread and butter, milk, crackers, fruit, cake, and coffee. Water and food also were taken to the front gate for hungry passers-by. When Taylor, a guest of the George Higginsons', stopped at the Hubbards' house, he was given special treatment. He had become exhausted while helping the Higginsons prepare for flight. Hubbard dosed him with sherry.

Grandmother Hubbard was sent to safety at the home of her grandson, near Jefferson Park. She wore a poplin dress over her finest silk gown, a winter coat over the dresses, and a mink cap on her head. She carried a muff, a black silk dress pattern, and a bundle of umbrellas. When Ann Hubbard helped hoist the old woman into a pony phaeton, the sight left her weak from laughter.

"She looked like an elephant," Ann later recalled, "and when she got into the phaeton she filled the whole seat."

Hubbard drove his mother to his son's house, the phaeton suffering minor damage on the way when another vehicle ran into it. He brought his father back to help move out, with the elder Hubbard's horse tied behind the buggy.

It was morning. Workmen from the packing plant helped the Hubbards get ready to leave, as did a nephew, George, who had dropped in for a week's visit. George saved a white wax cross, covered with sprigs of fuchsias, in a glass case. Dr. Cooper, rector of the neighborhood Episcopal church, carried out a fourteen-foot French mirror, valued at three hundred dollars. Alice Tinkham left behind her most expensive winter suit, of royal purple, and a matching velvet hat whose long feather cost fourteen dollars.

The Hubbards were ready to leave about 10 A.M., when a strange woman arrived with her baby. The panic-stricken mother said she had no idea what to do. Mrs. Hubbard told the woman to go north or be burned alive.

Three hired wagons were loaded with the best of the Hubbards' furniture and car-

THE THREE-STORY HOME OF MAHLON OGDEN, BROTHER OF CHICAGO'S FIRST MAYOR, OCCUPIED A BLOCK ON LAFAYETTE PLACE (NOW WALTON), THE PRESENT SITE OF THE NEWBERRY LIBRARY. AFTER A QUICK TRIP TO HIS DOWNTOWN OFFICE TO SAVE SOME PAPERS, OGDEN RETURNED TO FIND HE HAD PLENTY OF HELP IN THE FIGHT TO SAVE HIS HOUSE BECAUSE MANY PEOPLE HAD CHOSEN HIS SPACIOUS YARD AS A REFUGE. CARPETS SOAKED IN WATER, ROOF-WATCHERS WITH WATER AND BROOMS, A PATROL TO KEEP THE WOODEN SIDEWALK FROM BURNING, AND A FORTUNATE SHIFT IN THE WIND ALL GAVE ADDED PROTECTION. BUT SINCE MOST OF HIS NEIGHBORS HAD LOST THEIR HOMES, OGDEN BECAME THE TARGET OF JEALOUS ANGER. HE AND HIS FAMILY RECEIVED THREATS FOR WEEKS AFTER THE GREAT FIRE. (JACK LEVIN COLLECTION)

pets. Virtually everything was stolen by the drivers.

The Hubbards were just pulling away in their buggy when a sister of their second maid came up and asked for a seat. The young woman was pregnant. The buggy was full and the house already burning, and for once Mrs. Hubbard's sense of hospitality deserted her. But Alice and Mary Clark, much to their aunt's annoyance, jumped out and gave their places to the expectant mother who, Mrs. Hubbard felt, could have been taken to safety by her own family.

The Hubbards had left without eating or drinking, despite their generosity to the refugees. Hubbard grew extremely thirsty. He stopped in a place on Division Street for something to drink. There was no water, and the shopkeeper refused to give him beer when he learned that Hubbard had no money with him. Mrs. Hubbard was highly indignant, and expressed great satisfaction

on learning later that the fire had taken over the fellow's premises, beer and all.

The pregnant girl was deposited at the Woman's Home on Jackson near Halsted. The matron was reluctant to take her in. Mrs. Hubbard settled the matter in a hurry when she reminded the matron that she had sold the Home some adjoining property, and had given it a year's interest—six hundred dollars—free.

The Hubbards reached the West Side in safety. Mary and Alice showed up some time later. They had ridden part of the way on the Madison Street horsecar and were surprised to be charged only the regular five-cent fare.

The three-story frame residence of Mahlon Ogden stood on Lafayette Place, facing Washington Park, a short distance northeast of Hubbard's. The grounds covered the entire block. The house had a wide front porch with a railing, and the fenced-in yard held several outbuildings and many large elm trees. The house was twelve years old.

Ogden was awakened about 1 A.M. Monday by the watchman, and went at once to his insurance office at 162 Lake Street. He brought back a buggy loaded with papers. Next he tried to save the home of his brother-in-law, Ezra Butler McCagg, who was in Europe.

The McCagg mansion, considered one of the city's most handsome, stood opposite the southwest corner of Washington Park at the intersection of Clark and White. It also occupied a full block, its extensive grounds accommodating a fine garden, stables, and two large greenhouses. The house was surrounded by tall trees and neatly trimmed hedges. The owner was especially proud of his large skylighted library, with shelves to

T.M.AVERY LUMBER

Chicago A
the princip
Side. So in
uncommo
houses still

The fir
in this part
whose eyes
could barel
and got son
some four-
to be ready
the river.

Mayor
Milwaukee
from Mayo
CHICAG
WHOLE DEF

Luding
tried to ord
equipment,
jammed, ar
cleared. Th
however, ar
were sent. I
two others,
Citizens we

the ceiling containing his splendid collection of books.

Ogden soon decided there was little he could do to protect the house. It was directly exposed to the onslaught of the flames. But after reaching home it occurred to him that McCagg's aged mother might be in the house. He hurried back and found her sitting with her daughter Carrie in perfect composure, although the fire was very near.

Ogden hurried the two women outdoors, and they walked to the nearest main thoroughfare, Chicago Avenue, two blocks south. It was oppressively hot, and Mrs. McCagg's strength gave out. Ogden, who could not abandon her, was on the verge of despair until a friend chanced to pass by in a wagon and took the three to Ogden's house.

The McCagg house and stables went very quickly. But through some thermal freak the two greenhouses survived without damage. McCagg's safe—perhaps carried out and abandoned by a hurried thief—was found in the street with its contents burned around the edges but otherwise intact. Apparently some thoughtful passer-by—or the thief—seeing smoke coming from the keyhole, had taken time from his own affairs to stuff the opening with mud, which baked hard and smothered the flames.

Ogden's house—like almost everyone else's still standing—was crammed with friends and refugees from the fire. The grounds were filled with wagons, livestock, and furniture.

Ogden and a swarm of helpers worked frantically to save the house. Judge Andrew J. Brown of Evanston, who had already lost three North Side houses, was among them. They tore up carpets, soaked

them in the cistern, and hung them down the sides of the house and barn. Another group of men stood on the mansard roof with buckets and brooms, sweeping off sparks. The fence caught several times, but alert patrols repelled each attack.

Suddenly the wind proved an unexpected ally. When the flames were very near, the wind died down and the fire burned vertically for several minutes. When the gale sprang up again, the flames were less intense. Much of what they had been feeding on was consumed during the calm. Then, when the sidewalk along Dearborn caught, the wind blew the flames away from the house.

The heat from the blocks to the east made it uncomfortable to sit at breakfast near the windows. The grounds were jammed with possessions brought from all

THE RUINS OF C[...]
HARRISON STRE[...]
MICHIGAN AVEN[...]
PAUL'S UNIVERS[...]
AVENUE AT VAN [...]
PROMINENT CHIC[...]
THIS AREA. (CHI[...]
SOCIETY)

Shortly after the engines arrived from Milwaukee, anxious citizens searched out Marshal Williams to urge that he have streams played on coal piles or safes which were close enough to water to be reached by the hoses.

Williams was worn out. His eyes were torturing him, and his clothes were soaked through. During the morning he left the fire briefly and drove to where his wife had taken refuge on the upper West Side. He changed clothes and drank a cup of tea. He tried to eat some bread, but took two bites and was unable to swallow them. He then returned to the battle.

George Rau, foreman of the *Protection* hook and ladder, reached Chicago Avenue some time after daylight Monday. About a hundred worried citizens surrounded him and said he was the only fireman they had seen. Rau's first thought was that he was to be lynched. But all the mob wanted was to have him tear down a couple of buildings. He and scores of volunteers began demolishing a packing plant at the corner of Chicago and Franklin Street, But as the fire approached, his assistants began to drift away. Rau finally gave up and left.

Dennis Swenie was still with the *Coventry*, alongside a steamer from Milwaukee, near the Chicago Avenue Bridge. The fire was checked in that neighborhood but it was evident that the flames could not long be kept from taking the bridge. The *Coventry* crew rolled up their hose and crossed over.

The fire was coming up Roberts Street along the river. Swenie, who had remained behind with the engine, told everyone he saw to cross the river at once or it would be too late. He then took the *Coventry* to the West Side.

Wayne Chatfield, owner of a lumberyard on the east side of the river, three blocks below the Chicago Avenue Bridge, saw that his yards were sure to burn. He and his superintendent began moving the office safe, believing it would be in less danger in the yard. They struggled with it as far as the front door, where it upset, but couldn't move it any farther. They appealed for aid from passers-by, but in vain. Chatfield then brought out a basket of fine wine for bait. The safe was outdoors in no time at all.

The wind was scorching, and the fire had reached the river both above and below the lumberyard. The superintendent suggested they each use a bundle of shingles as a life buoy, and make their way across the river. Chatfield refused, because he couldn't swim. Instead he ran to the bridge, where he found the approaches already gone. The stone abutment was about twelve feet high, and when he tried to climb it he fell back. He made it on a second attempt with the aid of the iron supports which held the planking. They were so hot his hands were permanently scarred.

Shortly after Chatfield's flight, a burning vessel drifted into the bridge, turned it sideways, and set it afire. The means of escape for a considerable number of refugees was thus cut off. Several bodies were found at the foot of the bridge, near the *Gund* engine house.

Many others lost their lives as they tried to turn north again from Chicago Avenue. The fire pursued them into a bewildering maze of dead-end alleys leading from Townsend and Wesson Streets, and trapped them there.

R. B. Roseman, a former San Francisco fireman, managed to save three men and a woman from the North Side, stranded when the bridge burned. He and two other men procured a boat and rowed across the river. They were showered with a hail of burning debris, lost an oar, and floated under the span. A falling timber broke Roseman's arm. Nevertheless, they brought the refugees back to the West Side unhurt.

In the middle of the afternoon, the triumphant Hildreth, his work on the South Side ended, came up to the North Side with his powder wagon to put his talents to use. He was accompanied by a driver and a young man he didn't know. He did not get the reception he wished for.

He stopped several men as they hurried by, to enlist their help. None would have any part of his plans. "I grabbed hold of them," he complained later, "took right hold of them with more force than if I'd been sheriff . . . but they would leave me, just as soon as I would take my hands off them, and cut. The word 'powder,'" he added, as if surprised, "was a terror to them."

Weary and hungry, with apparently no more wards to conquer, Hildreth finally gave up and went home.

Twelve-year-old Willys Warner Baird and his friend Paul Blatchford lived next door to each other on La Salle Street near Oak. When it seemed certain that their homes would go, they loaded their communal cave in the back yard—six feet square by five feet deep and covered with planks and sod—with playthings, kitchen utensils, and an iron kettle filled with soap. Everything burned but the soap.

When the Bairds left home, one of the youngsters wore three hats, one on top of

the other. His father, Lyman Baird, suddenly realized he was wearing his best silk topper in the midst of the flying sparks. He rushed into the house, hung it up, and put on an old one, leaving his new hat for the flames.

Mary Blatchford, whose husband was out of town attending a religious conference, organized the retreat for herself, her four children, and the servants. Before they left, they had breakfast, complete with their favorite graham gems which the Swedish cook-laundress had prepared. They also took time to dump the goldfish from the aquarium on the ground, to save them from the crueler fate of being slowly boiled to death. Amy and Fanny Blatchford carried between them a wastebasket filled with dolls.

Ulmenheim, as the Blatchford home

THE EXPERTISE WITH WHICH CHICAGO'S FIRE DEPARTMENT MET THE FORMIDABLE CHALLENGE OF THE GREAT FIRE MAY BE STUDIED IN THIS PICTURE OF LAKE STREET ABLAZE. THREE STEAMERS AND TWO HOSE CARTS ARE ON HAND; SIX STREAMS OF WATER ARE BEING THROWN, FIVE FROM THE GROUND AND ONE FROM A VANTAGE POINT ON THE ROOF. AT LEAST TWO BULL-HORNS ARE IN USE. (CHICAGO PUBLIC LIBRARY)

was known, burned half an hour after its occupants left. The destruction was hurried by the explosion of some gunpowder in a third-floor closet.

Mrs. Christiane Fischer, a widow with six young daughters, lived in a white two-story house with a high porch on Flori-mond Street, two blocks above North Avenue near Lincoln Park. Her husband had been a custom bootmaker, who supplied ballet shoes to Crosby's Opera House until his death five months before. The six daughters did not lack strong discipline in the absence of their father, however; Mrs. Fischer made them toe the line in the traditional German way.

Hours before the fire reached Flori-mond Street, Mrs. Fischer was rousing her children from their slumbers. "Children, get up!" she told them in German. "There is a great fire!"

A neighbor's three sons dug a hole in the back yard, and Mrs. Fischer was invited to store in it her most valuable possessions. She made her choice with great care. Into the hole went an engraving, *The Apple Gatherers,* which her late husband won in a raffle, another picture, *Carnival,* brought over from Germany, a mirror, the family atlas and some other books, and—most important of all—her Wilson and Wheeler sewing machine, which was not yet paid for. All these were later removed unharmed.

Friends and relatives began arriving from other parts of town, each believing the Fischer home was too far north to burn. Among them were some close friends, Guido and Julia Guilsdorf, who thought the rest of their family was following them, and an aunt, Mrs. Anna Burkhart, who carried her two-year-old son Henry and a picture of her nephew who lived in California.

The remainder of the Guilsdorf family failed to arrive, and Julia tried to slip away several times toward Wells Street in search of them. Mrs. Fischer, whose sense of responsibility weighed heavily upon her, finally lost patience:

"Julia, *wenn du nicht bei mir bleibst muss ich dich festbinden!*" ("Julia, if you don't stay with me, I'll have to tie you!")

The Fischers and their guests remained in the house until early afternoon. Then they started for Clybourne Street Bridge and the West Side. Mrs. Fischer took along some fresh-baked crullers. The six sisters wore puffed-sleeved dresses made by their mother. These departed from current fashion in that their petticoats—on orders from Mama—did not show beneath their skirts. Minnie brought a small basket filled with clothespins. Aunt Anna, weary of carrying her nephew's picture, hung it over Lina's neck. The picture bobbed up and down as she walked, hitting her gently on the back.

The procession went west on Center Street. Horses, wagons, and people were jammed tightly against each other on Clybourne Bridge, and they crossed very slowly. Emma, who had a deathly fear of horses, walked directly under the head of one, and remembered this feat of daring all the rest of her life.

During the last week in September Mrs. Julia Lemos, a widow who lived on North Wells Street with her parents and worked as an artist at a lithographer's, had tearfully placed four of her five children in the Half-Orphan Asylum, on Wisconsin Street. Her mother, Mrs. Eustace Wyszynski, was in poor health.

THE CLUSTER OF MASTS BELONG TO SHIPS WHOSE SKIPPERS WERE UNABLE TO REACH THE LAKE. BEYOND THE SHIPS IS OLCOTT'S COAL YARD, WHICH SEEMS TO HAVE ESCAPED UNSCATHED. THIS IS A VIEW FROM FRANKLIN STREET. (CHICAGO TRIBUNE)

THIS VIEW OF THE WEST DIVISION, WHERE THE FIRE BEGAN, DEPICTS THE DEVASTATION OF THE AREA. THE FIRE'S HEAT WAS SO INTENSE THAT STEEL BEAMS MELTED, STONE FLAKED, AND MARBLE WAS REDUCED TO POWDER. IRONICALLY, ONE OF THE FEW BUILDINGS TO SURVIVE IN THE WEST DIVISION WAS THE O'LEARY HOUSE. THIS IS A PANEL FROM THE GROSS CYCLORAMA. (LIBRARY OF CONGRESS)

Watching five youngsters while her daughter was at work had proved too much for her. So all but the baby were sent to the nursery.

On Sunday afternoon, the separation had proved more than Mrs. Lemos could stand. She hurried to the institution, where she was paying seven dollars a week for board, and said she wanted the children home again. The matron told her it was against the rules to dismiss them until Monday morning. Mrs. Lemos went disconsolately home. She then paid twelve dollars for a month's advance rent to her landlord, who lived next door.

The baby was asleep early. By nine o'clock Mrs. Lemos also went to bed. As she pulled the solid shutters over the windows to make the room completely dark, she noticed how hard the wind was blowing, and thought to herself it would be a bad night for a fire.

She was awakened about 5 A.M. by a commotion outside, and opened the shutters to find the streets crowded with people. A neighbor saw her:

herself hastened to the corner of Wisconsin and Franklin Streets and found the matron, Mrs. E. L. Hobson, preparing to set out with her seventy charges, a dozen of whom were infants. Mrs. Hobson said the Lemos children would be all right, but their mother wasn't to be turned away again. She took them at once, even though they wore ragged garments instead of the good clothes she had sent with them.

They all hurried home and had breakfast. Her father suggested she ask the landlord to return the twelve dollars she had paid him. She went next door on this errand, but the landlord refused. He had a wagon, however, and offered to take one load of whatever they wished to the prairies, in place of returning the money. They sent two trunks, a mattress, and a feather bed. Their names were on the trunks and they hoped their belongings would be safe.

Mrs. Lemos was impatient to leave. Her father kept insisting the wind would change. People streamed by as Mrs. Lemos stood in the doorway, the baby in her arms and the other children behind her. A woman jogged along, with three youngsters panting to keep pace, and jolted Mrs. Lemos into action.

"Madam," she cried sharply, "ain't you going to save those children?"

Mrs. Lemos persuaded her parents to flee. Her mother put some bread and a pound of coffee into a valise, and brought along a little tin kettle. Her father was accompanied by his valuable hunting dog, on a chain, and also carried his gun and a large round clock. They went into the prairie to the north, and luckily found their trunks. It was almost evening. Wyszynski put the bedding down and covered the children with a cloak.

"You just getting up?"

"Yes," said Mrs. Lemos. "What's the matter?"

"The city has been burning all night, and the fire is coming to the North Side."

Mrs. Lemos darted to the rear of the house and woke her parents. Wyszynski's first thought was for his grandchildren. He began wringing his hands.

"The children! The children!" he cried. "I must go for them!"

His daughter reminded him that he didn't know where the asylum was. She

An hour later wind-blown debris fired some of the piles of salvage, and the grass also caught. Mrs. Lemos and her parents hastily awoke the children and they all fled, leaving all they had saved behind. They felt the heat on their backs as they ran. Some distance farther north, Wyszynski tore some boards from a fence and the children lay on them, under the cloak. Mrs. Lemos sat on the grass, holding the baby. Nine-year-old Willie slept with his head in her lap.

The sky began to cloud over and grow dark. Mrs. Lemos could see the flames and a distant church steeple topple over. Willie suddenly awoke, and began weeping. She tried to comfort him:

"Willie, Mother is here. Do not cry!"

"Yes, but, Mama," said Willie, a faithful Sunday school scholar, "isn't this the Last Day?"

One of the very few individuals who successfully defied the flames was a newly married policeman named Richard Bellinger, who lived on Lincoln Place, near Lincoln Park.

Aided by his brother-in-law, another

policeman, Bellinger made full preparations to repel an attack. He had plenty of time to plan his offensive, since his home was at the northern end of the city. He raked up all the leaves, and ripped up the wooden sidewalk, the picket fence, and the front steps. These he took to a vacant lot and burned.

He covered the roof of the small white cottage, recently built for his bride, with wet blankets and rugs. A ladder was placed against the side of the house, and buckets of water gathered at hand.

Bellinger and his brother-in-law fought a long and arduous battle against embers which landed on the roof and yard. This modest dwelling and Mahlon Ogden's fine one were the only two which survived in the burned area on the North Side.

The 230 acres of Lincoln Park provided an emergency refuge for about thirty thousand homeless people Monday night. The park, much of which was still simply wilderness, contained a few small lakes, miles of winding drives, and a zoo. The park proper was just above the old German and Catholic cemeteries, which were side

A PANORAMIC VIEW OF THE NORTHEASTERN PART OF THE SOUTH DIVISION SHOWS CLEAN-UP CREWS AT WORK. FOUR OR FIVE MEN BEYOND THE HORSE-DRAWN CARTS ARE TUGGING AT A ROPE IN HOPES OF TOPPLING A WALL OF THE BUILDING IN THE CENTER. 1 ELEVATOR A 2 ELEVATOR 2, SHOWING FIFTY FEET OF BURNING WHEAT 3 MICHIGAN AVENUE 4 RUINS OF MICHIGAN CENTRAL DEPOT 5 MICHIGAN AVENUE TERRACE 6 TRINITY CHURCH 7 FIRST NATIONAL BANK 8 COURTHOUSE 9 POST OFFICE AND CUSTOMHOUSE 10 ST. PAUL'S CHURCH 11 MCVICKER'S THEATER 12 OPERA HOUSE 13 WABASH AVENUE 14 LAKE PARK (R.R. DONNELLEY & SONS CO.)

by side on Schiller Street. The majority of the graves had been moved elsewhere, but a few—mostly those of strangers or the very poor—remained.

The wooden grave markers burned, with their carved or painted inscriptions, and some of the stone vaults cracked open. Part of the fence between the park and Clark Street caught fire, as did trees and bushes, and piles of clothing and furniture. A contemporary account says a group of concert singers from a German saloon, still in their evening clothes, sat to windward of one of the tombstones and sang, while a group of Methodists held a prayer meeting close by.

Among those who took refuge in Lincoln Park was H. August Kirchhoff, an importer, who lost both his Lake Street store and his home on La Salle Street. He saved a few of his possessions, such as a marble-topped table, dragged to the park at the end of a rope by a servant girl.

That evening Kirchhoff, his wife, and the girl began walking toward Evanston. A farmer in a buggy gave them a lift. Kirchhoff offered his sole remaining possession— a gold watch—in payment. Their benefactor refused, saying he would collect five dollars "when the time comes." It wasn't until several years later that he dropped into Kirchhoff's new store and got his money.

All during the later stages of the fire, when it seemed the flames would burn themselves out at last for lack of fuel, there was one dread thought in everyone's mind: The wind might change, and the enemy return again to the West Side.

The fire did manage to force its way against the wind in numerous places, but not with the speed it displayed when allied with the wind. Finally, late that Monday night, came the end of the long dry spell which had made the destruction of the city possible.

Rain began to fall in a cold drizzle, in some places as early as 11 P.M. Even those who lay wet and chilled in Lincoln Park, on the prairies, and at the Lake shore offered thanks to Providence. Without the rain, if the wind had shifted, the Great Chicago Fire might well have continued until nothing at all remained of the city.

Mary Fales, one of those made homeless on the North Side, summed up the general reaction:

"I never felt so grateful in my life," she said, "as to hear the rain pour down."

CHAPTER 20

When we lay down, away from the crowd, and I knew I had my husband and children safe, I felt so rich—I have never in my life felt so rich!

—MRS. CHARLES FORSBERG

THE CITIZENS of the stricken city were planning for the future long before the flames burned themselves out at Fullerton Avenue in the North Division.

Josiah W. Preston, president of the Board of Trade, returned from New York on Monday to find the city in flames. He promptly rented rooms on the West Side for temporary offices.

The story was told that early Monday morning, even before the *Tribune* building had burned, a man was seen poking about in the ruins of the nearby Reynolds block, feeling the bricks to see whether they had cooled sufficiently to be used again.

Monday afternoon Mayor Mason began organizing a relief program for the city. His first proclamation showed special sensitivity to the problems involved:

"In consequence of the great calamity that has befallen our city, and for the preservation of good order, it is ordered by the Mayor and Common Council of Chicago that no liquor be sold in any saloon until further orders. The Board of Police are charged with the execution of this order."

Mason took over the First Congregational Church, at Washington and Ann Streets, as a temporary city hall and relief headquarters. Melville Stone, who reached his West Side home about noon, took horse and buggy and toured the prairies, telling refugees to go to the church for food and clothing.

The mayor appointed O. W. Clapp, a commission merchant, to distribute whatever supplies came in on the South Side in the way of "charities from the unknown to the unknown." Mason wrote the authorization for Clapp in pencil on the back of an old envelope, and gave Clapp a policeman's star.

Clapp proved energetic and efficient. He started out by obtaining the use of Tobey and Booth's packing house, at Eighteenth Street and the river, for a warehouse, and told railroad switchmen to start unloading relief trains there.

Clapp returned briefly to his home at 23 Twenty-sixth Street, where he found his coachman in a towering rage. The latter had hitched the carriage horses to a wagon and gone to the Lake with all available buckets, pans, and other containers, to bring water for the Clapps and their neighbors. One housewife used the precious stuff for her Monday wash!

Mayor Oakley Hall of New York promptly issued a proclamation there, calling on all citizens to aid Chicago. Contributions of food or clothing taken to the Erie or New York Central stations would be carried to Chicago free through the generosity of Jay Gould and William Vanderbilt. Jim Fiske and Jay Gould themselves sent a special trainload of food and bedding Monday night.

Whatever intercity jealousies had existed vanished with the flames. Cincinnati raised $160,000 for Chicago relief by sunset Monday; and Governors Lucius Fairchild of Wisconsin, Henry Baldwin of Michigan, Samuel Merrill of Iowa, and Rutherford Hayes of Ohio issued proclamations urging immediate help.

Governor John Palmer of Illinois called a special session of the Legislature for Friday, to appropriate money for relief, and took other steps at once. Monday afternoon he sent his secretary, Gen. E. B. Harlan, to report to Mason, and to guarantee the governor's help and cooperation. Palmer also wired to ask if food were needed. Mason replied that cheese, bread, and cooked provisions would be welcome, as well as tents for the homeless. Palmer had handbills printed and distributed throughout Springfield listing these needs.

At 8 P.M. Monday he again wired Mason, telling him three carloads of provisions had been sent and more were to come.

Tuesday morning, awe-stricken citizens explored the ruins of the heart of their city. The burned-over area was roughly one mile across and four miles in length. Many build-

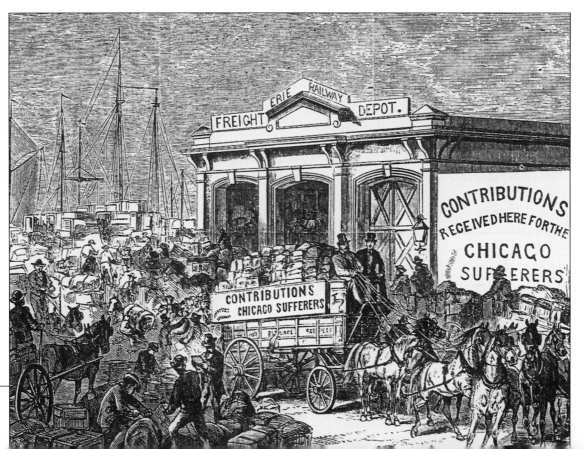

CONTRIBUTIONS FOR CHICAGO'S NEEDY WERE COLLECTED AT THE ERIE FERRY HOUSE IN NEW YORK CITY. HELP POURED IN FROM GENEROUS, CARING PEOPLE ALL OVER THE GLOBE. (R.R. DONNELLEY & SONS CO.)

ings had vanished so completely there was no evidence that they had ever existed. Nearly 100,000 persons were made homeless, and 73 miles of streets and 17,500 buildings of all kinds destroyed.

For mile after mile no sign of the city remained but the built-up roadways, which resembled lonely highroads designed solely to permit passage through some otherwise impassable desert. In some areas there was "not a sound to break the solitude, not a building to change the blackened landscape. . . ."

Where wooden buildings had stood, "the work of destruction was as complete as if the whole had been caught up and borne away. . . . Block after block would reveal no evidences of there having existed civilization, save the excavations of the cellars and a thin layer of ashes. . . . Wood was reduced to an impalpable dust, and all metals shrank away in liquid rivulets and disappeared."

Several hundred tons of pig iron in the McCormick reaper factory yard, and anchors and cables on warehouse sidewalks, ran together like taffy in the sun. Granite blocks cracked and flaked, and pieces of stone lying in the street were split through. The heat turned slabs of marble and limestone to powder. Iron railings and columns warped or liquefied.

In the business district it was rare to find four walls of any building standing, or even a single wall or chimney taller than twenty feet or so. Sightseers who climbed to the top of an omnibus on the North Side gazed across the main streets of the South Division—across what had been the heart of the business district—and saw men standing on the ground three miles away.

One articulate observer left this description:

"Nearly every brick and stone wall has tumbled to the ground. The Courthouse and Post Office walls mostly stand, although entirely gutted. Here and there a tall jagged piece of wall limps its form above the chaotic mass of brick and stone. These ghastly obelisks are the only signboard to tell the stroller among the ruins where he is. In groping among the ruins, one has to ask where such and such a street *was* in order to get his bearings."

Joseph Medill told of "more widespread, soul-sickening desolation than mortal eye ever beheld since the destruction of Jerusalem. The proud and stately city of yesterday for miles around had sunk into cellars and basements. What had hours before been the mart of commerce was now an indescribable chaos of broken columns, fallen walls, streets covered with debris, melted metal, charred and blackened trees standing up like spectres. Thousands of columns of smoke and enveloping tongues of flame still rose out of the tumbling ruins that crashed to earth, throwing up clouds of dust. Great elevators had disappeared. The tall spires of churches, the Courthouse dome, the stately blocks that were the pride of the city and the admiration of visitors, the noted landmarks . . . everything had disappeared."

On Clark Street, in the North Division, the trees had been burned to the ground. Twin rows of Lombardy poplars along North Avenue to Lincoln Park were now lines of black spots beside the street.

An improvised morgue was set up Tuesday in a livery stable at 64 Milwaukee Avenue and the doors guarded by policemen, who admitted groups of ten persons each minute or so during the day. About seventy bodies, some burned beyond recog-

FIRE!

Destruction of Chicago!

2,600 Acres of Buildings Destroyed.

Eighty Thousand People Burned Out.

All the Hotels, Banks, Public Buildings, Newspaper Offices and Great Business Blocks Swept Away.

Over a Hundred Dead Bodies Recovered from the Debris.

Incendiaries and Ruffians Shot and Hanged by Citizens.

FAST WORK ENABLED THE CHICAGO TRIBUNE TO PUBLISH A STORY ABOUT THE FIRE ON OCTOBER 11. THE HEADLINES COMBINE FACT AND THE FALSE RUMOR ABOUT VIGILANTE LYNCHINGS.

1 Lind Block

2 Grand Pacific

3 Court House

4 Post Office

12 Clark Street

5 First National Bank

13 4th Avenue

6 SECOND PRESBYTERIAN CHURCH 7 CENTRAL ELEVATOR "B" 8 TRINITY EPISCOPAL CHURCH 10 FIRST PRESBYTERIAN CHURCH

11 KNIGHT'S BLOCK, HARRISON STREET 15 STATE STREET 9 ST. PAUL'S UNIVERSALIST CHURCH

14 DEARBORN STREET 16 WABASH AVENUE

CHICAGO, AS SEEN AFTER THE GREAT CONFLAGRATION.

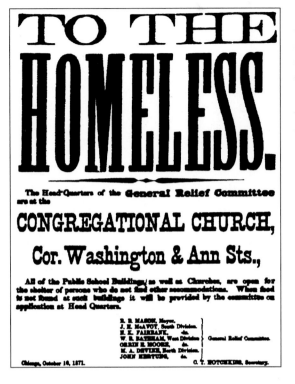

TO THE HOMELESS.

The Head Quarters of the **General Relief Committee** are at the

CONGREGATIONAL CHURCH,

Cor. Washington & Ann Sts.,

All of the Public School Buildings, as well as Churches, are open for the shelter of persons who do not find other accommodations. When food is not found at such buildings it will be provided by the committee on application at Head Quarters.

R. B. MASON, Mayor.
J. E. McAVOY, South Division.
E. K. FAIRBANK, do.
W. B. BATEHAM, West Division.
ORRIN R. MOORE, do.
M. A. DEVINE, North Division.
JOHN HERTUNG, do.

General Relief Committee

Chicago, October 10, 1871.

C. T. HOTCHKISS, Secretary.

nition and others bearing no sign of injury, were laid out in rows on the floor. The only illumination came through the cobwebbed windows. A pile of pine coffins stood near-by for use when bodies were identified.

No one ever knew how many died. Only 120 bodies were recovered after the fire but official guesses of the number of dead ranged from 200–300. Some undoubt-edly slipped into the river, and their bodies never were found. Others must have been consumed completely.

Most of the dead were from the neigh-borhood of Chicago Avenue and the river, or from the narrow dead-end streets near Wesson and Townsend, a little farther north. When the Chicago Avenue Bridge was closed to traffic, many vehicles and pedestrians turned toward Division and were trapped on those streets.

An unknown number of foolhardy, unlucky, or intoxicated persons also were trapped and killed in the South Division. The roster there included McDevitt, the billiards champion, and John Donovan and Henry J. Ullman of the banking firm of Wrenn, Ullman and Company. Ullman kept his date with death on Clark Street, near Monroe, apparently while trying to reach his office to save money and securities.

In the ruins of Bookseller's Row on State Street, all that was legible of the stock of more than a million books, according to one report, was a scorched page from the Bible, containing the first chapter of the Lamentations of Jeremiah:

"How doth the city sit solitary, that was full of people! how is she become as a widow! she that was great among the nations. . . . She weepeth sore in the night, and her tears are on her cheeks. . . ."

At daylight Tuesday several thousand men, women, and children began preparing breakfast of sorts on the prairies north of town. The rations were so meager that a single biscuit and weak tea composed the entire bill of fare for some.

Mrs. Miller had the horses hitched, and left to try to find her father. Miller, his aching eyes covered by a blue veil, accom-panied her. They drove first to the Lake, where a buggy they had left with their coachman stood half-burned. They poked in the drifted sand and found the bed. It was smoking, but enough down was saved to make a couple of pillows. They also uncovered some white enamel jewelry, set with pearls, which had been Miller's first gift to his wife.

After a prolonged search they came upon Mrs. Miller's father, standing near the Randolph Street Bridge. When the fire

moved toward his office, a nearby druggist had given him a cane and a crutch. Since he had to walk or die, he walked.

Julia Lemos and her children awoke early and drank a pitcher of milk which her father brought from a farmhouse. The little group also divided half a loaf of bread she carried in her bag. The Wyszynskis, searching without hope for their trunks, found they had been buried by a thoughtful policeman and were intact. The entire family found shelter in a German Lutheran church on Sedgwick. They took over two pews, and subsisted on supplies sent in by the city.

The church janitor made an unappetizing brew of "coffee" from parched rye. Mrs. Wyszynski, who had clung to the coffee and pot she had brought from home, got permission to make her own, three times daily.

When the first potful was brewed, a lady wearing a silk dress and diamond ear-

rings, and carrying a poodle in her arms, came down hopefully from the pulpit. The aroma, she said, was irresistible. Could she have a cup? Mrs. Lemos invited her to share the coffee with them each time they made a fresh supply.

When her husband found her the next day the stranger bade Mrs. Lemos a grateful farewell. "We may never meet again," she said fervently, "but we will meet in heaven."

The third day after the fire, the whole family received free railroad passes and left to join relatives in New York. The janitor drove them to the station with their few belongings, in return for the gift of Wyszynski's hunting dog.

Goodwin, who had finally reached his Lake View home only to discover that it was also menaced by flying embers, guarded it until the rains came. Then he went to bed. In the morning he borrowed a buggy and a horse, and left in search of provisions. On the road he met Isaac Arnold, worn and

LEFT: THE CURIOUS AND THOSE WHO HAD BEEN BURNED OUT WASTED LITTLE TIME BEFORE EXAMINING THE DISASTER SCENE. PERHAPS THE THREE MEN IN TOP HATS ARE DECIDING HOW SOON THEY CAN REBUILD. (CROMIE COLLECTION)

ABOVE: BOOKSELLER'S ROW, ON STATE STREET BETWEEN WASHINGTON AND MADISON, HOUSED A NUMBER OF THE 68 BOOK DEALERS DOING BUSINESS IN CHICAGO IN THE 1870S. (JACK LEVIN COLLECTION)

anxious, still searching for his wife and daughter. Arnold asked for a lift into town.

They reached Erie and Pine Streets, where Arnold's house had been. Not even a chimney was standing. They then went down State to Indiana Street, where they met the first buggy they had seen since starting out. In it was Arnold's family.

Reports of the fire reached Henry Hamilton in Cleveland, Illinois, on Monday. He called at the office of a Rock Island newspaper and found them true. He took the night train for Chicago, arriving at 6 A.M. Tuesday. Several of the cars carried relief supplies. Hamilton got off at 22d Street on the South Side and walked to State, where he waited hopefully for a horsecar. When none came, he continued walking north and discovered why no horsecars were running. The tracks were bent and twisted from the heat.

State Street Bridge was gone, and he went to the tunnel at La Salle. A stranger was arguing with a policeman who was trying to stop him from entering the tunnel.

There were no lights, and the condition of the interior was not known. The other traveler was eager to search for a brother who had been attending Rush Medical College. He and Hamilton finally overrode the policeman's arguments and started through the tube with locked arms. They lighted matches to find their way, but continually stumbled over boxes and debris. They were bruised and exhausted when they reached daylight.

Hamilton found no sign of his home, although he saw his kitchen range buried beneath the walls of the church across the street. He walked up to White Street and saw Gurdon Hubbard's house in ruins. At Dr. Williams's place the story was the same. He recognized his damaged household furnishings in the yard, along with some piano legs and half-burned pedals.

Hamilton was tired and hungry, and had no notion of what had happened to his family. He decided to sit and wait. He rested on a large stone for an hour or so. Then a buggy came up Sedgwick Street. It was driven by his wife.

Clapp wasted no time getting organized for his relief work. Early Tuesday he found the Eighteenth Street warehouse cleaned and cleared, and was told some railroad cars were expected before noon. He went to the Plymouth Church on Wabash Avenue and asked for volunteers among the refugees to help unload them. Twenty men responded. Clapp commandeered a Farwell truck and one from Field and Leiter's to take the men to the Eighteenth Street warehouse.

Signs had been placed in all the churches telling where food, bedding, clothing, and shelter were available. By evening Clapp had supervised the distribution of ten carloads of supplies. The only complaint Clapp heard during the early rush was from the clergyman of a fashionable church, who asked for supplies of better quality because he had "high class parishioners."

Fifty carloads of food and clothing arrived before the sun went down Tuesday. Milwaukee made up a special train, and schools there were closed and business virtually suspended as everyone helped with the collection.

St. Louis had a relief train on the way Tuesday. In New York City wagons went up and down Fifth Avenue and other streets with signs on the sides which read: GIVE US CLOTHING FOR THE FIRE SUFFERERS!

A visitor from Chicago in New York saw people run from their homes and throw garments into the wagons as they rolled slowly by.

Some citizens fled town as soon as they could arrange transportation. The railroads provided free passes for several days. But most citizens stayed on, rebuilding their homes and businesses as best they could.

Margaret O'Toole, who sold chestnuts on Lake Street, was at her regular stand Tuesday morning, an incongruous sight amidst the wreckage. She was the first merchant in the stricken area to open for business.

At the Merchants' Insurance building a number of Western Union employees, Loesch among them, perched on the tumbled debris until a messenger told them to report to the new office at State and Sixteenth Streets. The others decided not to go, but Loesch promptly headed for the new quarters via Clark Street. At Twelfth

THOSE WITHOUT ENOUGH CLOTHING WERE WELCOME AT DISTRIBUTION CENTERS SUCH AS THIS. NOTE THE PILE OF SHOES IN THE LEFT CORNER, WAITING FOR THE RIGHT-SIZED FEET TO COME ALONG. (R.R. DONNELLEY & SONS CO.)

Street he paused to price an apple pie in a bakery window. He expected to be asked at least two dollars but it was only twenty cents. He bought and ate it on the spot.

Western Union had moved into a brick warehouse, with boards laid across barrels serving as desks. Persons waiting to send telegrams were lined up for a block and a half when Loesch arrived. They stood side by side in the street, using the raised sidewalks to write on. Loesch sent a wire of his own to Buffalo, listing the names of former Buffalo residents he knew to be alive. Then he began taking telegrams, all of which were sent free that day.

Sam Greeley drove to town during the morning and stood in line for half an hour to wire some friends in Boston. Later in the day he asked a wealthy citizen for a loan. He was handed a dime, which he used to buy some crackers.

ON TUESDAY MORNING, THE GENERAL
RELIEF COMMITTEE BEGAN DISTRIBUTING
RAILROAD PASSES FOR ANYONE WANTING
TO LEAVE CHICAGO. THE LINE OF APPLI-
CANTS EXTENDED FOR NEARLY A BLOCK ON
WASHINGTON STREET. IT WAS THOUGHT
THAT 15,000 PEOPLE LEFT CHICAGO ON
MONDAY AND 15,000 MORE ON TUESDAY.
(ANDREAS)

RAIL ROAD PASS.

Head Quarters Gen'l Relief Committee,

Chicago, --------------------1871.

--------------------------------Rail Road Pass

--------------------------------A Sufferer by

the late Fire to.........................

ORREN E. MOORE,

Attest; *[signature]* Chairman Relief Com.

..............................Secretary

One local merchant sent the following telegram Tuesday morning to his wife, who was visiting in New York:

STORE AND CONTENTS, DWELLING AND EVERYTHING LOST. INSURANCE WORTHLESS. SEE SMITH IMMEDIATELY; TELL HIM TO BUY ALL THE COFFEE HE CAN AND SHIP THIS AFTERNOON BY EXPRESS. DON'T CRY.

John S. Wright, editor, author, and real-estate dealer, who had escaped from the South Division only minutes ahead of the flames, was walking at Wabash and Congress Streets Monday when he met D. H. Horton, whose firm had published Wright's book, *Chicago, Past, Present, and Future.*

"What do you think of the future of Chicago?" Horton asked wryly.

Wright had a ready answer:

"I will tell you what it is, Horton. Chicago will have more men, more money, more business within five years than she would have had without this fire."

CHAPTER 21

I have seen only one complainer and that was a millionaire.

—MRS. AURELIA KING

IT IS believed that the fire has spent its force," said one of the mayor's proclamations cautiously on Tuesday, "and soon all will be well." Mason also urged the citizens to use "great caution in the use of fire in their dwellings and not to use kerosene lights at present, as the city will be without a full supply of water for two or three days." This warning was no doubt superfluous for most Chicagoans.

Actually, water of sorts was available sooner than Mason had hoped. Steam from a locomotive boiler was used to pump river water directly into the mains starting at midnight Tuesday. Those who had a sample pronounced it "smoky but good." It was not, however, particularly healthful. One tragic consequence of the fire was a minor epidemic of typhoid in the weeks following.

Repairs on the waterworks also began Tuesday, when the ruins had barely cooled. The engines proved to be in bad shape, but the damage to the boilers was slight. All available men—even without experience—were put to work making steampipe. Two hundred and fifty men were kept busy for several days. A cookhouse was hastily erected, and meals provided by Clapp's relief committee.

The first engine was started at 8:20 P.M., October 27, and water was available without interruption thereafter, even though the other pumps were not in operating condition until November.

The brave response of the business community to its losses reflected the basic confidence that the city had in itself. Very few businessmen were despondent, and most got back to work very swiftly, making do with what could be saved from the ashes, and credit.

The last building burned early Tuesday morning. The first load of lumber was delivered to the South Side Tuesday afternoon.

Cyrus McCormick went to meet his wife at the station Tuesday wearing a half-burned hat and overcoat. They went at once to the ruins of the reaper works, where McCormick told the gathered employees that a new factory would be built as soon as possible.

A carefully planned program of recovery was prepared by cashier Harlow Higinbotham for Field and Leiter's store. Field found an available building, an old brick horse barn at State and Twentieth Streets, while Leiter began an inventory of the salvage. Meanwhile, a warehouse was rented in Valparaiso, Indiana, to which shipments from the East were sidetracked until the "store" was ready. Higinbotham himself took his family and that of Levi Leiter to his mother's home in Joliet, where he and the company's bookkeepers put the books in shape. Field and Leiter's opened within three weeks.

Stores and offices were set up in houses on Michigan and Wabash Avenues and State Street, below the burned-out area. One church was divided into offices, another became a watch factory, and a third an express office. The basement of one house was a shoe store, the main floor a button factory, and the bedrooms served as offices for doctors, lawyers, and insurance men. A telegraph office occupied the upper dormer.

Throughout the city, sign painters were sure of steady work, whether they could spell or not. The sign for one shoe store, for example, read "SHOOES."

Moore and Goes, whose sign-painting shop had been on Madison Street, moved to the West Side. They left a sign giving their new address together with an estimate of their financial condition: "Capital, $000,000.30."

On top of the tumbled wreckage of Woods' museum was a notice reading: "COL. WOODS' MUSEUM—Standing Room Only. R. Marsh, treasurer." Carl Pretzel, publisher of a humor magazine written in German-English dialect, left a note on what had been his office: "Carl Pretzel, gon avay."

William Kerfoot, a real-estate man, threw up a hasty shack office among the South Side debris. Emblazoned on it was the assertion: "All gone but wife, children, and energy."

OPTIMISM WAS DISPLAYED BY WILLIAM D. KERFOOT, A REAL ESTATE AGENT WHO, WITH TWO OTHER MEN, PUT UP A WOODEN SHACK, 12 FEET BY 16 FEET, BETWEEN CLARK AND DEARBORN ON THE MORNING OF OCTOBER 10. HE CALLED IT THE "KERFOOT BLOCK" AND ADDED THIS TO HIS SIGN: "ALL GONE BUT WIFE, CHILDREN, AND ENERGY." THIS WAS THE FIRST NEW BUILDING TO GO UP IN THE BURNED OUT BUSINESS DISTRICT AND KERFOOT'S STATEMENT BECAME ONE OF THE MOST QUOTED IN CHICAGO HISTORY. (ANDREAS)

Bankers were left in suspense for several days concerning the condition of their safes and vaults. For some time the brick or steel of which they were made was too hot to handle. There was also the fear that the contents might have become superheated, and would ignite, if they had not burned already, when exposed to the air.

Early in the week, a group of worried bankers was considering paying depositors twenty-five cents on the dollar, but Chauncy Blair, president of Merchants' National, talked them out of it.

"If a dollar," he said, "is found in the vaults of the Merchants' National Bank when they are reached and opened, that dollar belongs to the depositors!"

The vaults and safes were finally opened Friday and Saturday. The contents of some safes, especially the smaller ones, did indeed flare and burn as soon as the doors were opened. But in many instances the contents were found unharmed. Four of the brick vaults in the city hall were intact, though two were smashed by falling walls. None of the banks which opened their vaults Saturday lost what was in them. This was of inestimable importance in getting the city back on its financial feet.

The post-office vaults were opened Saturday, in the presence of Treasury Department representatives and troops of the Fifth Infantry. One corner of the inner iron box had been opened when the Depository vault fell into the basement, and everything inside was burned except some gold coins. There had been $1,500,000 in currency in the vault, but the only papers recovered were some fragments of gold certificates worth $19,000, which were redeemed for $16,500.

In an old safe in one corner of the Depository, however, $37,172 was found untouched. The total loss in currency and coin certificates was $1,034,300, for which McLean, the collector of the port, was responsible. Congress, however, later passed a special act, relieving him of the necessity of repaying it.

H. R. Hurlburd, comptroller of the currency, met with bank officials Sunday, and warned the national banks that any not resuming on a pay-in-full basis by Tuesday would be thrown into receivership. But all banks opened for business in normal fashion, greatly to the benefit of the city's prestige.

Samuel Greeley, who had gone to Boston to borrow money for new surveying instruments, returned to Chicago in time to make a badly needed survey October 24. His bankbooks had been destroyed in the fire, but he got his money from one bank by simply telling the banker—from memory—how much he had on deposit.

An uncommon degree of personal integrity was displayed by Albert C. Lane, county superintendent of schools and custodian of school funds. The Franklin Bank failed as a result of the fire, and a private bondsman had to make up the amount of school funds lost in the bank. Lane—while by no stretch of the imagination responsible—spent years repaying the bondsman.

One business was unable to respond to the situation with much resilience or enthusiasm: The fire insurance companies were left reeling from a blow that many never got over. Three hundred and forty-one had claims to meet. Fifty-seven were sent out of business. Fourteen of the twenty Chicago companies involved went under, some paying only three cents on the dollar. When all claims were paid, $45 million had

THE CHICAGO TRIBUNE FOR OCTOBER 18 CARRIED A NOTICE TO LIGHTEN SOME HEAVY HEARTS. THE LIVERPOOL & LONDON & GLOBE INSURANCE CO. NOT ONLY WOULD PAY IN FULL ALL LEGITIMATE CLAIMS, BUT WAS STILL SELLING FIRE INSURANCE, DESPITE HAVING LOST ABOUT $3 MILLION AS A RESULT OF THE CHICAGO CLAIMS.

APPROPRIATELY ENOUGH, THIS INSURANCE CHECK FOR $4,000 TO HART, ASTEN & CO., THE FIRST ONE PAID AFTER THE DISASTER, SHOWS A FIREMAN ON A LADDER WITH A BULLHORN. THE CHECK WAS DATED OCTOBER 12, 1871. (ANDREAS)

been given policyholders of $88 million due.

Robert S. Critchell, Chicago representative for the Phoenix Insurance Company, wired his home office immediately after the fire that their losses would be about $400,000. He requested that someone be sent at once with $30,000 in cash to start paying out claims.

Critchell rented an office on Canal Street Wednesday, and on Friday Frank Williams, cashier of the New York office, and T. R. Burch, acting general agent, arrived. Williams wore a buckskin belt with $10,000 in it. Shortly thereafter, Critchell met the proprietor of a destroyed grain-bag factory on the street and offered him $3,500 to settle a $4,000 policy. The offer was accepted, and Critchell gave him a draft for the amount on the spot. This was probably the first insurance claim paid after the fire.

The newspapers of Chicago had the greatest story of the day right at their doorsteps—or rather, in most cases, occupying the whole house. It is not surprising that they should have gone back into operation promptly.

Monday morning, while the fire was still burning, Joseph Medill went in search of a new office for the Tribune. He had had only two hours' sleep since leaving the building to the flames. He finally found a small printing shop on the West Side and rented it. It had neither steam presses nor an engine, and the type was composed mainly of capitals and numerals.

That afternoon this limited equipment was loaned to the Journal, which had established headquarters next door. The Journal put out an extra, four by six inches in size, printed on one side of the paper.

The Post also managed to get out an edition, under the headline A NIGHT OF HORROR NEVER BEFORE EQUALED ON THE CONTINENT!

Medill and Bross spent Tuesday getting their new office in order. Medill took charge of gathering material for the paper, while Bross attended to cleaning up the place.

Bross also took charge of procuring stoves for the offices. He found four in a store on Halsted Street. They cost sixteen dollars each.

Bross told the storekeeper he wanted them for the Tribune, and instructed him to start cutting pipe for them. He said they would be paid for as soon as the Tribune vaults were opened. The storekeeper demanded cash on delivery.

"On Saturday," commented Bross, "our note would have been good for $100,000. On Tuesday we could not buy four stoves and the fixtures on credit."

Bross took the storekeeper back to the office to measure the pipes, assuring him the money would be forthcoming. Then he went in quest of cash. He stopped all the friends he saw on the street. The tenth man, Edward Cowles, asked how much he needed.

"All you can spare," Bross said.

Cowles gave him sixty dollars. Bross took it to the store, promising he would soon have the remainder. At the office once more, he was able to borrow a hundred dollars from another friend.

By midafternoon Charles Lowell, one of the clerks, said people were asking to insert advertisements for lost friends and relatives.

"Take them and the cash," Bross replied. A windowsill and a dirty box were the only desks available.

A man entered with a business proposition. "I haven't a morsel of food for my wife and children tonight," he said, "and not a cent to buy any: May I paint 'Tribune' over your door?"

Bross said he could, and they agreed on a fee. The enterprising stranger earned $3.75.

The stoves were up—and paid for—by four o'clock. Clerks were taking ads, and paper was being loaded into the basement. The first issue was printed Wednesday morning at the *Journal,* which had acquired a steam press.

Col. H. W. Farrar of the *Journal* was on a train for Cincinnati while the fire was still burning. There he bought a four-cylinder rotary press, dismantled it, and boxed it. Meanwhile, Charles Wilson, owner of the paper, was having a foundation dug for the press in the cellar of the temporary office.

Murat Halstead of the Cincinnati *Commercial* loaded up a lot of old type and shipped it to the *Tribune.* Medill, hearing of an available rotary press in Baltimore, bought it by telegraph and had it forwarded at once. The dimensions were sent by wire

and while the press was en route a foundation was being made ready.

The *Times* was the last of the major dailies to resume publication. Its owner, Wilbur Storey, was one of the few businessmen in town who seemed beaten by the fire.

"The *Times* is dead," he said. "Chicago is gone, and I'm all through." Storey figured he might retrieve $80,000 from the wreckage and retire.

But his despondency lifted. He found some old type in a barn behind his house and borrowed money from some friends. The *Times* came back to life on October 18.

The newspapers, it must be admitted, evidently felt that a plain unvarnished tale of the recent catastrophe failed to do it complete justice. Not only were the early issues filled with descriptions of the fire and its aftermath, embellished with a good deal of fulsome rhetoric; they also contained a good many stories based on rumor, as well as outright fabrications. The story of Mrs. O'Leary and her cow received its major impetus in this fashion. There were also accounts, some them purportedly by eyewitnesses, of the lynchings of incendiaries, and other acts of individual and collective violence, none of which appears to have had any basis in fact. These flights of journalistic fancy had rather unfortunate consequences later on.

The papers were also filled with personal advertisements—containing both pathetic appeals and reassuring information.

"Rev. J. T. Goodrich, stopping at the Metropolitan Hotel at the time of the fire, is anxiously inquired after by his son, J. C. Goodrich, Tradesmen's National Bank, Philadelphia."

CHICAGO CHILDREN RECEIVED SPECIAL ATTENTION FROM YOUNG SOCIETY WOMEN OF THE TOWN. SOME MADE SANDWICHES FOR HUNGRY YOUNGSTERS AT VARIOUS DISTRIBUTION POINTS. MATTRESSES OF HAY, CORNHUSKS, OR EXCELSIOR WERE ALSO PROVIDED, AND J.L. PICKARD, SUPERINTENDENT OF SCHOOLS, DIRECTED ALL TEACHERS TO DETERMINE WHICH ABSENTEES STAYED HOME BECAUSE THEY HAD NOTHING TO WEAR. THOSE IN NEED WERE GIVEN MONEY AND GARMENTS. (CHICAGO PUBLIC LIBRARY)

"Mr. McLogan, 228 Laflin, has a boy 2 or 3 years old—speaks French."

"If Mr. Biscoff, formerly barber on North-av., will call at 165 Waubansia, he will find one or two pictures saved from the fire, and supposed to be his. J. Netterville."

"Will the gentleman who gave me the clock and picture on State st. Oct. 9 call at 258 Cottage Grove-av. Dr. Steere."

"PERSONAL-INFORMATION WANTED OF George Norman Beresford, who was in Chicago at the time of the fire. If this meets his eye, he is earnestly requested to communicate with his friends, who are in deep anxiety. . . . If he is in want of funds, or wishes to return home, money has been placed to his credit with E. M. Archibald, British Consul, New York. Any one who can give information would confer a favor by addressing Claudius De La Poer Beresford, Ravenscliffe, Lancashire, England."

Hotelkeepers, realizing the demand for lodgings that would develop among both local residents and sightseers, worked feverishly to get ready for the invasion.

George W. Gage bought the Gault House on the West Side, the only large hotel left in that division. He met Marshall Field on the street and told him he wanted carpeting. Field protested that he didn't know whether he had "a cent in the world."

"Neither do I," said Gage calmly, "but there are thousands of people coming to see these ruins and I'm going to have a place to take care of them."

John Drake dropped by the Michigan Avenue Hotel the week after the fire and offered the balance of the money due on his purchase agreement. The proprietor refused to conclude the deal and Drake left, returning in a few moments with several friends. Then he laid a watch on the other's table and said he wanted possession in five minutes or the other man would be thrown into the Lake.

Drake renamed it the Tremont House.

The first Sunday after the fire was a clear mild day. Excursion trains filled with sightseers pulled into town. Residents of nearby communities also hitched up and drove into town. Despite the hazard of falling walls, there was a constant procession of the curious through the burned districts. John Jex Bardwell, a Detroit photographer, made a special trip to Chicago to get pictures of the ruins.

The Reverend Robert Collyer, like many other ministers that Sunday, held services in front of the remains of his church that day. The gray-haired pastor stood on a broken pillar and told his congregation that he had been "endeavoring all week to reach such a spiritual height as to be able to look down upon all the devastation and thank God for all." He added that he had not yet been able to do so, but that "God would not demand this today . . . all this in good time."

Collyer promised to remain with his parishioners, telling them he didn't think they could find "a cheaper pastor." He said he had preached one year for seventy-five cents and could do so again. If all else failed, he added, he "could still make as good a horseshoe as any blacksmith in Chicago."

The generosity of the rest of the world made a very substantial contribution to the city's swift recovery.

A wide assortment of food arrived for some days after the fire: bread, live fowls, crackers, flour, sugar, cabbage, beef, pork, coffee, bacon, doughnuts, cheese, sauerkraut, cake, and fruit. Among the clothes contributed—aside from simply utilitarian items—were ball gowns, theatrical costumes, brocaded silks, white vests, and lavender gloves. The Ohio Female College forwarded sixty complete suits of ladies' underwear.

President Grant sent $1,000 as a personal contribution. The Cincinnati Elastic Sponge Mattress Company donated 100 mattresses, Cincinnati newsboys two days' earnings, and the Jane Coombs Comedy Company their gate receipts for one performance. Washington, D.C., hackmen turned over a day's fares, and the crew of the U.S.S. *Vermont* a day's pay. Police departments from Quebec to Louisville chipped in to aid their fellow policemen in the Garden City, most of whom were burned out.

The final total of money given was $4,820,148.16, of which $973,897.80 came

from twenty-nine foreign countries. The manufacturing town of Furth, Bavaria, sent $2,302.31; the Common Council of London, England, 1,000 guineas; Boston, $400,000; Buffalo, $100,000; New York, $600,000; and Lafayette, Indiana, $10,000. Ninety dollars came from residents of the "Dacotah" Territory.

In England, Thomas Hughes, author of *Tom Brown's School Days,* began collecting books for a Chicago public library. Donors included Charles Kingsley, John Stuart Mill, Dante Gabriel Rossetti, Disraeli, and Queen Victoria.

Contributions in goods included two items of considerable usefulness: sixteen dozen packages of Shield's eyewash and 600 boxes of burn salve.

Eastern firms telegraphed their Chicago

customers with offers of unlimited credit. Carloads of stock for store and warehouse poured in right behind the relief trains.

The owner of the Townsend House in Oconomowoc, Wisconsin, came to Chicago two days after the fire. He asked that all former patrons and their friends who wished to come to his hotel leave letters to this effect at the *Journal* office. They were welcome to remain free of charge until they could find other quarters.

STATE OF MICHIGAN, EXECUTIVE OFFICE, LANSING, *October* 9.

The city of Chicago, in the neighboring State of Illinois, has been visited, in the providence of Almighty God, with a calamity almost unequalled in the annals of history. A large portion of that beautiful and most prosperous city has been reduced to ashes and is now in ruins. Many millions of dollars in property, the accumulation of years of industry and toil, have been swept away in a moment. The rich have been reduced to penury, the poor have lost the little they possessed, and many thousands of people rendered homeless and houseless, and are now without the absolute necessaries of life. I, therefore, earnestly call upon the citizens of every portion of Michigan to take immediate measures for alleviating the pressing wants of that fearfully afflicted city by collecting and forwarding to the Mayor, or proper authorities of Chicago, supplies of food as well as liberal collections of money. Let this sore calamity of our neighbors remind us of the uncertainty of earthly possessions, and that when one member suffers all the members should suffer with it. I cannot doubt that the whole people of the State will most gladly, and most promptly, and most liberally respond to this urgent demand upon their sympathy; but no words of mine can plead so strongly as the calamity itself.

HENRY P. BALDWIN,
Governor of Michigan.

A letter in the *Tribune,* from A. Hitzfeld of Curlew, Nebraska, offered free lots to anyone wishing to build a home in that town, which had been founded only the previous June. The letter said that lumber was only $16 a thousand feet, and Hitzfeld promised that no one would starve.

Out-of-town fire engines began returning home the day after the fire, since many had left their own citizens virtually without protection. But the Amoskeag Manufacturing Company of Manchester, New Hampshire, and the Silsby Manufacturing Company, Seneca Falls, New York, loaned the city two steamers for several weeks without payment while the Chicago engines were being repaired.

Some relief groups from other cities paid personal visits to Chicago. By October 20, Phoebe Cozzens of St. Louis had been to town twice with supplies from the Ladies' Christian Society of St. Louis. A relief committee from Boston arrived after a 55½-hour train ride and put up at the Michigan Avenue Hotel. The city of Cincinnati sponsored a soup kitchen, run by Eli Johnson, "as thorough a gentleman as ever made a dish of soup." This fed 3,500 daily at the corner of Green and Carroll Streets. It was still in operation in December.

A month after the fire, relief authorities were caring for more than 60,000 persons at regular distributing points. The Ladies' Relief Society, organized October 19 at the home of Mrs. Wirt Dexter, was running at full capacity. One of its main objectives was to find those in need who were too proud to apply, and to help them with a minimum of embarrassment. The society also tried to supply persons needing clothing, and kept thirty to fifty seamstresses at work at this task.

Of the approximately 100,000 homeless, it was estimated that 20,000 had gone out of town and 15,000 others were being cared for by friends. This left about 13,000 families who needed complete or partial assistance. The purchase of sewing machines to enable women to help support themselves and their families was a major item. Within a few weeks, 4,389 machines had been bought outright for fire sufferers and 1,837 others partly paid for.

When the schools reopened October 23, Superintendent J. L. Pickard told his teachers to observe their pupils' clothing and inquire whether any children were staying home for lack of something to wear. Teachers were given clothing and money to help such students. A public-spirited citizen, R. F. Queal, offered to lend money to teachers without any interest charge.

When bread from out of town arrived in moldy condition, because of having been shipped while it was still warm, those Chicago bakers still in business began providing 10,000 to 20,000 loaves daily. Mattresses of hay, excelsior, and corn husks were made at the rate of 300 to 400 dozen daily by local upholsterers for the relief society.

The weather was excellent throughout most of the fall, but neither rain nor, later, snow could halt the rebuilding. Workmen were able to command wages which would have been thought fantastic before the fire, and they were willing to work no matter what the weather was like. When the harvests were over, farmers came from as far as 150 miles away to get temporary jobs. Laborers were getting the munificent sum (in 1871) of two dollars a day, and carpenters and bricklayers from four to six dollars. John Farwell paid seven dollars for dawn-to-dusk labor without a noon break.

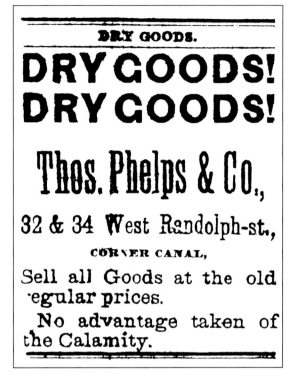

DRY GOODS.

DRY GOODS!
DRY GOODS!

Thos. Phelps & Co.,

32 & 34 West Randolph-st.,

CORNER CANAL,

Sell all Goods at the old regular prices.
No advantage taken of the Calamity.

Inflation in wages came as a shock to Potter Palmer when he asked bids from contractors to clear the wreckage at Field and Leiter's. The lowest bid was $5,000, although a fair price before the fire would have been no more than $1,000. Palmer finally hired the workmen himself.

Inflation—or rather, gouging—unhappily spread to other fields. Hotels sometimes asked as much as eight dollars a day for a small room. A small house, which earlier would have rented for twelve dollars a month, was snapped up at seventy-five. In a few instances tenants were dispossessed to make room for others willing to pay more.

Some grocers doubled the prices of hard-to-get staples, such as meat and sugar. Stocks of bread, cheese, and milk quickly ran out despite spiraling prices. Good Lake water sold as high as five dollars a barrel for a time, especially in areas away from the supply.

Not all merchants tried to charge what the traffic would bear. A grocery store run by Pat O'Connell in the West Division carried a sign reading, "All Parties Without Money Can Have Meat Here." W. K. Nixon, whose building in the South Division was completed in November, cut the rent 10 percent below what his leases called for.

The demand for newspapers was abnormally heavy, with the first issues scalped for as much as a dollar apiece. The *Tribune* was able to print fewer than 20,000 copies daily, and could have sold three times as many.

Fire relics also had a brisk sale. Pieces of the courthouse bell were especially popular. Some of the metal had already been melted and made into souvenir rings and scarf pins when the 7,200-pound remainder was sold at auction, for the same purpose, to Thomas Bryan. He paid 62½ cents a pound for it.

Barracks and tents were erected immediately to help accommodate the homeless. Stoves were in short supply, and three weeks after the fire only a few of these temporary shelters were heated. Smallpox cases, as well as typhoid from the use of dubious water, were common. The *Mail* of October 19 warned its readers to boil water before use. Overcrowding contributed to the danger. In mid-November a dozen cases of smallpox were found in a boardinghouse on Canal, where 150 immigrants were living.

The building committee of the relief society gave out lumber to erect one-room houses. These came in two sizes: twelve-by-sixteen feet and sixteen-by-twenty. All that was required was a place to put the shanty and the ability to nail it together.

The city leased ground on the east side of Michigan Avenue at $500 per 25 feet, for temporary shacks. Such structures were also put up in other parts of the business district. The resultant architectural hodgepodge badly dismayed one fastidious lady, who wrote a friend in Europe:

"To see the lines of rough sheds which are taking the places of all the magnificent buildings destroyed is simply heartbreaking. . . . I for one do not expect to see it [the city] restored to where it was a few short weeks ago. The men of Chicago are heroes; their energy and cheerfulness and determination almost sublime; but I fear many a brave heart will sink under difficulties almost insurmountable."

By the year's end 6,000 small shanties, 2,000 fairly sound frame buildings, and 500 really substantial ones of brick or stone were finished or nearing completion. Within two years vacant property in the business area was worth more than the same land *and* its building had been before the fire.

Unfortunately not everyone in the city set to with a will in the efforts toward recovery. A *Tribune* editorial, October 21, urged a "no-work, no-eat policy," for able-bodied men who hung around the churches, smoking their pipes, and waiting for relief supplies to be handed them.

The relief society was plagued by applicants whose homes were intact. And unscrupulous persons who were not Chicago residents applied to the railroads, which provided passes to refugees who could find homes elsewhere, for free rides. The system had to be suspended for two days, until Eliphalet Blatchford came up with a simple solution to the problem. At the three issuing offices, one clerk took down the name and address of each applicant, and this information was passed on to a second clerk, behind a screen, who had a copy of

the newest city directory. The directory was often, as Blatchford put it "a most surprising witness." It proved necessary to keep a policeman on hand, since some of the would-be travelers proved violently resentful. In a few days, only one office was needed.

Even outside Chicago, freeloaders learned the material value of posing as fire victims. A Philadelphia paper carried this acid comment:

"Chicago was probably the most populous city in the world, previous to the conflagration. Some 14,000,000 of her 'destitute citizens' have passed through this city in the past three weeks. You can't throw a cat in any direction without hitting a 'sufferer.'"

There were plenty of honest sufferers, however, for a long time after the fire.

Many persons were in hospitals with injuries suffered during the fire. The list included Charles Ketteling, burned at the Lake Shore stables; Charles McIntyre, burned in Metropolitan Hall; Thomas McQuinan, burned at 123 West Kinzie; James Divaro, whose feet were severely burned while he was trying to save his furniture; Henry Gaylord, whose hands and face were burned in his home on North State Street; and three crewmen of the schooner *Ellsworth,* which burned on the river near Twelfth Street.

The ruins yielded a sad harvest as the rubble was cleared away. Mrs. Barbara Innis was found at 295 East Indiana, her jewelry mingled with her bones. Andrew Monahan was found at 115 North Market, where he had last been seen "very drunk" at the time of the fire. An unidentified body was found

than a month after the fire of overwork. It was said that he "took neither sleep nor rest from the night of the fire until he died."

A very few killed themselves. Among these were W. E. Longworthy, a master builder, whose shop behind Heath and Milligan's was wiped out by the flames.

According to the *Evening Mail* for October 23, Longworthy "committed suicide yesterday by putting the muzzle of a seven-shooting revolver in his mouth and firing upwards. . . . He [earlier] sought to drown his cares in drink. . . ."

Laborers in the ruins ran considerable risk, and several were killed. Three men died on Friday the 13th when a wall fell on them at 151 South Water Street. Others were crushed to death during work at the *Tribune* and at the Butters building on Michigan Avenue.

By and large, however, the city revived from its wounds and its losses with speed and energy which amazed the rest of the country. One exuberant writer in *The Nation* describing this progress, employed a nautical metaphor until it ran aground. "Chicago," he said, "is under jury masts, and yet carries her ensign down, but she answers her helm, lays her course, is making fair headway, and her crew, though on short allowance and sore tried, is thoroughly sober and knows its stations."

in the Briggs House wreckage, and that of James Thompson (identified by bankbooks nearby) on Clark Street on the North Side. The drowned body of Martin Lunt, assistant tender of the Erie Street Bridge, was taken from the river. He had reportedly leaped into the water, for some unknown reason, from a boat containing his household goods.

The fire claimed other victims indirectly.

David Green, the punctilious night superintendent of the post office, died less

CHAPTER 22

*Who is this General Sheridan? Is he some imperial satrap
in whose favor the city of Chicago or the state of Illinois have
abdicated their functions?*

—CHICAGO TIMES

ONE SEQUENCE of events marred the admirable record of the city's progress. This was the comedy of errors—with one unfortunately very tragic consequence—concerning the preservation of law and order.

There had been a good deal of looting during the fire—and some violence. Many citizens were fearful that really serious outbreaks of lawlessness might spring up in the jungle of the ruins. Ugly rumors along this line began to spread before the flames were out. The newspapers were none too careful about separating fact from conjecture in these matters, and inadvertently helped foster this anxiety.

Many of those in authority favored a get-tough policy to maintain order. As early as Monday, Allan Pinkerton issued a directive to his large force of private policemen, entrusting them, on his authority, with the security of the ruins of the business section.

"Any person stealing or seeking to steal any of the property in my charge," it warned, "or attempt to break open the safes, as the men cannot make arrests at the present time, they shall kill the persons by

my orders. No mercy shall be shown them, but death shall be their fate."

At about the same time General Sheridan called on Mason and suggested bringing in troops, to calm the populace and protect public property. Mason agreed.

Thieves & Burglars!

OFFICE OF

Pinkerton's Police.

Orders are hereby given to the Captains. Lieutenants Sergeants and Men of Pinkerton's Preventive Police. that they are in charge of the Burned District from Polk Street, from the River to the Lake and to the Chicago River. Any person Stealing or seeking to steal. any of the property in my charge or attempt to break open the Safes. as the men cannot make arrests at the present time, they shall

Kill the Persons by my orders, no Mercy Shall be shown them, but Death shall be their fate.

Allan Pinkerton.

THIS BLOOD-AND-THUNDER WARNING FROM ALLAN PINKERTON WAS PRESUMABLY INTENDED TO FRIGHTEN POTENTIAL THIEVES. SO FAR AS IS KNOWN, PINKERTON'S MEN NEVER SHOT ANYONE DURING THE FIRE OR AFTERWARD. (CHICAGO PUBLIC LIBRARY)

Sheridan then wired General Belknap, Secretary of War. He pointed out that the fire could properly be considered a national calamity. He also told Belknap he had ordered rations from St. Louis, tents from Jeffersonville, and a couple of companies of infantry from Omaha—all in Belknap's name. This determined but impetuous action was characteristic of the peppery cavalry general.

Rumors of a wave of lawlessness spread faster than the fire itself. Stories of an invasion of the city by out-of-town criminals, and horrifying tales of incendiaries and the fate being meted out to them, were run as factual stories in the city's papers.

Readers with anything left to lose quickly became stirred up. On Tuesday, a delegation which included Col. Thomas W. Grosvenor, the city prosecutor, waited on General Sheridan and urged him to put the city under martial law. Pressure also was brought on Mayor Mason, who was equally alarmed and agreed readily. He issued this far-reaching proclamation Wednesday:

"The preservation of the good order and peace of the city is hereby entrusted to the Lieut. General P. H. Sheridan, U.S. Army.

"The Police will act in conjunction with the Lieut. General in the preservation of the peace and quiet of the city, and the Superintendent of Police will consult with him to that end.

"The intent hereof being to preserve the peace of the city, without interfering with the functions of the City Government."

Governor Palmer was ignorant of this development, but concerned about the rumors which quickly reached Springfield. He had received a wire Tuesday from Gen. Anson Stager, a Chicago businessman, declaring that "great consternation and anxiety exists on account of the presence of roughs and thieves." He passed this on to Mason, together with the erroneous information that two incendiaries had been shot the night before, and asked if troops were needed.

He was told Mason would like some sent. Palmer then ordered Col. H. Dilger to take a company of militia and a thousand muskets to Chicago. Dilger arrived at 4 A.M. Wednesday, with 200 armed men and many boxes of extra muskets. By 4 P.M. he had 516 men and a battery of four guns on duty.

Dilger, after surveying the situation, informed the governor that the rumors of trouble were untrue. He also passed on

PROCLAMATION!

The preservation of the good order and peace of the city is hereby entrusted to Lieut. General P. H. Sheridan, U. S. Army.

The Police will act in conjunction with the Lieut. General in the preservation of the peace and quiet of the city, and the Superintendent of Police will consult with him to that end.

The intent hereof being to preserve the peace of the city, without interfering with the functions of the City Government.

Given under my hand this 11th day of October, 1871.

R. B. MASON, Mayor.

other very pertinent information: that Mason knew nothing of the request for state troops, and that Sheridan had 700 men of his own in town.

Palmer evidently did not discern that Sheridan was in effective command of the city. He simply told Dilger to return as soon as his services were no longer required. Sheridan told Palmer that seven companies of army troops were in town or coming, a regiment was being organized from former soldiers in the city, and that he would free the state militia in a day or so.

Governor Palmer came to Chicago Thursday and conferred with Mason and Sheridan. He was told things were quiet, and left with the belief that both the state militia and the regular army troops soon would be withdrawn. No one mentioned martial law. As Palmer said later, with considerable heat, "I did not imagine I was con-

ferring with him [Sheridan] as a military officer of the United States. . . . I could not, therefore, imagine that he was exercising the illegal authority he afterwards asserted."

Meanwhile the troops were being used as guards and sentinels, with special attention to bank vaults and property in the business district.

On Thursday also, General Sheridan reported to Mason:

"I am happy to state that no case of outbreak or disorder has been reported. No authenticated case of incendiarism has reached me, and the people of the city are calm, quiet, and well-disposed."

On October 17 Palmer found out at last that Chicago was under martial law. He was surprised and furious. He gave Mason two days to remedy the situation and then sent him a note pungently summarizing his views.

"It . . . has occasioned me the pro-
foundest mortification that you failed to
inform me . . . of the necessity, in your
judgment, for the employment of military
force for the protection of the city; and it
has pained me quite as deeply that you
should have thought it proper, without
consultation with me . . . to have practically
abdicated your functions as Mayor. Happily
there is no necessity, either real or imagi-
nary, for the longer continuance of this
anomalous state of affairs.

"The United States troops are now in
Chicago in violation of law. Every act of the
officers and soldiers of the United States
Army that operates to restrain or control the
people, is illegal, and their presence in the
city—except for the purposes of the United
States—ought to be no longer continued."

But Mason continued to place his trust
in Sheridan, and Sheridan continued to
deploy his little army on the streets of
Chicago. Next day what had been a minor
squabble among politicians turned deadly
serious.

Colonel Grosvenor, the public prosecutor, who himself had suggested putting the
town under martial law, was walking home
shortly after midnight from the home of
Judge Augustus Banyon on Harrison Street.
There had been a party, but it was steadfast-
ly asserted later that the only refreshment
had been a little claret.

Grosvenor reached University Place, on
Cottage Grove. He was challenged by a
sentry, Theodore Treat, a nineteen-year-old
Chicago University student. Treat was a
member of the First Regiment of Chicago
Volunteers, recruited by Sheridan for twenty days of service. He had never loaded or
fired a gun before.

Grosvenor's reply to the challenge has

become lost in the darkness of years. Treat said that Grosvenor answered, "'Go to hell and bang away,'" and kept on walking. He thought from his language he "must be a rough." General Sheridan sprang to the defense of his subordinate, and later charged that Grosvenor had used bad language, was intoxicated, and pulled a pistol.

Whatever was said, Treat fired at Grosvenor from across the street. Grosvenor staggered and fell.

"I am shot," he cried, "I am killed. Oh, God! Oh, God! My wife! My wife!"

The wounded man then managed to stumble to his feet, and ran a few clumsy steps. He collapsed in a ditch. An unloaded pistol was found in his coat pocket.

Firemen from a nearby engine house, who had heard his cries, carried him to the station and then home to his wife.

"I was coming along," he told her. "I heard someone say, 'Halt! Halt!' and I halted and said, 'I am going home,' and I started. Then he shot me and ran."

Grosvenor "called for his little boy and kissed him good night, asked for a glass of water, drank it, and died."

Treat, whom the *Tribune* described as "a high-toned and extremely conscientious young man," was arrested, but defended himself stoutly.

"I did not know he was an influential man. I did not know but he was a rough. It was dark and I could not exactly see what sort of looking man he was."

The *Times* took a strong stand in an editorial the next day. It called Sheridan "the generalissimo whom the valiant college boys have regarded as the authority for their lawless proceedings."

"Who is General Sheridan?" it thundered on. "Is he some imperial satrap in

whose favor the City of Chicago or the State of Illinois have abdicated their functions? . . . The man called General Sheridan has no more authority in the City of Chicago than any other person whom an imbecile board of police may have appointed as a special policeman. If the mayor were not an old idiot, and if his coadjutors on the police board were not as near as possible to nonentities, they would have put a stop long ago to the arming of boys to shoot down peaceable citizens."

The "imbecile" police board members sent a formal note of protest to Mason:

". . . The presence in the inhabited portion of the city, of military bodies under arms, and patrolling the streets, drinking in saloons, and disgusting citizens, is a measure fraught with evil consequences, and . . . all but regular troops should be relieved of further duty within the city. . . ."

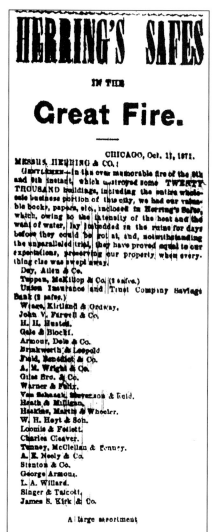

The volunteers were disbanded Monday, October 23, and martial law was declared at an end.

Governor Palmer, however, was still furious. He wrote the attorney general and Charles H. Reed, state's attorney for the Seventh Judicial District, urging the indictment of Treat, General Sheridan, Frank Sherman, and Mason for the killing. A coroner's jury did indeed call Grosvenor's death murder, but Treat was released, and no further action was taken.

Even after martial law was ended, a group of citizens, including Joseph Medill, wrote Sheridan to suggest bringing four companies of infantry to guard at least the relief depots.

Sheridan relayed the request to Washington, which approved it. Palmer promptly wrote an angry note to President Grant protesting this new "interference" with the affairs of Illinois. Grant replied soothingly that Sheridan had been told to do nothing not in harmony with the Constitution of the United States or the laws of Illinois.

The final blast at Sheridan's actions came when a legislative committee—named by Palmer—turned in its report on martial law in Chicago. A dissenting report called the military actions justified, but the majority said:

"It is shown by the evidence that all the violent acts, and riotous conduct, with a single exception, occurring in the city from the time of the fire to the 11th of December, had been committed by soldiers of General Sheridan's command."

The report also charged that the soldiers were drunk, interfered with the police, reopened saloons closed by order of the mayor, stopped citizens without cause, and drove home neighborhood fire patrols. The soldiers, the report concluded, were "more detriment than service."

Soon after, Police Sergeant Ed Hood of the South Branch precinct was acquitted of a charge of conduct unbecoming a police officer. Hood had arrested a corporal and three privates for terrorizing citizens. The principal witness against him, Gen. Philip Sheridan, did not appear.

CHAPTER 23

Let the Watchword henceforth be: Chicago Shall Rise Again.

—JOSEPH MEDILL

LATE IN November the board of police and fire commissioners held a two-week inquiry concerning the fire. Specifically they tried to establish the causes of the fire, and to evaluate the behavior of the departments. They heard dozens of witnesses, including the O'Learys and their neighbors, and numerous firemen from Marshal Williams on down. But, in their report, no cause was assigned and no blame fixed. Perhaps this is as is should be.

There was no lack, however, of unofficial explanations of the fire to choose from. Mrs. O'Leary's cow was, of course, the most popular culprit. There were as many versions of this story as there were people to tell them, but they all agreed on one point: that the cow had kicked over the lamp. There were some who maintained that Mrs. O'Leary was not herself involved in the late milking, but the belief was general that she had taken the lamp to the barn.

The *Times* one day carried a long story crediting the *Société Internationale,* an anarchist group, both with starting the fire and keeping it going. According to another account, a fire extinguisher salesman, angered at poor sales in Chicago, decided to demonstrate to the unappreciative citizens

just how much his product was needed.

Several observers—mostly outside the city—maintained that the destruction of Chicago was a punishment from heaven. One of these confident interpreters of the ways of God to man, the Reverend Granville Moody of Cincinnati, was sure the fire was sent because Chicago had recently voted to permit saloons to be open on Sundays. The Sons of Temperance of Urbana, Illinois, concurred in this view.

The Rushville, Indiana, *Democrat* claimed the fire was divine retribution for the burning of Atlanta by Sherman's forces. "God adjusts balances," was its pious comment. "Maybe with Chicago the books are now squared."

A Southerner who lived on the route of Sherman's march wrote to offer 100 bales of hay to the cow which was rumored to have kicked over that fatal lantern.

In the aftermath of the fire the O'Learys received considerable attention in the local press. The *Tribune* gently though somewhat inaccurately described them as "the worthy old couple who owned the cow stable." But the *Times* of October 18 let vituperative imagination run wild. Mrs. O'Leary was called "an old hag . . . whose very appearance indicated great poverty. She apparently

THE CHICAGO HISTORICAL SOCIETY PLACED TWO COMMEMORATIVE MARKERS ON THE DE KOVEN STREET PROPERTY WHERE THE GREAT FIRE BEGAN. THE FIRST ONE WAS DEDICATED IN 1881 — TEN YEARS AFTER THE FIRE — AND THE SECOND IN 1937. (CHICAGO TODAY)

was about seventy years of age and was bent almost double with the weight of many years of toil, and trouble, and privation." The story asserted—with bland disregard for accuracy—that Mrs. O'Leary had been removed from the relief rolls after years of being "a pensioner of the county," and had sworn revenge "on a city that would deny her a bit of wood or a pound of bacon. How well she kept her word is not known, but there are those who insist the woman set the barn and thus inaugurated the most terrible calamity in the history of nations. . . ."

The *Times* then quoted her as having said that she went to the stable at 9:30 Sunday night (the fire was then at least forty-five minutes old) and that the cow kicked over the lamp.

During the inquiry the same paper took an equally colorful and equally malicious approach—but the description was otherwise quite different.

"She is a tall, stout, Irish woman with no intelligence," said the reporter on December 3, "and acted as if she believed the city wanted her to pay every cent of the losses created by the fire. . . . During her testimony the infant [she held] . . . kicked its bare legs around and drew nourishment from mammoth reservoirs."

The *Times* also attacked her husband. "Leary knew even less than she did." It portrayed him as a "fast talker with a rich brogue" and said he was a "stupid-looking sort of a man, who acknowledged himself that he could neither read nor write."

The *Journal* of October 21 apparently came closest to objectivity, picturing Mrs. O'Leary as a "stout Irish woman, some 35 years of age" who denied ever getting relief. One of her other comments also has the ring of truth. When the reporter suggested that the fire must have been pretty rough on her, she replied, "Rough! Why, my God, man, it was a terror to the world!"

The O'Learys, with justification, felt themselves persecuted by free-wheeling newspaper stories. But journalism of the time was very personal indeed, and others also received a good share of abuse.

"If Mr. Norman Gasette," said the *Mail* in a vitriolic piece on October 25, "had been half as zealous in attending to his duties as County Recorder as he was in getting his friends into office, he would have saved the priceless records of the Courthouse. A moderate amount of energy and sense would have secured the services of a hundred men at the cost, if necessary, of ten thousand dollars, and had every book conveyed to a place of safety. But a fire is very different from a ward meeting."

On December 5, when water had not yet been turned on in its new Lind block office, the *Mail* again found it necessary to chide the city administration.

"We have borne this infamous treatment patiently and quietly as long as we shall," it said righteously, "and we denounce these men, McArthur, Carter, Prindiville, and the full-paid, do-nothing satellites connected with the Board of Public Works, as promise-breaking, imbecilic, decency-defying nincompoops."

At the inquiry, Marshal Williams rehearsed once more his vain attempts to expand the fire department. He mentioned again his proposal for at least one fire boat on the river, and suggested that pipes be run under the pavement from the hydrants directly either to the river or the Lake.

Williams indirectly gave a very cogent explanation of why the fire had got out of hand. "[Strike] it before it gets the start of you. That is the only secret in putting out fires. If the fire gets the start of you, you have to work very hard. One thing I would state. One great reason that the Chicago department has had such good success as they have had in this wooden city—it is nothing more or less—they have been right on their taps and on it before it got started."

Out of charity or tact, he made no mention of how the mix-up in alarms had prevented the department from doing just that on October 8.

The inquiry also brought out that several firemen were rewarded after the disaster, although not—it was always declared—for any special services.

The foreman of Ryerson's lumberyard,

which lay on the fringes of the West Side fire and was therefore saved, paid Benner $300. Eight fire companies received $200 to $300 each. The money came from Ryerson's, the Chicago Dock Company, and other grateful firms whose buildings survived the holocaust.

Bullwinkle said he had received a $5 or $10 present from someone whose trunk he didn't know he was saving—it was thrown on the wagon without his knowledge. Foreman Mullen got $50 from the Pittsburgh and Fort Wayne railroad, a sum which he generously split with his company, $8.30 per man.

Conway made a point of mentioning that he had seen no firemen drunk—only citizens with firemen's hats on. He said that

IN 1956, WITH LITTLE REGARD FOR HISTORIC PRESERVATION, THE DE KOVEN STREET PROPERTY AND THE MARKERS WERE TORN DOWN IN ORDER TO BUILD THE CHICAGO FIRE ACADEMY, A TRAINING SCHOOL FOR CITY FIREMEN. (CHICAGO SUN TIMES)

A FASCINATING LINK WITH THE GREAT FIRE WAS THE RELIC HOUSE, WHICH WAS BUILT WITH MATERIALS SALVAGED FROM THE RUINS OF THE FIRE. THIS POPULAR BEER GARDEN AND MUSEUM STOOD ON CLARK STREET ACROSS FROM LINCOLN PARK. IT WAS TORN DOWN IN 1930. (CROMIE COLLECTION)

he, too, had been rewarded after the fire. The donor was Baker, who had offered $200 if Conway would change the stream and put it on his property.

Baker, Conway said, gave him two cigars.

Fuller, the night fire-alarm telegraph operator, gave the most telling answer to the charge that some of the firemen might have been under the influence of liquor:

"Intoxicated?" he said. "I do not believe they had time to become intoxicated. They had all they could do to save themselves and their apparatus from being burned up."

Concerning responsibility for the fire,

J. W. Foster, in an article published shortly after, presents the most convincing conclusions.

"Cool headed residents of Chicago," he wrote, "are far less inclined to attribute this overwhelming catastrophe to the judgment of God than to the folly of man. When human agency lays the train and fires the match, it evinces an overweening confidence in Divine Providence to expect that it shall intervene to prevent the explosion. . . . When we shall have eliminated from this grand catastrophe all the elements chargeable to private greed and public incompetency, there will be little or nothing to be carried to the account of Divine Providence."

And Joseph Medill's robust editorial in the *Tribune,* three days after the fire, proved to be the most accurate appraisal of the future of the city.

"All is not lost. Though four hundred million dollars worth of property has been destroyed, Chicago still exists. She was not a mere collection of stones, and bricks, and lumber. . . . The great natural resources are all in existence: the lake, with its navies, the spacious harbor, the vast empire of production extending westward to the Pacific . . . the great arteries of trade and commerce, all remain unimpaired, undiminished, and all ready for immediate resumption. . . .

"We have lost money, but we have saved life, health, vigor and industry. . . .

"Let the Watchword henceforth be: *Chicago Shall Rise Again.*"

That November the voters of Chicago elected Joseph Medill mayor. He ran on the "Fireproof" ticket.

POSTSCRIPT

Even though much of Chicago was destroyed in one of the worst disasters America has ever seen, the most amazing thing was the speed with which the city recovered. In some areas, building owners were inspecting and counting the reusable bricks before they were cool. Margaret O'Toole, a chestnut seller, was at her regular place of business Tuesday morning. John S. Wright, a real estate dealer, author, and editor who had been driven from the South Side by the blaze, said of the city's future, "Chicago will have more men, more money, more business within five years than she would have had without the fire." And, in an editorial in the Chicago *Tribune*, Joseph Medill said, "All is not lost. Though four hundred million dollars worth of property has been destroyed, Chicago still exists. The lake, the spacious harbor, the vast empire of production, the great arteries of trade and commerce all remain. We have lost money, but we have saved life, health, vigor, and industry." Chicagoans rebuilt their city in a style more bold and more grand than it had been before. And a short 22 years later, it invited the world to come to see it by hosting the World's Columbian Exposition, which celebrated the 400th anniversary of the discovery of America by Christopher Columbus.

CHICAGO WAS PROUD OF ITS HOTELS. THE
TREMONT (RIGHT), WHICH BECAME A REN-
DEZVOUS FOR THEATRICAL FOLK, THE
GRAND PACIFIC (BOTTOM LEFT), AND THE
PALMER HOUSE (BOTTOM RIGHT) WERE
ALL REBUILT VERY QUICKLY.

THE PALMER HOUSE, WITH ITS UNUSUALLY LARGE ROOMS AND MARBLE AND GOLD TRIMMINGS, ILLUSTRATES THE ELEGANCE OF CHICAGO'S REBUILT HOTELS. THE WORLD FAMOUS BARBERSHOP (LEFT) HAD SILVER DOLLARS IMBEDDED IN ITS FLOOR AND THE GRAND PARLOR (BELOW) DEMONSTRATES THE GRANDEUR OF THE HOTEL.

THE SAME DAY THE FIRE BURNED ITSELF
OUT, THE FIRST LOAD OF LUMBER WAS
DELIVERED TO REBUILD THE CITY. WITHIN A
MONTH, BUILDINGS OF BRICK AND STONE
WERE GOING UP. THE PHOTOGRAPH BELOW
SHOWS THE WHITE STONE MARINE
BUILDING AT LAKE STREET LOOKING EAST
FROM LA SALLE STREET. (CHICAGO
HISTORICAL SOCIETY) THE INTERIOR OF
THE NEW COURTHOUSE (BELOW RIGHT)
SHOWS THE ELEGANCE OF THE NEW CITY.
(ANDREAS) AND THE NEW MARSHALL FIELD
STORE (SHOWN IN 1893) WAS A TRIBUTE
TO THE CITY'S SPIRIT. (MARSHALL FIELD
ARCHIVES)

TWENTY-TWO YEARS AFTER THE GREAT FIRE, THE 1893 WORLD'S COLUMBIAN EXPOSITION SPREAD OVER 680 ACRES OF CHICAGO. THE FAIR ATTRACTED MORE THAN 21 MILLION VISITORS AND INTRODUCED PEOPLE TO THE FERRIS WHEEL (LEFT), THE MOTION PICTURE CAMERA, AND ELECTRICITY, WHICH WAS PRESENTED AT THE 1889 PARIS EXPOSITION BUT WAS LARGELY UNKNOWN TO AMERICANS. THE PLEDGE OF ALLEGIANCE WAS WRITTEN FOR THE EXPOSITION'S DEDICATION. PICTURED BELOW IS THE FAIR'S MAIN BUILDING. (ANDREAS)